J. M. TEDDER and **A. NECHVATAL**
Queen's College, Dundee, Scotland

Basic
Organic
Chemistry

A Mechanistic Approach

1966
John Wiley and Sons
London   New York   Sydney   Toronto

Library of Congress catalog card no. 66-17112

ISBN 0 471 85011 X

First published May 1966

Reprinted October 1968

Reprinted July 1970

Reprinted August 1971

Text set in Monotype Modern Extended Number 1, 10 on 11½ point.

Reprinted by offset lithography by Dawson & Goodall Ltd.,

The Mendip Press, Bath

Foreword

This volume is based on a series of lectures given to the first B.Sc. Class at Queen's College, Dundee, Scotland. The reaction of the students was favourable, but they protested that the lectures appeared to bear no relation to any of the organic chemistry in the recommended textbooks. To overcome this difficulty, the lectures were dictated into a tape-recorder, and a stencil was made *verbatim* from the recording; stencilled copies were then prepared and handed out to the class. This was done originally with no thought of publication. In preparing the present book from these lecture notes, the text has been reworded in many places in order to avoid the grossest colloquialisms sometimes used in class, but the content remains unchanged.

Traditionally organic chemistry is taught as a list of preparations and properties of different classes of compounds. As a result the student is presented with a huge collection of facts to which a little theory may subsequently be added as a piquant sauce to make the indigestible mass a little more palatable. However, it is ideas and not facts that the student wishes to learn. If the traditional approach is adopted, methane is a logical choice as a first compound to discuss. It hardly makes sense, however, to describe its preparation by the dry distillation of sodium acetate when carboxylic acids are not discussed until Chapter 6 or 7. (This is a bad reaction to introduce early in the course in any case, as its mechanism is complicated and it is by no means a general reaction.) A more serious disadvantage of the traditional approach is that it leads to a number of generalizations which are by no means true; for example, it is frequently said that an alkyl halide treated with aqueous sodium hydroxide yields an alcohol, treated with alcoholic potash yields an olefin, and treated with sodium ethoxide in alcohol yields an ether. The greatest disadvantage of the traditional approach is that the chemistry of carbon appears to be quite unrelated to the chemistry of the remaining 91 naturally occurring elements.

The objection often raised to suggestions that organic chemistry should be taught from a theoretical basis is that the student who is taught this way will not know how to ascend the homologous series or how to convert an acid into its ester. We have sought to avoid this in two ways. Firstly, by giving a few questions illustrating 'useful reactions' at the end of each chapter. Secondly, by including methods of preparation after the reactions themselves have been described. We have not neglected natural products, but have preferred to discuss these almost at the end of the course when the students are in a position 'to appreciate the structures and reactions involved.

We have not discussed the latest experimental techniques, e.g. spectroscopy. Our feeling is that it may well be reasonable to introduce infrared, nuclear magnetic resonance, and ultraviolet spectroscopy almost as soon as melting point and boiling point are introduced; but just as these latter techniques are introduced in the laboratory so spectroscopy must be introduced into organic chemistry as part of the practical training.

This book is based on a so-called mechanistic approach and some readers may be surprised therefore that we have restricted our discussion to the Lewis theory of valency. We believe that the indiscriminate drawing of 'balloons' and 'sausages' without an understanding of what these represent would be completely reprehensible. If all we mean by saying that a carbon atom is sp^3 hybridized is that the atoms bonded to it are distributed round it in a tetrahedral fashion, surely it is better to say so rather than introduce a meaningless terminology.

This book covers much of the ground of the syllabuses for the examinations leading to the Certificate of Education at Advanced Level in England and Wales. There are, however, some gaps. For instance, most of the Advanced Level syllabuses include addition to unsymmetric olefins, dibasic acids, and acetoacetic ester. We do not consider these topics suitable for students of this level.

Although no knowledge of organic chemistry is assumed, a good grounding in general chemistry is taken for granted. We assume that the student is familiar with the Lewis theory of valency, with the basic concepts of equilibrium, thermochemistry, and the Brønsted–Lowry theory of acids. It is most important, in our opinion, that the student should realize that the division into physical, inorganic, and organic chemistry is purely one of administrative convenience. It is meaningless to consider the chemistry of one element in isolation and it is pointless to try and understand the reactions of carbon compounds without understanding the basic principles of thermodynamics.

We believe the way organic chemistry is treated in this book is the best way to introduce the subject to a student for the first time. We are aware that there are still many teachers who are convinced that the traditional approach remains the best method. We hope that students taught traditionally may still benefit from the present book. We recommend that such students should not attempt to assimilate the two approaches simultaneously but read this book *after* they have completed one year of the traditional approach.

Preface

This book is an attempt to develop the ideas on which current thinking in organic chemistry is based. The arguments developed in one chapter depend on all those developed in previous chapters and the book is meaningless unless read consecutively. The chemistry of carbon compounds must not be regarded as something separate from the rest of chemistry and the present book is intended to be read in conjunction with similar courses on physical and inorganic chemistry.

Chemistry is an experimental science and experience in the laboratory is an essential part of any student's training. The techniques of chemistry—for instance, crystallization or distillation—can only be learned in the laboratory and are not therefore discussed in the present book.

Although this book is an attempt to get across ideas rather than facts it is still important that the student can use these ideas to answer the types of question he is likely to encounter in the laboratory. In order to exemplify this point there are one or two problems at the end of most chapters. Only by doing problems can a student make sure he has grasped the ideas which he has been reading about. At the end of some chapters there is, in smaller type, a section on nomenclature. These sections are not intended to be worked through in the first reading of the book. On the other hand, when the first reading of the book is completed we hope the student will start the book again and on this occasion read the nomenclature sections carefully. Nomenclature in isolation is a dull and difficult subject; nomenclature considered in conjunction with the chemistry of the compounds being named becomes logical,

interesting, and a useful way of revising some of the ideas developed in the main part of the chapter.

Acknowledgements

We would like to express our indebtedness to the very many
colleagues who read through our original lecture notes and gave us
much encouragement and advice. As well as our colleagues in this
department we are indebted to colleagues in eight other univer-
sities. We also acknowledge very considerable assistance from the
editorial staff of the London office of John Wiley and Sons. Above
all else we are indebted to the First B.Sc. Class at Queen's College
in the session 1964–65 to whom the lectures were first given and
whose enthusiastic response provided the stimulus to carry the
work through.

August, 1965

We wish to thank many friends and colleagues who have
suggested minor alterations to the first printing.

June, 1966   J.M.T.
                                                                          A.N.

Contents

Introduction

Organic chemistry is the study of carbon compounds, and the question immediately arises as to why we separate the chemistry of one element from that of all the other 91 naturally occurring elements. The answer is two-fold. Firstly, for every chemical compound known containing no carbon, there are many dozens containing carbon. The second reason is related to the first; what we call life is a highly complex series of chemical processes and these invariably involve compounds of carbon. Further than this, any form of life, wherever it may exist, must involve the chemistry of carbon. Only by utilizing carbon compounds is it possible to build up systems complex enough to support life. It does not matter whether the Martians are little green men with horns or, as H. G. Wells pictured them, octopus-like creatures, the crucial point is that only by using carbon compounds is it possible to create an organism complex enough to represent what we mean by life. Having established that carbon is unique among the elements the next question is, why is it unique?

For the present discussion we shall make use of Lewis's theory of valency according to which chemical bonds are formed by atoms sharing electrons to form electron pairs, each atom concerned tending to produce the shell corresponding to the inert gas nearest to it in the periodic table.

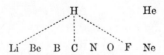

Thus in the diagram above, which represents the first row of the periodic table, lithium tends to lose an electron to form Li^+, a lithium cation, in which the lithium nucleus is surrounded by two electrons, as in helium. At the other end of the first row of the elements is fluorine, which tends to gain an electron so that it has 8 electrons in its outer shell like the inert gas neon. Let us now compare the compounds formed by hydrogen with lithium, carbon, and fluorine. Lithium hydride is an ionic solid best represented as Li^+H^-. It is extremely reactive, almost explosively so, with water:

$$LiH + H_2O \longrightarrow Li^+ + H_2\uparrow + OH^-$$

Hydrogen fluoride is a low-boiling liquid which also reacts violently with water:

$$HF + H_2O \longrightarrow H_3O^+ + F^-$$

Carbon tetrahydride, CH_4, normally called **methane**, is a gas which is completely immiscible and inert with water. Methane in many ways resembles molecular hydrogen. A molecule of hydrogen does not ionize readily:

$$H:H \;\longrightarrow\!\!\!\!/\; H^+ + H:^-$$

and it does not react with water. The H—H bond in hydrogen is a typical non-polar covalent bond: the two electrons forming it are shared equally between two hydrogen atoms, whereas in lithium hydride the hydrogen has a bigger share of the electrons and in hydrogen fluoride the fluorine atom has the bigger share; this can be represented by the simplified picture shown below.

$$Li \; :H \qquad H:H \qquad F: \; H$$

Lithium hydride and hydrogen fluoride are polar molecules whereas molecular hydrogen is not. Methane is very similar to molecular hydrogen in that the electrons forming the bonds between the carbon atom and the hydrogen atom are equally shared between the carbon atom and the four hydrogen atoms.

$$H:\overset{\displaystyle ..}{\underset{\displaystyle ..}{C}}:H$$

Metallic lithium reacts violently with hydrogen fluoride to form hydrogen and the salt lithium fluoride, Li^+F^-. It also reacts violently with water to form hydrogen and lithium hydroxide, Li^+OH^-, which is also a polar salt. Lithium dissolves in liquid ammonia, NH_3, reacting gently to give a salt, lithium amide, $Li^+NH_2^-$, and hydrogen. Lithium does not react with methane at normal temperatures. Notice the decreasing reactivity in this series:

$$Li + HF \longrightarrow Li^+F^- + \tfrac{1}{2} H_2 \quad \text{very violent}$$
$$Li + H_2O \longrightarrow Li^+OH^- + \tfrac{1}{2} H_2 \quad \text{rapid}$$
$$Li + NH_3 \longrightarrow Li^+NH_2^- + \tfrac{1}{2} H_2 \quad \text{slow}$$
$$Li + CH_4 \longrightarrow \text{no reaction at normal temperatures}$$

We have likened the C—H bond in methane to the H—H bond in molecular hydrogen and this suggests that hydrogen could be replaced in a molecule H—X by carbon or, specifically, by carbon surrounded by three hydrogen atoms, CH_3 (methyl group), to produce a further molecule CH_3—X. Table 1.1 shows such a parallelism between some inorganic compounds H—X and their methyl analogues CH_3—X.

Table 1.1

	H—X	CH_3—X
Hydrogen chloride (fluoride, bromide, iodide)	H—Cl (F,Br,I)	CH_3—Cl (F,Br,I) Methyl chloride (fluoride, bromide, iodide)
Water	H—OH	CH_3—OH Methanol (Methyl alcohol)
Ammonia	H—NH_2	CH_3—NH_2 Methylamine
Hydrogen sulphide	H—SH	CH_3—SH Methyl mercaptan
Formaldehyde	H—CHO	CH_3—CHO Acetaldehyde
Formic acid	H—COOH	CH_3—COOH Acetic acid
Hydrogen cyanide (Prussic acid)	H—CN	CH_3—CN Methyl cyanide (Acetonitrile)
Sulphuric acid	H—OSO_3H	CH_3—OSO_3H Methyl hydrogen sulphate

This process can be extended further in water and ammonia, since there is more than one hydrogen atom which can be replaced by CH_3.

2

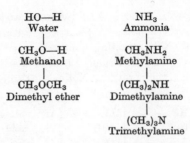

HO—H	NH$_3$
Water	Ammonia
│	│
CH$_3$O—H	CH$_3$NH$_2$
Methanol	Methylamine
│	│
CH$_3$OCH$_3$	(CH$_3$)$_2$NH
Dimethyl ether	Dimethylamine
	│
	(CH$_3$)$_3$N
	Trimethylamine

Hydrogen attached to carbon can also be replaced by methyl, giving series such as that shown below.

HCHO	HCOOH
Formaldehyde	Formic acid
│	│
CH$_3$CHO	CH$_3$COOH
Acetaldehyde	Acetic acid
│	│
CH$_3$COCH$_3$	CH$_3$COOCH$_3$
Acetone	Methyl acetate

What about the hydrogen atoms in methane? Clearly we can do just the same as illustrated in the scheme below.

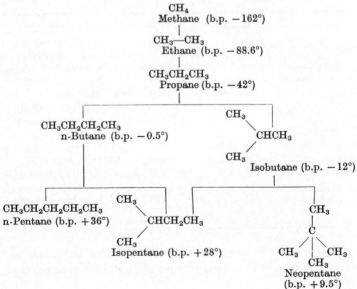

Two molecules with the same molecular formula but different structures are called **isomers**. How many isomers of hexane (C_6H_{14}) are there? (cf. Problem 1 and its answer).

This process can be contined *ad nauseum*, e.g. the common plastic polythene (sometimes called 'Alkathene') consists of very long chains of carbon atoms surrounded by hydrogens, i.e. $H(CH_2)_nH$ where n is a very large number. The first four compounds in the above scheme are gases; the pentanes are low-boiling colourless liquids and the longer the carbon chain the higher the boiling point. When the chain contains sixteen carbon atoms in a row the boiling point has reached 280° and the hydrocarbon is no longer a liquid but a low-melting solid (or wax). Similarly, hydrogen chloride can yield not only methyl chloride, but a whole series of chlorides with carbon chains attached to the chlorine atom; similarly from water a series of alcohols and ethers can be built up by successive replacement of hydrogen atoms by methyl groups as shown in the next scheme.

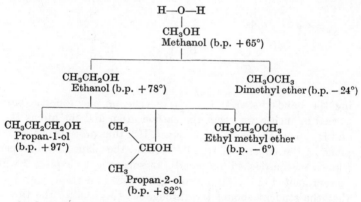

Such series are called **homologous series** (C_nH_{2n+2}, the alkanes; $C_nH_{2n+1}OH$, the alcohols; $C_nH_{2n+1}CO_2H$, the carboxylic acids, are all general members of homologous series where n can be any integer). In all homologous series there is a gradation of physical properties, and in general the boiling points and melting points increase with increasing chain length. Usually a compound with a branched chain has a lower boiling point than its straight-chain isomer.

Thus we can build up long straight chains of carbon atoms, or, alternatively, branched chains with as many branches as we like. The next question is, is it possible to make a chain bite its own tail, i.e. can there be cyclic chains of carbon atoms? The answer is 'yes', but before considering this we must go back and consider the actual shape of the methane molecule. So far it has been drawn as though it were flat, with the carbon atom in the centre linked to four hydrogen atoms, making the whole molecule a square. This has only been done for convenience in drawing. Since the bonds between carbon and hydrogen consist of pairs of electrons, and since electrons repel each other, each of the bonds would be expected to be as far away from the other three bonds as possible in methane. This will occur when the bonds from carbon to hydrogen subtend an angle of $109° 28'$ to each other. This represents the tetrahedral distribution, i.e. each hydrogen atom can be regarded as being at the apex of a tetrahedron in which the carbon atom is at the centre, as in **1**. **2** represents methane show-

(1)   (2)   (3)

ing the bonds between the atoms. The tetrahedron has been turned in such a way that the carbon atom and the atoms $H_{(a)}$ and $H_{(b)}$ lie in the plane of the paper. $H_{(c)}$ thus projects out of the plane of the paper and $H_{(d)}$ lies behind the plane of the paper (shown with a dashed-line bond). In subsequent chapters **2** will be represented in the simplified form **3**. It is important, however, that the student should try throughout to visualize the three-dimensional nature of chemistry.

This tetrahedral arrangement of the bonds around the carbon atom means that molecules which we have described above as linear, e.g. the linear hydrocarbons, are, strictly speaking, not linear but zigzag. The direction of the bonds is fixed but free rotation about a bond joining two atoms is possible. Thus, there is only one 1,2-dichloroethane, positional isomer **5**; this can be converted into **4** simply by rotation of the C—C bond. When we now try to make the cyclic hydrocarbons but keep the bonds between the carbon atoms at exactly 109° 28', we find that only rings of six carbon atoms or larger can be made. 5-, 4-, and 3-membered rings can be

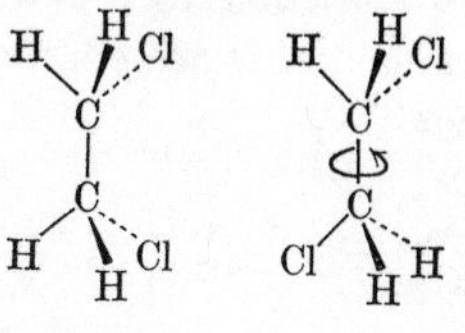

(4)   (5)

5 can be converted into **4** by rotation about the carbon–carbon bond

Bonds in the plane of the paper C—H

Bonds behind the plane of the paper C----H

Bonds in front of the plane of the paper C ◄ H

made only by sacrificing the tetrahedral angle; the extent of the sacrifice becoming, of course, greater as the ring becomes smaller.

Cyclohexane, C_6H_{12}, has a puckered ring in which the tetrahedral angle is perfectly preserved, and the same is true for any larger ring system. Cyclopentane is almost planar and the bonds are

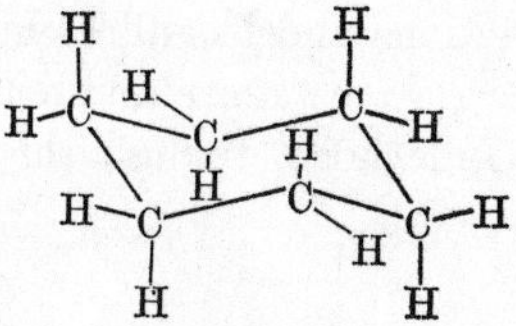

Cyclohexane

only slightly distorted from the tetrahedral angle. In cyclobutane and cyclopropane, however, distortion is considerable. This introduces what is called **strain**. For the moment we can best interpret this in terms of energy and regard strain as the energy required to move the bond from its tetrahedral angle. This strain energy will have to be taken away from the energy of the bond and therefore

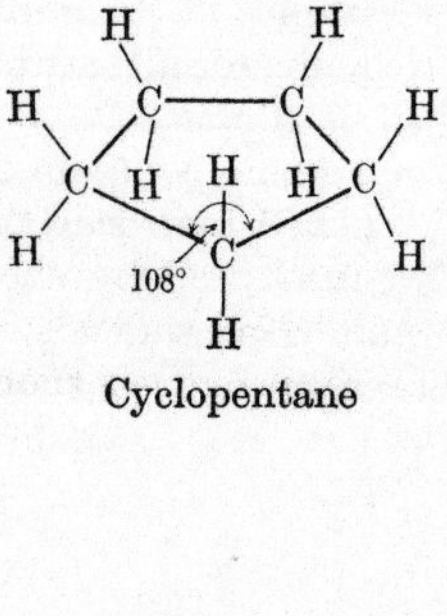

Cyclopentane 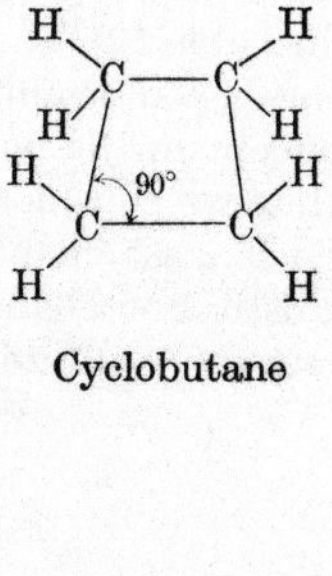   Cyclobutane 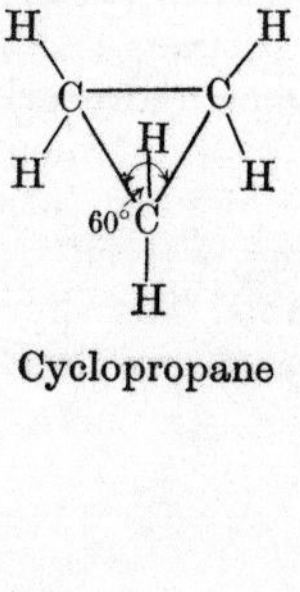   Cyclopropane

a strained bond will be weaker than a non-strained one. Further discussion of cyclic compounds will be postponed until later.

There is one further consequence of the tetrahedral arrangement of the bonds around the carbon atom which must be mentioned here briefly. If we consider a carbon atom attached to four different atoms or groups we see that two arrangements are possible, one of which is a mirror image of the other.

(6)   (7)

Stereoisomers of lactic acid

These two mirror images, **6** and **7**, are like a left-handed glove and a right-handed glove and are not superimposable on one another. From a chemical point of view, these two compounds will have identical chemical reactions and it suffices here to say that these two isomers, called *stereoisomers*, are distinct species and can be separated by physical methods, though this matter will be discussed in Chapter 15.

Nomenclature

We have laid stress on the great number and variety of compounds built up of carbon atoms. It is extremely important, therefore, that we have some systematic method of nomenclature. Such a system has been worked out by a commission appointed by the International Union of Pure and Applied Chemistry. The following are some of the most important rules for the naming of acyclic open-chain hydrocarbons with the general formula C_nH_{2n+2}. The first four such unbranched hydrocarbons are called methane, ethane, propane, and butane. Names of the higher members of this series consist of a numerical prefix and a termination '-ane'. Examples of the numerical prefixes are shown in Table 1.2. The generic name for all saturated acyclic hydrocarbons, branched or unbranched, is alkane.

The fundamental concept in the naming of organic compounds is one of substitution. Thus we consider the branched hydrocarbon as being derived from the longest chain in it, substituted by shorter chains. The shorter substituent chains are named as radicals. The radicals are derived from the saturated unbranched hydrocarbon by

Table 1.2. Nomenclature for straight-chain hydrocarbons C_nH_{2n+2}

$n =$					
1	Methane	11	Undecane	32	Dotriacontane
2	Ethane	12	Dodecane	33	Tritriacontane
3	Propane	13	Tridecane	40	Tetracontane
4	Butane	14	Tetradecane	50	Pentacontane
5	Pentane	20	Eicosane	60	Hexacontane
6	Hexane	21	Heneicosane	70	Heptacontane
7	Heptane	22	Docosane	80	Octacontane
8	Octane	23	Tricosane	90	Nonacontane
9	Nonane	30	Triacontane	100	Hectane
10	Decane	31	Hentriacontane	132	Dotriacontahectane

the removal of a hydrogen atom from the terminal carbon and are named by replacing the ending '-ane' of the name of the hydrocarbon by '-yl', e.g.

CH_3— methyl from CH_4 methane;

$CH_3CH_2CH_2CH_2$— butyl from $CH_3CH_2CH_2CH_3$ butane;

$CH_3(CH_2)_9CH_2$— undecyl from $CH_3(CH_2)_9CH_3$ undecane.

We are now in a position to name a branched-chain hydrocarbon. The name of the longest chain present in the molecule is prefixed by the names of the side chains, e.g.

$$CH_3CH_2CHCH_2CH_3$$
$$|$$
$$CH_3$$
Methylpentane

Clearly this name is ambiguous for the following molecule is also methylpentane.

$$CH_3CHCH_2CH_2CH_3$$
$$|$$
$$CH_3$$
Methylpentane

To distinguish between these two molecules, the carbon atoms of the longest chain, that is the five carbon atoms of the pentane molecule, are numbered from one end to the other with arabic numerals, the direction of numbering being chosen so as to give the lowest possible number to the side chain. Thus our two examples become 3-methylpentane and 2-methylpentane.

$$\overset{5}{C}H_3\overset{4}{C}H_2\overset{3}{C}H\overset{2}{C}H_2\overset{1}{C}H_3$$
$$|$$
$$CH_3$$
3-Methylpentane

$$\overset{1}{C}H_3\overset{2}{C}H\overset{3}{C}H_2\overset{4}{C}H_2\overset{5}{C}H_3$$
$$|$$
$$CH_3$$
2-Methylpentane

Many small common molecules have a common 'semi-systematic' name as well as the systematic name; 2-methylpentane is also known as isohexane, 'iso' denoting the presence of a $(CH_3)_2C$ group in a hydrocarbon. If two or more side-chains of a different nature occur, they are cited in alphabetical order, multiplying prefixes 'di-', 'tri-', etc., being ignored.

$$CH_3CH_2 \quad CH_3$$
$$\quad | \qquad \quad |$$
$$CH_3CH_2CH_2CH—CCH_2CH_3$$
$$\qquad \qquad \qquad \quad |$$
$$\qquad \qquad \qquad CH_3$$

4-Ethyl-3,3-dimethylheptane

The cyclic hydrocarbons of the general formula C_nH_{2n} are named by prefixing 'cyclo-' to the name of the straight-chain compound with the same number of atoms. Some examples are given below.

Cyclohexane   Cyclopropane   1-Ethyl-3-methyl-
                                               cyclopentane

There are additional rules to deal with more complicated molecules but the above are sufficient to deal with any hydrocarbons which we are likely to meet here. We would advise the student to have a little practice at naming some hydrocarbons (cf. Problem 1).

Problems

1. Draw out all the possible isomers of molecular formula C_7H_{16}. Name them.

2. In the text a particular shape (*conformation*) of cyclohexane is shown. Draw the possible conformations of methylcyclohexane, $CH_3C_6H_{11}$, in which the tetrahedral arrangement of carbon atoms is maintained.

CHAPTER 2

The Carbon–Hydrogen Bond

Before we can consider any chemical reactions of the carbon–hydrogen bond we must remember why a chemical bond is formed in the first place. Two hydrogen atoms combine to form a hydrogen molecule because the hydrogen molecule has a lower energy than two separate hydrogen atoms (or a proton and a hydride anion). This means that when two hydrogen atoms come together to form a molecule, energy is released. Similarly, in order to break the hydrogen molecule into its two constituent atoms we must supply energy. This energy required to break a bond is called the **bond-dissociation energy**. It is normally written $D(\text{H—H})$ and is expressed in kilocalories per mole, e.g. $D(\text{H—H}) = 103$ kcal mole^{-1}. In methane the carbon–hydrogen bond has a dissociation energy of 102 kcal mole^{-1} $[D(\text{CH}_3\text{—H}) = 102$ kcal mole$^{-1}]$. (Notice that this is the bond-dissociation energy for a single carbon–hydrogen bond in methane; it is not the bond-dissociation energy of a carbon–hydrogen bond in a methyl radical, which is slightly less. The average energy required to strip all four hydrogen atoms from carbon is called the bond energy; it is not the same as the bond-dissociation energy, which refers specifically to one carbon–hydrogen bond in methane.)

If we take a mixture of methane and chlorine in the gas phase at room temperature in the dark, no reaction occurs. In the presence of light, however, a rapid reaction ensues and with an excess of methane the main products are methyl chloride and hydrogen chloride, the excess of methane remaining unchanged. The function of the light is to dissociate the chlorine molecule into chlorine atoms. The chlorine molecule absorbs visible light at the violet end of the visible spectrum and near-ultraviolet light. The

11

energy of light in this region of the spectrum is far greater than
that necessary to dissociate molecular chlorine, the bond-dissociation energy of which is approximately 67 kcal mole^{-1}. The
sequence of reactions that then occurs is shown in the following
set of equations:

$$Cl_2 + h\nu \xrightarrow{\;\;1\;\;} 2\,Cl\cdot \qquad\qquad \text{Initiation}$$

$$\left. \begin{array}{l} Cl\cdot + CH_4 \xrightarrow{\;\;2\;\;} CH_3\cdot + HCl \\[2ex] CH_3\cdot + Cl_2 \xrightarrow{\;\;3\;\;} CH_3Cl + Cl\cdot \end{array} \right\} \text{Propagation} \qquad \begin{array}{l} \Delta H = -2 \text{ kcal} \\ \qquad\quad \text{mole}^{-1} \\[1ex] \Delta H = -23 \text{ kcal} \\ \qquad\quad \text{mole}^{-1} \end{array}$$

The first feature to notice about these reactions is that as soon as
reaction 1 has occurred once, reactions 2 and 3 are self-propa-
gating, so that one quantum of light absorbed by one chlorine
molecule would apparently be sufficient to initiate chlorination of
all the methane present. In practice, however, this sequence of
reactions, called a **chain reaction**, can be terminated by three possible steps:

$$\left. \begin{array}{l} Cl\cdot + Cl\cdot + M \xrightarrow{\;\;4\;\;} Cl_2 + M^* \\[2ex] CH_3\cdot + Cl\cdot \xrightarrow{\;\;5\;\;} CH_3Cl \\[2ex] CH_3\cdot + CH_3\cdot \xrightarrow{\;\;6\;\;} C_2H_6 \end{array} \right\} \text{Termination}$$

In the reaction between methane and chlorine the chain length†
can be as long as 10^6 although most reaction chains are much
shorter. At present we are most concerned with the thermochemistry of the reactions. The enthalpy of reaction, ΔH, for
reaction 2 is -2 kcal mole^{-1} and the enthalpy of reaction for

---

* Two chlorine atoms coming together do not stay bound unless they can
lose the excess 67 kcal. They can lose this energy by collision with another
molecule M (which could be Cl_2, CH_4, or $CHCl_3$, etc.). Two methyl radicals
do not require a 'third body', as M is called, because the energy can be
partly dispersed in internal vibrations.

† In the last chapter we used the term *chain length* to refer to the number
of carbon atoms joined together in a linear hydrocarbon; e.g. in butane,
$CH_3CH_2CH_2CH_3$, the carbon chain is four atoms long. Unfortunately, the
same term is used in reaction kinetics to describe the number of times a
repetitive cycle of reactions occurs. Thus reaction 2 followed by reaction 3
is considered to be a unit of the chain reaction, and 'chain length' in this
context refers to the number of times reactions 2 and 3 are repeated before
the chain is terminated by reactions 4, 5, or 6.

reaction 3 is -23 kcal mole^{-1}. Notice that both these enthalpies of reaction are negative, i.e. the reaction is exothermic, heat being given out during the reaction. This means that as regards energy the reaction is going downhill; that is, it is a favourable process. Now let us compare chlorination with bromination:

$$Br_2 + h\nu \xrightarrow{1} 2\ Br\cdot$$

$$Br\cdot + CH_4 \xrightarrow{2} CH_3\cdot + HBr \quad \Delta H = +13\ \text{kcal mole}^{-1}$$

$$CH_3\cdot + Br_2 \xrightarrow{3} CH_3Br + Br\cdot \quad \Delta H = -26\ \text{kcal mole}^{-1}$$

(Only the chain-propagating steps are shown here.) It is plain that reaction 2 in bromination is an *endothermic* process, i.e. heat is absorbed during the reaction. On the other hand, reaction 3 is exothermic, as it was in chlorination. The overall process of converting one molecule of methane and one molecule of bromine into one molecule of methyl bromide and one molecule of hydrogen bromide is exothermic. Experimentally we find that if a mixture of methane and bromine are illuminated at room temperature, reaction takes place, but only very slowly. This reflects the fact that reaction 2 is an endothermic reaction, i.e. this part of that reaction is energetically an uphill process. In order that bromination of methane may occur at a reasonable rate, it is necessary to heat the reactants to provide the necessary energy.

Fluorination, on the other hand, is extremely rapid, even at low temperatures; the reason for this becomes apparent from the following equations:

$$F_2 + h\nu \xrightarrow{1} 2\ F\cdot$$

$$F\cdot + CH_4 \xrightarrow{2} CH_3\cdot + HF \quad \Delta H = -36\ \text{kcal mole}^{-1}$$

$$CH_3\cdot + F_2 \xrightarrow{3} CH_3F + F\cdot \quad \Delta H = -67\ \text{kcal mole}^{-1}$$

Here, both propagating steps are highly exothermic and the conversion of one molecule of methane into one molecule of methyl fluoride is accompanied by the liberation of 103 kcal. This massive release of energy together with the fact that the bond-dissociation energy of fluorine is only 37 kcal mole^{-1}, results in *thermal branching* (meaning that additional molecules of fluorine are dissociated thermally, so starting off new chains). It is easy to see that this thermal branching is a self-increasing process and ultimately fluorination results in an explosion unless a great excess of some inert gas such as nitrogen is also present to absorb the heat evolved.

In all these halogenation processes reaction 2 is the rate-determining step. We have argued that bromination proceeds only very slowly at room temperature because reaction 2 is endothermic. However, although chlorination is rapid at room temperature it is accelerated by raising the temperature; and even though fluorination is so rapid at room temperature, it becomes faster still if the temperature is raised. This suggests that although the reaction is exothermic it still requires a supply of energy before it will take place. We can illustrate this by the following scheme which represents three stages in the reaction:

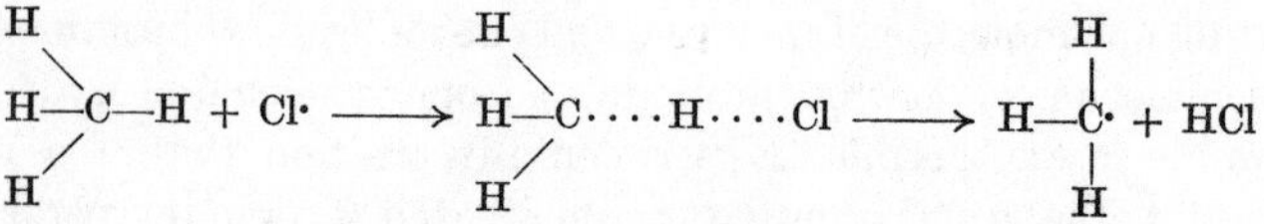

$$
\begin{array}{ccc}
\text{H} & \text{H} & \text{H} \\
\text{H}-\text{C}-\text{H} + \text{Cl}\cdot \longrightarrow & \text{H}-\text{C}\cdots\text{H}\cdots\text{Cl} \longrightarrow & \text{H}-\text{C}\cdot + \text{HCl} \\
\text{H} & \text{H} & \text{H}
\end{array}
$$

First we have a methane molecule and a chlorine atom; next a hydrogen atom half-bonded to a methyl radical and half-bonded to a chlorine atom; and finally a methyl radical and a molecule of hydrogen chloride. As the chlorine atom approaches the methane molecule there will be electronic repulsion which will increase as the chlorine atom approaches closer. Finally, the stage is reached when the electrons forming the carbon–hydrogen bond are uncoupled and the new bond is formed between the hydrogen atom and the chlorine atom. But let us consider the reverse process, i.e. the interaction between a methyl radical and a hydrogen chloride molecule. Here, again, as the methyl radical approaches the hydrogen chloride molecule it will be repelled, the repulsion increasing as the species come closer together. Thus, the intermediate species in the three-step reaction sequence above represents a state of high energy. This can be depicted by plotting the energy of the system against the reaction coordinate, the latter representing the progress of the reaction between one molecule of methane and one chlorine atom (Figure 1). The difference in energy between the initial state and the final state is equal to ΔH, the heat of reaction. The difference in energy between the initial state and the transition state is equal to E, the activation energy. This is the energy that must be supplied before the reaction occurs. Figures 2 and 3 represent, respectively, the

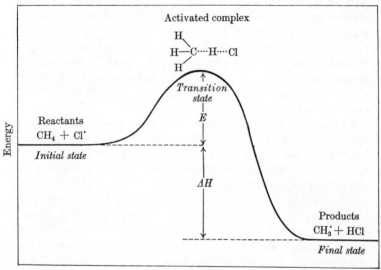

Reaction coordinate
Figure 1

potential energy situation in reaction 2 for bromination (an endothermic reaction) and in reaction 2 for fluorination (a highly exothermic reaction). Notice that in bromination ΔH is positive

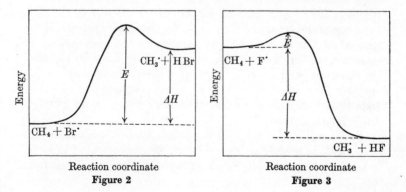

Reaction coordinate   Reaction coordinate
Figure 2   **Figure 3**

and the activation energy, E, is very large. In fluorination, on the other hand, ΔH is large and negative and the activation energy is very small. Reactions that involve only the making of bonds, such as the recombination of chlorine atoms (reaction 4 in the chlorination chain mechanism) have no activation energy and the rate of this reaction is independent of the temperature. All reactions which involve the breaking as well as the making of bonds have an activation energy, even though they are extremely exothermic as in the case of fluorination, and these reactions will all be accelerated by raising the temperature, no matter how fast they may be.

The rate of a chemical reaction depends upon the electronic energy situation, but also on the probability that the reactants will collide and, what is more, collide with an orientation relative to one another that enables them to react. When discussing the electronic energy situation as represented by Figures 2 and 3, we are considering a methane molecule and a halogen atom isolated in free space; but ordinary practice is concerned with a large number of methane molecules and a large number of chlorine atoms mixed together, and the rate of the reaction then depends upon the properties of the whole system. In any chemical reaction there is an energy barrier between the reactants and products; because we are always concerned with a large number of molecules with different rotational, vibrational, and translational degrees of freedom, the energy barrier we are concerned with is a *free energy* barrier.

A discussion on the significance of free energy is outside the scope of the present chapter. At present we will simply regard it as a composite term including both the electronic energy and the probability. It is only valid to consider the electronic energy in isolation, as was done above, when reactions occur by identical mechanisms, and even here the probability term may be important. For reactions that occur by different mechanisms their relative exothermicity or endothermicity can give no guide to their relative rates.

So far we have considered the chlorination of methane which can yield, as initial product, only one monochlorinated product, namely methyl chloride. Similarly there is only one product from the monochlorination of ethane, ethyl chloride. But with propane, two products are possible:

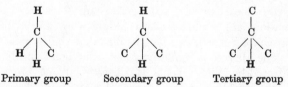

This is a very common situation in organic chemistry. Here, having a reaction from which more than one product is possible, we are interested to know which of the isomeric chloropropanes will be formed. From the discussion concerning heats of reactions, we should expect that the chlorine atom would abstract the most weakly bound hydrogen atom. In practice the reaction yields approximately equal amounts of the two propyl chlorides, but there are only two hydrogen atoms on the central carbon atom whereas there are six identical hydrogen atoms on the two terminal primary carbon atoms. (A CH_3 group is called a primary group, a CH_2 group is called a secondary group, and a CH group is called a tertiary group.) Generally, in saturated hydrocarbons primary carbon–hydrogen bonds are stronger than secondary bonds which are stronger than tertiary bonds. Thus a chlorine

Primary group   Secondary group   Tertiary group

atom abstracts the more weakly bound secondary hydrogen atoms in propane three times faster than it abstracts primary hydrogen. In bromination, reaction 2 is endothermic and the strength of the C—H bond which is being broken will have a much greater effect on the course of the reaction; as a result bromination is very much more selective. In bromination at 150°

the ratio 2-bromopropane:1-bromopropane is of the order of 30:1 (i.e. the rate of replacement of the hydrogen on the secondary carbon atom is approximately 90 times faster than the rate of replacement of a hydrogen atom on a primary carbon). In fluorination the reaction is highly exothermic and very unselective; slightly more 1-fluoropropane than 2-fluoropropane is obtained but only because the statistical probability of 3:1 in favour of primary attack outweighs the actual relative rates of attack which is only $1\frac{1}{2}$:1 in favour of the secondary position.

The only reactions discussed above for the aliphatic hydrocarbons are halogenations. The ordinary powerful chemical reagents, such as sulphuric acid, nitric acid, hydrochloric acid, sodium hydroxide, etc., have no effect on alkanes at normal temperatures. This is because they are ionic reagents and the C—H bond does not break ionically at all readily. Consider a molecule AB where the two atoms A and B are bound together by the sharing of a pair of electrons; this can break in three ways as depicted in the following diagram:

$$A:B \longrightarrow A^+ + :B^- \left.\begin{array}{l}\\\\\end{array}\right\} \textbf{Heterolysis } \text{giving ions}$$
$$A:B \longrightarrow A:^- + B^+$$
$$A:B \longrightarrow A\cdot + B\cdot \qquad \textbf{Homolysis } \text{giving free radicals}$$

Sulphuric acid and sodium hydroxide readily undergo heterolysis giving ions, and the common reactions of these reagents are ionic reactions. It was emphasized in the previous chapter that the carbon–hydrogen bond is non-polar, and does not undergo ionic reactions. It does, however, undergo **free-radical** reactions and the halogenations are examples of this. From what was said in the previous chapter it will also be apparent that the carbon–carbon bond in the alkanes is similarly a non-polar bond and likely to be unaffected by ionic reagents. It is because alkanes are unaffected by the normal ionic reagents that they are often described in textbooks as being chemically inert. In fact this is not really true. The alkanes are not attacked by ionic reagents but they react readily with free radicals and atoms. The normal combustion process by which, for example, petroleum is consumed in an internal combustion engine, is principally a free-radical process and the main constituents of petroleum are saturated hydrocarbons. Hydrocarbons are not inert substances but extremely reactive ones in the appropriate kind of reaction and this shows how important it is to understand the mechanism of any reactions discussed. Throughout this book we shall consider reactions, how they occur, and why.

Nomenclature

A halogen derivative is designated by taking the name of the hydrocarbon from which it is derived and preceding it by prefixes indicating the nature and number of the halogen atoms. Arabic numbers indicate the position(s) of the substituent(s). Three examples are given below:

$CH_3CH_2CH_2CH_2Cl$ 1-Chlorobutane
$CF_3CH_2CH_2CH_2CH_3$ 1,1,1-Trifluoropentane
$CH_3CHBrCH_2CHClCH_2CH_2F$ 2-Bromo-4-chloro-6-fluorohexane

Problems

1. Suggest a mechanism for the iodination of ethane, clearly distinguishing between initiation, propagation, and termination steps. The approximate bond-dissociation energies are: $D(H—I)$, 71 kcal mole^{-1}; $D(C—I)$, 50 kcal mole^{-1}; $D(I—I)$, 36 kcal mole^{-1}. On the basis of this information what would you predict about the feasibility of the iodination of ethane at room temperature?

2. Predict the principal product from the monobromination and monofluorination of butane and isobutane.

3

CHAPTER 3

The Carbon–Halogen Bond

The most important feature of the carbon–hydrogen bond is that it is completely non-polar.

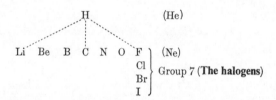

If we look again at the diagram of the first row of the periodic table, and remember that lithium hydride is polarized in the form Li^+H^- while hydrogen fluoride is polarized in the direction H^+F^-, we may expect the carbon–chloride bond to be polarized in the direction C^+Cl^-. In the first chapter we emphasized the fact that carbon does not readily form stable anions or cations: the carbon–chloride bond in methyl chloride is thus not ionized but only partly polarized as follows:

$$
\begin{array}{c}
\text{H} \\
\text{C}^{\delta+} \\
\text{H} \quad | \quad \text{Cl}^{\delta-} \\
\text{H}
\end{array}
$$

In the last chapter the lack of reactivity of alkanes towards ionic reactions such as sulphuric acid and sodium hydroxide was attributed to the fact that carbon–carbon and carbon–hydrogen bonds were non-polar. In *monohaloalkanes* (**alkyl halides**) we find that the carbon atom attached to halogen carries a small positive charge. Thus an alkyl halide is attacked by species with a negative charge, that is, by anions. The anion we are most familiar with is hydroxyl, OH^-. If a hydroxyl ion, OH^-, attacks the carbon atom of methyl chloride, then a chloride anion, Cl^-, will be ejected.

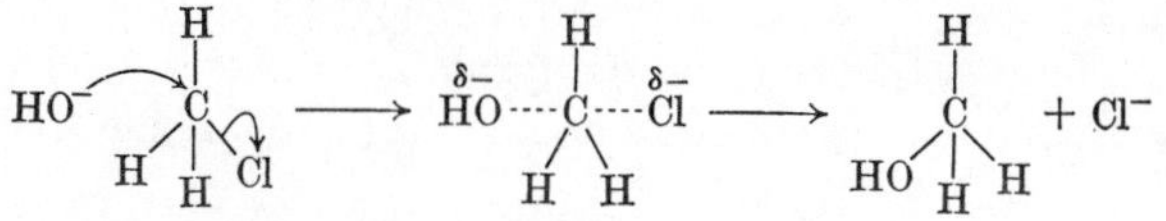

In the diagram the curved arrow from the minus sign on the OH ion to the carbon atom is to indicate that the hydroxyl anion provides a pair of electrons to form a new carbon–oxygen bond. The curved arrow from the bond between carbon and chlorine indicates that the two electrons in the carbon–chlorine bond are both to be donated to the chlorine atom to form a chloride anion. Next we have the activated complex which represents the hydroxyl ion coming in on one side of the carbon atom and the chloride anion departing from the other. In the activated complex the three bonds from carbon to hydrogen are approximately planar, at right angles to the plane of the paper. Finally we have the products of the reaction, methyl alcohol (or methanol) together with a chloride anion. This is a general reaction, so that others can be written, such as:

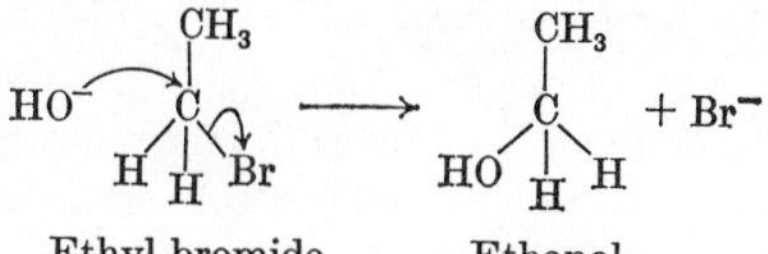

Ethyl bromide   Ethanol

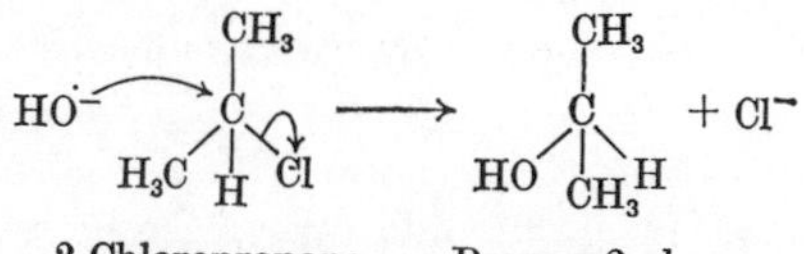

2-Chloropropane   Propan-2-ol

Here again curved arrows are used, so let us define what they represent. A curved arrow represents the *transfer of a pair of electrons* during a reaction process. In some older textbooks curved arrows represent partial donation or polarization of electrons in the ground state of a molecule, but in this text curved arrows will not be used in this fashion.

We began by saying that we should expect that the carbon atom attached to a halogen in an alkyl halide would be susceptible to attack by anions, and have shown that when the anion is a hydroxyl anion this leads to the formation of alcohols. Table 3.1 includes some of the common anions. Let us examine the halide

Table 3.1. Some common anions

Acid	Anion	Acid	Anion	Acid	Anion
HCl	Cl^-	HOH	HO^-	HCN	CN^-
HBr	Br^-	CH_3OH	CH_3O^-	HSH	SH^-
HF	F^-	C_2H_5OH	$C_2H_5O^-$	H_2SO_4	HSO_4^-
HI	I^-	CH_3COOH	CH_3COO^-	$HClO_4$	ClO_4^-

anions first. Since the halide anions are similar to one another we should expect the reaction between a fluoride anion and butyl chloride to be a reversible reaction yielding butyl fluoride and a chloride anion:

$$C_4H_9Cl + F^- \rightleftarrows C_4H_9F + Cl^-$$

Now we know from the previous chapter that the carbon–fluorine bond is stronger than a carbon–chlorine bond and we might therefore expect the reaction between a fluoride anion and butyl chloride forming butyl fluoride and a chloride anion to be exothermic. However, this argument does not take into account the extent to which the chloride and fluoride anions may be bound by the solvent. In practice a fluoride anion in aqueous solution is very tightly bound by water molecules. (Such binding of ions by a solvent is called *solvation*.) This solvation of a fluoride ion is so strong that the fluoride ion becomes extremely unreactive and no reaction could take place between an aqueous solution of sodium fluoride and butyl chloride. However, we should expect the reaction to take place in a solvent which binds (*solvates*) ions less readily and this is true for dry glycol (glycol has the structure $HOCH_2CH_2OH$). Thus butyl chloride can be converted into butyl fluoride by heating the former with potassium fluoride in dry glycol:

$$C_4H_9Cl + KF \xrightarrow[\text{glycol}]{\text{Dry}} C_4H_9F + KCl$$

Notice that the mechanism of this reaction is the same as that of the replacement of a chlorine atom by a hydroxyl:

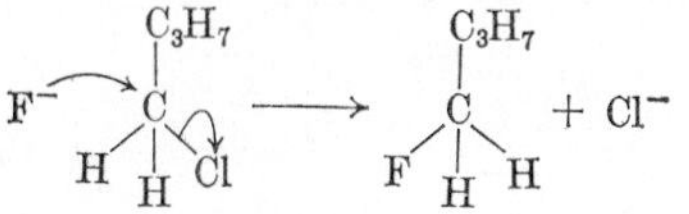

The replacement of chlorine by fluorine is an exothermic process, but that of chlorine by iodine would be endothermic (energetically an uphill reaction):

$$C_5H_{11}Cl + NaI \rightleftharpoons C_5H_{11}I + NaCl$$

Just as the reaction between butyl chloride and a fluoride anion is reversible, so a reaction between pentyl chloride and sodium iodide would be reversible. But on energetic grounds we should expect the equilibrium to lie very much on the side of pentyl chloride and sodium iodide; that is, the equilibrium constant, K, is much less than 1:

$$K = \frac{[C_5H_{11}I][NaCl]}{[C_5H_{11}Cl][NaI]}$$

But K is a constant, so that if sodium chloride (NaCl) is removed by some process, then more pentyl iodide must be formed to maintain the equilibrium. Sodium iodide is soluble in acetone, but sodium chloride is not. If we reflux pentyl chloride and sodium iodide in acetone, then, even though at the start the equilibrium is very much in favour of the reactants, as soon as any sodium chloride is formed it will be precipitated, and ultimately the reaction is forced in the direction of pentyl iodide and sodium chloride.

Now, in the third column of Table 3.1, the first acid listed is water and we have already considered the reaction between an alkyl halide and a hydroxyl anion. Just as the hydrogen atom in water can formally be replaced by a methyl (CH_3) group to give methanol (CH_3OH), so can the hydrogen atom in the hydroxyl anion be replaced by an alkyl radical to give, in the case of methyl, a methoxide anion (CH_3O^-) and of ethyl an ethoxide anion ($C_2H_5O^-$). These anions react in the same fashion as the hydroxyl anion:

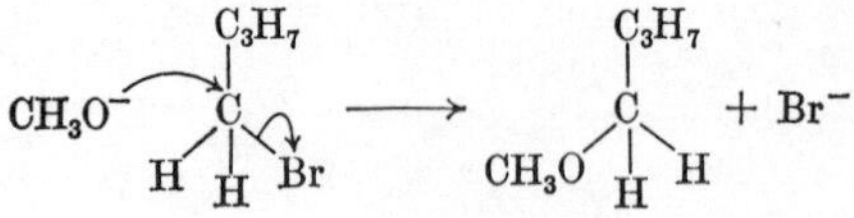

Butyl methyl ether

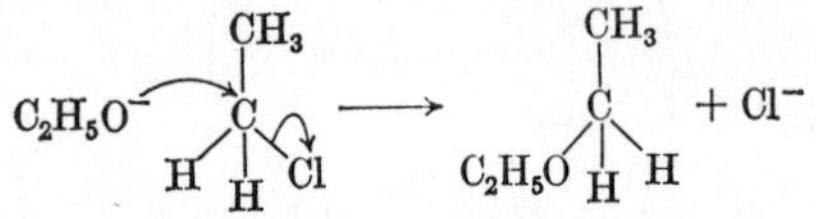

Diethyl ether

These reactions are quite general.

The hydrogen sulphide anion reacts similarly (the product of this reaction is called a mercaptan, or according to systematic nomenclature, a thiol):

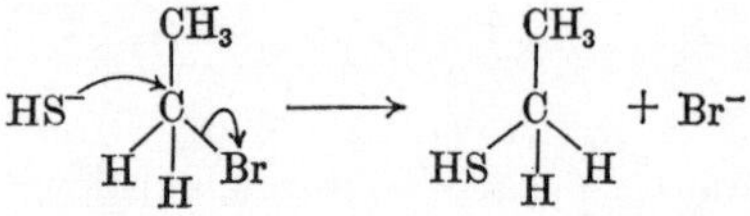

Ethanethiol

The cyanide anion also displaces a halogen in a similar reaction and the product in this case, an alkyl cyanide, is of particular interest because a new carbon–carbon bond is formed.

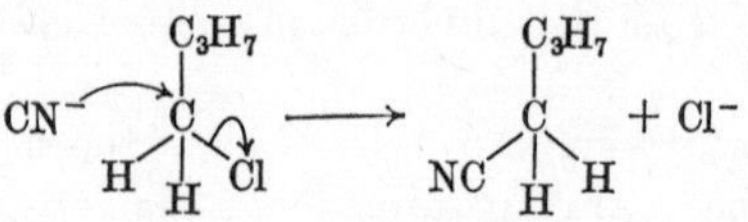

Butyl cyanide

This is an extremely important reaction in the synthesis of organic compounds and can be generalized in the following form:

$$K^+CN^- \quad R - X \xrightarrow[\text{Solvent}]{C_2H_5OH} RCN + K^+X^-$$

where R represents any alkyl group, potassium cyanide a source of cyanide ions, and X any halogen.

The acetate anion also displaces a halogen anion:

$$Na^+CH_3COO^- \quad C_3H_7 - I \longrightarrow CH_3COOC_3H_7 + Na^+I^-$$

Propyl acetate

This still leaves two anions from Table 3.1 whose displacement reaction has not yet been described. The reason for this is that these are anions of strong acids while the others (except the halogen anions) are anions of weak acids. Perchloric acid is a very strong acid because the perchlorate anion firmly holds the pair of electrons which form the oxygen–hydrogen bond in undissociated acid. The stronger the acid the more firmly the anions hold this electron pair. All the displacement reactions described involve the donation of an electron pair to the slightly electropositive carbon atom attached to the halogen atom in the alkyl halide. The stronger the acid from which the anion is derived, the less readily will that anion donate its electron pair. In general, therefore, it is only the anions of weak acids which will displace halogen anions from the alkyl halides.*

We have been careful to emphasize that it is the electron pair which the incoming anion donates; thus we could depict the displacement reaction as:

$$[H:\ddot{O}:]^- \quad C \quad Cl \longrightarrow H:\ddot{O}: C + [:\ddot{C}l:]^-$$

If this is correct, it is the availability of an electron pair which is important rather than the negative charge; thus a compound such

---

* This discussion should not be taken to imply anything about the rate of substitution reaction with different ions. The readiness of an anion to donate a pair of electrons is only one of a number of factors (e.g. we have already discussed the strength of the new bond being formed and also the solvation of the anion).

as ammonia which has an electron pair readily available for donation would undergo this kind of reaction:

$$H_3N: \overset{|}{\underset{|}{\overset{}{C}}} \overset{}{\underset{Cl}{\frown}} \longrightarrow H_3\overset{+}{N} \overset{|}{\underset{}{\overset{C}{\diagdown}}} + Cl^-$$

Now why does water, which has two non-bonded pairs of electrons on the oxygen atom, not displace the halogen anion in the same way? The answer is that ammonia is a strong base while water is only a weak one. Nitrogen is less electronegative than oxygen, and the lone pair on the nitrogen atom in ammonia is readily available for bonding with a proton whereas the two pairs of electrons on the more electronegative oxygen are not. Let us now look further into the reaction of ammonia with an alkyl halide:

$$\overset{\frown}{NH_3} \quad C_2H_5\overset{\frown}{-}Br \longrightarrow C_2H_5NH_3^+ + Br^-$$

$$C_2H_5NH_3^+ + NH_3 \rightleftharpoons C_2H_5NH_2 + NH_4^+$$
$$\text{Ethylamine}$$

The first product from the reaction of ammonia with ethyl bromide is ethylammonium bromide but in the presence of an excess of ammonia we may expect the proton on the ethylammonium ion to equilibrate with ammonia molecules to yield free ethylamine and the ammonium cation. Now ethylamine has a non-bonded pair of electrons, just as ammonia has, so we may expect further reactions:

$$C_2H_5\overset{\frown}{N}H_2 \quad C_2H_5\overset{\frown}{-}Br \longrightarrow (C_2H_5)_2NH_2^+ + Br^-$$

$$(C_2H_5)_2NH_2^+ + NH_3 \rightleftharpoons (C_2H_5)_2NH + NH_4^+$$
$$\text{Diethylamine}$$

The product of this reaction, diethylamine, also has a non-bonded pair of electrons and we may expect further reaction:

$$(C_2H_5)_2\overset{\frown}{N}H \quad C_2H_5\overset{\frown}{-}Br \longrightarrow (C_2H_5)_3NH^+ + Br^-$$

$$(C_2H_5)_3NH^+ + NH_3 \rightleftharpoons (C_2H_5)_3N + NH_4^+$$
$$\text{Triethylamine}$$

The product of this further reaction, triethylamine, still has a pair of non-bonded electrons and we must therefore expect yet a further reaction still:

$$(C_2H_5)_3\overset{\frown}{N} \quad \overset{\frown}{C_2H_5}\overset{\frown}{-}Br \longrightarrow (C_2H_5)_4N^+ \ Br^-$$

Tetraethylammonium bromide

The product of this last reaction, tetraethylammonium bromide, no longer has a pair of non-bonded electrons and the reaction can now proceed no further. The product of the first reaction, ethylamine, is a **primary amine.** That of the second stage, diethylamine, is a **secondary amine,** and that of the third stage of the reaction, triethylamine, is a **tertiary amine**, and the product of the final stage, tetraethylammonium bromide, is a **quaternary salt.** In general the reaction between an alkyl halide and ammonia will lead to a mixture of all four products.

We have now discussed at some length reactions in which a species with a pair of non-bonded electrons attacks the slightly electropositive carbon atom in an alkyl halide and ejects the halogen atom as a halide anion:

$$Y: + \ R—X \longrightarrow Y\cdots R\cdots X \longrightarrow Y—R + X:$$

We began this discussion by saying that carbon did not readily form a carbonium ion and that, although the carbon–halogen bond was polarized, no free ions were formed. In solvents of high dielectric constant, separation of charge is facilitated and we can expect a greater degree of ionization. Under these circumstances and provided that the anion comes from a very strong acid and that the alkyl group contains substituents to stabilize a positive charge, ionization may occur to a very limited degree. The difficulties in forming a carbonium ion suggests that it is a high-energy species, i.e. a most reactive entity. Once formed, it will react extremely rapidly with any species able to donate an electron pair. We can thus visualize a two-step process:

$$R\overset{\frown}{-}X \underset{\text{Fast}}{\overset{\text{Slow}}{\rightleftharpoons}} R^+ + X^-$$

$$R^+ + Y^- \xrightarrow{\text{Fast}} R—Y$$

Substitution of an alkyl halide by this mechanism is rare among primary alkyl halides and most common with tertiary alkyl halides. This is because the stability of aliphatic carbonium ions is in the order tertiary more stable than secondary more stable than primary, with a methyl ion least stable. An example of this reaction is hydrolysis of *tert*-butyl bromide:

$$
\begin{array}{c}
CH_3 \\
| \\
CH_3 - C - Br \\
| \\
CH_3
\end{array}
\underset{Fast}{\overset{Slow}{\rightleftharpoons}}
\begin{array}{c}
CH_3 \\
| \\
CH_3 - C^+ \\
| \\
CH_3
\end{array}
+ \; Br^-
$$

$$
\begin{array}{c}
CH_3 \\
| \\
CH_3 - C^+ \\
| \\
CH_3
\end{array}
+ \; OH^-
\xrightarrow{Fast}
\begin{array}{c}
CH_3 \\
| \\
CH_3 - C - OH \\
| \\
CH_3
\end{array}
$$

tert-Butyl alcohol

Now, the free carbonium has only *a transient existence*. It is most important to appreciate the difference between these carbonium ions which have a transient existence in a reaction process from the stable ions such as hydroxonium, chloride, etc. Displacement reactions involving a carbonium ion are much less common than the displacement reactions discussed earlier in this chapter. The former occur when the alkyl halide is tertiary or when the displaced anion, instead of being a halogen is an anion of a stronger acid such as a sulphonic acid. Further discussion of this subject is outside the scope of the present chapter.

However, all these reactions have been concerned with replacement of a halogen atom by some species carrying a pair of non-bonded electrons. Such species are called *nucleophiles*, because they have an electron pair which is seeking a nucleus. These displacement reactions are therefore called *nucleophilic substitutions* and are denoted by the symbol S_N. We have discussed two mechanisms for this nucleophilic substitution. In the first, the nucleophile attacks the slightly electropositive carbon of the alkyl halide with its lone pair of electrons and ejects the halogen anion. The rate of such a reaction depends upon the concentration of the nucleophile and upon the concentration of the alkyl halide. It is a bimolecular reaction:

$$\text{Rate} = k_2[\text{Y}^-][-\overset{|}{\underset{|}{\text{C}}}-\text{X}]$$

In the second, less common mechanism the alkyl halide first ionizes to a very limited extent to give a carbonium ion, which once formed reacts extremely rapidly with the anion. The rate of this reaction therefore depends only upon the concentration of the alkyl halide and is independent of the concentration of the anion. It is a unimolecular reaction.

$$\text{Rate} = k_1[-\overset{|}{\underset{|}{\text{C}}}-\text{X}]$$

The common and more important reaction involving the push–pull transition state are called S_N2 reactions because two species are involved in the rate-determining step. The less common reaction involving a transient carbonium ion involves only one species in the rate-determining step and is therefore called an S_N1 reaction.

Problem

1. What reaction, if any, would you expect between ethyl bromide and the following species? Indicate any peculiarities about the conditions necessary for reaction.

(a) OH^-	(d) CN^-	(g) F^-
(b) H_3O^+	(e) NH_3	(h) $CH_3CH_2O^-$
(c) $Cl\cdot$	(f) HNO_3 (aqueous)	(i) I^-

CHAPTER 4

Alcohols and the OH Group
and Amines and the NH₂ Group

The first chapter showed how alcohols and amines could be formally considered to be built up by replacing the hydrogen atoms of water and ammonia by CH_3 groups and then replacing the hydrogen atoms on the CH_3 group by further CH_3 groups; e.g. from water

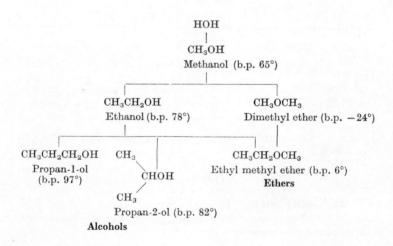

and from ammonia:

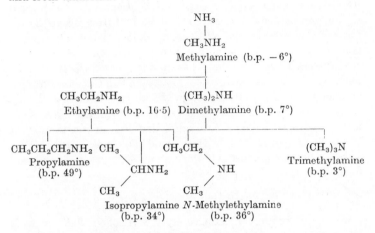

NH₃
|
CH₃NH₂
Methylamine (b.p. − 6°)

CH₃CH₂NH₂   (CH₃)₂NH
Ethylamine (b.p. 16·5)   Dimethylamine (b.p. 7°)

CH₃CH₂CH₂NH₂   CH₃   CH₃CH₂   (CH₃)₃N
Propylamine   \CHNH₂   \NH   Trimethylamine
(b.p. 49°)   /   /   (b.p. 3°)
                 CH₃   CH₃
            Isopropylamine N-Methylethylamine
               (b.p. 34°)   (b.p. 36°)

Before considering the chemistry of the OH and NH₂ groups attached to a carbon chain, we will briefly discuss the characteristic chemical properties of water and ammonia.

Among the hydrides of the elements of the first row of the periodic table, starting at the right with Group 7, there is hydrogen fluoride, a low-boiling extremely acidic liquid; in Group 6, water, boiling at 100°; in Group 5, ammonia, a low-boiling extremely basic liquid; and finally in Group 4, methane, a very low-boiling gas, inert to ionic reactions. In methane all the eight electrons in the outer shell of the carbon atom are shared with hydrogen. In ammonia there is one pair of non-bonded electrons. In water there are two pairs and in hydrogen fluoride three pairs of non-bonded electrons in the outer shell. The non-bonded electrons in hydrogen fluoride are so tightly held by the fluorine atom that they are not available for forming bonds; so that under no normal circumstances will hydrogen fluoride accept an additional proton to form H_2F^+; on the other hand, the proton in hydrogen fluoride itself can escape readily. Oxygen is less electronegative than fluorine, and water is a very much weaker acid (i.e. a proton escapes from the water molecule much less readily) than hydrogen fluoride; on the other hand, the two non-bonded pairs of electrons are available for forming bonds, and water is a much stronger base than hydrogen fluoride so that H_3O^+ is readily formed. Ammonia is only a very weak acid and under no normal circumstances does it donate one of its hydrogen atoms in the form of a proton; on the other hand, its lone pair of electrons is readily available for forming a bond, and ammonia is a very strong base. Finally, methane has no non-bonded electrons in its outer shell so that the carbon–hydrogen bond is non-polar in character as already discussed. In the alkyl halides the carbon–halogen bond was slightly polarized, but very much less so than in the hydrogen halides. We should therefore expect the extent of polarization in the alkyl–oxygen bond in alcohols and the alkyl–nitrogen bond in amines to be very small, i.e. there is *no* tendency for methanol to ionize as follows:

$$CH_3OH \longrightarrow CH_3^+ + OH^-$$

The main features of the chemistry of alcohols and amines is therefore not so much concerned with the carbon–oxygen bond in alcohols or the carbon–nitrogen bond in amines but rather with the reactions of the OH and NH_2 groups. In the first chapter and in the above diagram, we have formally regarded methanol as water in which one hydrogen atom had been substituted by a CH_3 group, and methylamine as ammonia in which one hydrogen atom had been substituted by a methyl group. We were solely concerned with indicating in a purely formal way how organic compounds can be regarded as being built up from familiar inorganic hydrides. The chemistry of methyl chloride has very little in common with the chemistry of hydrogen chloride and in this instance the relationship between methyl chloride and hydrogen chloride is purely formal. On the other hand, the chemistry of methanol and methylamine have a great deal in common with the chemistry of water and ammonia.

One of the most striking properties of water is its high boiling point (b.p. 100°). Comparing this with the boiling point of ammonia ($-30°$), methane ($-162°$), or hydrogen sulphide (b.p. $-61°$) shows how anomalous it is. One of the reasons for this high boiling point, and indeed one of the reasons for many of the other peculiarities of water, is the presence of hydrogen bonding. We can picture hydrogen bonding very qualitatively in the following way. One molecule of water readily transfers the proton to another molecule of water, so forming two ions OH^- and H_3O^+. Although this 'autoprotolysis' occurs only to a very small extent it does indicate that the oxygen–hydrogen bond in water must be strongly polarized in the direction $O^{\delta-}$—$H^{\delta+}$. We can thus visualize a weak bond between the oxygen atom of one molecule and the hydrogen atom of another. We make no attempt at the moment to describe the exact nature of this bonding beyond indicating that it may be of a polar nature:

Clearly in an alcohol the opportunities for hydrogen bonding are reduced by half, but nonetheless it is still important and affects the physical properties of alcohol quite considerably. For example, the boiling points of simple alcohols are as follows: methanol, 65°; ethanol, 78·5°; propanol, 97°. On the other hand, the boiling point of dimethyl ether, CH_3OCH_3, is $-24°$ and that of diethyl ether, $C_2H_5OC_2H_5$, is $+35°$. Alcohols are thus all liquids, their boiling points increasing with the length of the carbon chain. The lower members of the series methanol, ethanol, and propanol are completely miscible with water. The butanols are very soluble in water, but the higher members become increasingly less soluble as the number of carbon atoms increases. This gradation of properties is common to all homologous series (cf. Chapter 1).

The great feature of the chemistry of water is its amphoteric nature:

$HA + H_2O$	$\rightleftharpoons$	H_3O^+	$+ A^-$	Water as a base
		Hydroxonium ion		
$HA + C_2H_5OH$	$\rightleftharpoons$	$C_2H_5OH_2^+$	$+ A^-$	Alcohol as a base
		Ethyloxonium ion		
$B + H_2O$	$\rightleftharpoons$	$HB^+ +$	OH^-	Water as an acid
			Hydroxyl ion	
$B + C_2H_5OH$	$\rightleftharpoons$	$HB^+ +$	$C_2H_5O^-$	Alcohol as an acid
			Ethanolate ion	

The acid dissociation constant of water is 3×10^{-16}. Ethanol is a somewhat weaker acid, with $K_a = 10^{-18}$. The acidity of different alcohols differs only slightly though, in general, primary alcohols (RCH_2OH) are stronger acids than secondary alcohols (R_2CHOH), while tertiary alcohols (R_3COH) are the weakest. Since ethanol is a weaker acid than water, the sodium salt of ethanol cannot be made by treating it with sodium hydroxide; the easiest method for preparing sodium ethoxide is the direct reaction between sodium and ethanol. Sodium reacts with water so violently that the hydrogen evolved in the reaction may even ignite and explosions occur.

$$2\,Na + 2\,H_2O \longrightarrow 2\,Na^+ + 2\,OH^- + H_2 \uparrow$$
$$(NaOH = Sodium\ hydroxide)$$

With alcohol the reaction is very much less violent and alcohol can safely be treated directly with sodium:

$$2\,Na + 2\,C_2H_5OH \longrightarrow 2\,Na^+ + 2\,C_2H_5O^- + H_2 \uparrow$$
$$(NaOC_2H_5 = Sodium\ ethoxide)$$

The sodium salts of alcohols, called sodium **alkoxides**, are crystalline but they are very hygroscopic and hydrolyze in water to yield sodium hydroxide and the alcohol. The reaction of alkoxide anions with alkyl halides to yield ethers and a chloride anion was described in the last chapter:

$$RO^- \;\; R' \!-\! Cl \xrightarrow[\text{Solvent}]{\text{ROH}} ROR' + Cl^-$$

Alkoxide   Alkyl   Ether
 ion   halide

These reactions are carried out by using the alcohol from which the alkoxide ion is derived as solvent.

We noticed that the reaction of sodium with alcohol was exactly the same as the reaction of sodium with water except that it was much less violent. This is quite general; when an alcohol undergoes the same type of reaction as water, the alcohol reaction is usually much slower. Alcohol can replace water in many situations; for example, salts which crystallize with water of crystallization often, but not always, also crystallize with alcohol of crystallization. The hydroxyl group of an oxygen acid can be replaced by the alkoxyl group of an alcohol to yield an ester. These are reactions which can actually be carried out, but for the moment we shall consider them as purely formal steps in the same way that we have already considered the building-up of the carbon chain. Thus, with sulphuric acid we have:

$$\begin{array}{c} HO \\ \diagdown \\ SO_2 + CH_3OH \longrightarrow \\ \diagup \\ HO \end{array} \qquad \begin{array}{c} CH_3O \\ \diagdown \\ SO_2 + H_2O \\ \diagup \\ HO \end{array}$$

$$\text{Sulphuric acid} \qquad\qquad\qquad \text{Methyl hydrogen sulphate}$$

$$\begin{array}{c} CH_3O \\ \diagdown \\ SO_2 + CH_3OH \longrightarrow \\ \diagup \\ HO \end{array} \qquad \begin{array}{c} CH_3O \\ \diagdown \\ SO_2 + H_2O \\ \diagup \\ CH_3O \end{array}$$

$$\text{Dimethyl sulphate}$$

In a similar way a molecule of water can be eliminated from nitric acid and alcohol, giving ethyl nitrate and water:

$$HO-NO_2 + C_2H_5OH \longrightarrow C_2H_5O-NO_2 + H_2O$$
$$\text{Nitric acid} \qquad\qquad \text{Ethyl nitrate}$$

Nitrate esters are explosive: glycerol trinitrate is manufactured under the name 'nitroglycerine'; a mixture of glycerol trinitrate and kieselguhr (finely divided SiO_2) constitutes dynamite.

$$\begin{array}{c} CH_2OH \\ | \\ CHOH + 3\ HONO_2 \longrightarrow \\ | \\ CH_2OH \end{array} \qquad \begin{array}{c} CH_2ONO_2 \\ | \\ CHONO_2 + 3\ H_2O \\ | \\ CH_2ONO_2 \end{array}$$

$$\text{Glycerol} \qquad\qquad\qquad \text{Glyceryl trinitrate}$$

A particularly important class of esters is that formed between alcohols and organic acids by elimination of water, e.g. ethyl acetate formed by elimination of water from ethanol and acetic acid:

$$C_2H_5OH + HO-COCH_3 \rightleftharpoons C_2H_5O-COCH_3 + H_2O$$
$$\text{Ethanol} \quad \text{Acetic acid} \qquad\quad \text{Ethyl acetate}$$

Notice that this is a reversible reaction; in other words, ethyl acetate reacts with water to regenerate ethanol and acetic acid.

4

This particular reaction is a classical example of a reversible reaction.

$$K = \frac{[CH_3COOC_2H_5][H_2O]}{[CH_3COOH][C_2H_5OH]}$$

The equilibrium constant, K, at room temperature is here approximately 4. The reaction of an alcohol and an acid to form an ester is called *esterification* and the example shows that one way of preparing ethyl acetate in good yield would be to remove the water. The reverse reaction, i.e. the conversion of ethyl acetate and water into ethanol and acetic acid, is called *hydrolysis* and can be achieved by using a large excess of water. These reactions are normally carried out in the presence of a strong acid or base as catalyst, as will be discussed further in Chapter 8 (organic acids).

We began this chapter by emphasizing that the carbon–oxygen bond in alcohols was not very polar and that the principal reactions of alcohols were concerned with the OH group. We also mentioned how in the presence of a strong acid an alcohol can accept a proton, i.e. can behave as a base:

$$CH_3OH + HCl \rightleftharpoons CH_3\overset{+}{O}H_2 + Cl^-$$
Methyloxonium ion

Now although the carbon–oxygen bond in methanol is only very slightly polar, the carbon–oxygen bond in the methyloxonium ion is clearly much more polar and it is possible for an anion to attack the carbon atom:

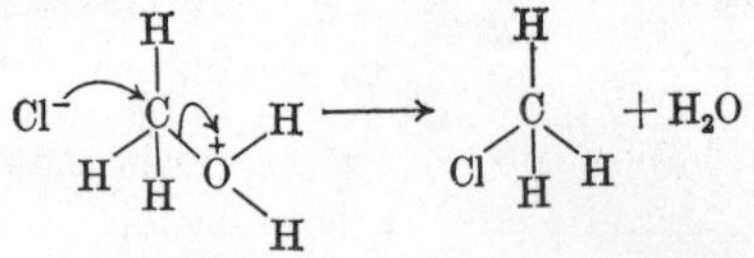

It would appear from the above two reactions that it would be possible to convert methanol into methyl chloride by treatment with hydrochloric acid. In fact this reaction does not occur in aqueous hydrochloric acid and is quite slow even when hydrogen chloride gas is dissolved in the methanol. However, by using phosphorus chlorides, PCl_3 or PCl_5, the water formed in the reaction is completely removed at the same time as the hydrogen chloride is generated. This is represented (rather crudely) in the equation:

$$3 \text{ ROH} + \text{PCl}_3 \longrightarrow 3 \text{ RCl} + \text{H}_3\text{PO}_3$$

Another way of obtaining the same result is to treat the alcohol with the sodium halide and sulphuric acid, the function of the acid being both to generate hydrogen chloride and so protonate the alcohol, and to remove the water as it is formed; for example, ethyl bromide can be prepared from ethanol, sodium bromide, and sulphuric acid:

$$\text{C}_2\text{H}_5\text{OH} + \text{Na}^+ \text{Br}^- + 2 \text{H}_2\text{SO}_4 \longrightarrow$$
$$\text{C}_2\text{H}_5\text{Br} + \text{Na}^+ + \text{H}_3\text{O}^+ + 2 \text{HSO}_4{}^-$$

In discussing the reactions of alcohols, we have emphasized the importance of the hydroxyl group rather than the carbon–oxygen bond, excepting only the reactions discussed directly above in which displacement can occur with oxonium ion. Ethers have two carbon–oxygen bonds and no oxygen–hydrogen bond, and, in general, the reactions of ethers are similar to those of the alkanes (saturated hydrocarbons) in that they do not react readily with ionic species. However, just as it is possible to add an additional proton to the oxygen in an alcohol, so it is possible to add a proton to the oxygen in an ether molecule to give an oxonium ion:

Diethyl ether   Diethyloxonium iodide

The oxonium is then capable of undergoing nucleophilic substitution, just as in the case of the oxonium ion from an alcohol:

Diethyloxonium iodide   Ethyl iodide   Ethanol

Here the diethyloxonium ion is written in a form that illustrates how the nucleophilic substitution is identical in type with the reactions discussed in the previous chapter.

Ammonia is a gas (b.p. $-33°$). The lowest number of the alkylamine series is methylamine, CH_3NH_2, which is a gas at normal temperature (b.p. $-7°$). The other lower alkylamines are low-boiling liquids: dimethylamine, $(CH_3)_2NH$, b.p. $7°$; trimethylamine, $(CH_3)_3N$, b.p. $4°$; and ethylamine, $C_2H_5NH_2$, b.p. $17°$.

Ammonia is a weak base; it is completely miscible with water with which it reacts to form an ammonium cation and a hydroxyl anion:

$$NH_3 + H_2O \rightleftharpoons NH_4^+ + OH^-$$

The alkylamines behave similarly although they are slightly stronger bases than ammonia; e.g. ammonia, $K_b = 2 \times 10^{-5}$; methylamine, $K_b = 4 \times 10^{-4}$; dimethylamine, $K_b = 5 \times 10^{-4}$, where

$$K_b = \frac{[RNH_3^+][OH^-]}{[RNH_2]}$$

The alkylamines form stable crystalline salts with the mineral acids corresponding to the salts that ammonia forms, such as ammonium chloride or ammonium sulphate.

Amine salts		
	$CH_3NH_3^+ \ Cl^-$	m.p. $226°$
	$C_2H_5NH_3^+ \ Br^-$	m.p. $160°$
	$(C_2H_5)_3NH^+ \ Cl^-$	m.p. $254°$

All these basic properties of the amines are due to the fact that the non-bonded pair of electrons on the nitrogen atom is readily available to yield a bond. We have already discussed the importance of this in a different kind of reaction in connexion with the reactions of the carbon–halogen bond. In the last chapter we discussed how the lone pair on the nitrogen atom of an amine would attack the carbon in an alkyl halide and eject the halide ion, as shown at the top of the next page.

The nitrogen–hydrogen bond in ammonia or an alkylamine, unlike that in the ammonium ion or quaternary ammonium salt, does not separate readily as a proton, i.e. ammonia and alkylamines are very weak acids. Sodamide, $NaNH_2$, can be made by dissolving sodium in liquid ammonia, and similarly the sodium salts of amines can be prepared by the direct interaction of metallic sodium with the amine. But since alkylamines are stronger bases than ammonia, they must be even weaker acids, and this reaction only occurs very slowly.

$$2\,RNH_2 + 2\,Na \longrightarrow 2\,R\bar{N}HNa^+ + H_2$$

Just as the OH group in oxygen acids can be replaced by the RO group of alcohols so it can by the RNH or the R_2N group, to yield amides; for example we can formally eliminate a molecule of water from methylamine and acetic acid to yield *N*-methylacetamide:

$$CH_3NH_2 + HOCOCH_3 \longrightarrow CH_3NHCOCH_3 + H_2O$$
N-Methylacetamide

At present we notice only the actual existence of these compounds; they will be discussed again in Chapter 8.

The Concept of a Functional Group

The last two chapters have surreptitiously introduced a basic concept in organic chemistry. This is the concept of a **functional group.** Particularly in the present chapter we have discussed the reactions of the OH group and the NH or the NH₂ groups, and have frequently disregarded the carbon chain. In the first chapter we discussed how long carbon chains can be built up; in the next chapter we described how the hydrocarbon chains were inert to ionic reactions. Thus an alkylamine reacts with water to form an alkylammonium ion and a hydroxyl ion, regardless of the length or complexity of the alkyl chain or chains attached to the nitrogen atom. Similarly, an alcohol reacts with sodium to form a sodium alkoxide and hydrogen, regardless of the length or complexity of the carbon chain attached to the oxygen. For these reactions we treat the OH group and the NH or NH_2 groups as the 'functional groups' of the molecule. This concept is somewhat old-fashioned and can be confusing; nonetheless the idea that for ionic reactions, at least, only the functional group of an organic molecule is important can be useful. Even with the reactions of organic halides which concern reaction at a carbon atom, it can still be useful to regard the halogen as a functional group because the remainder of the carbon chain is usually unaffected by ionic reactions. For example, in the reaction between 1-chlorobutane and sodium ethoxide to yield butyl ethyl ether only the carbon chain in the butyl group is completely unchanged by the reaction:

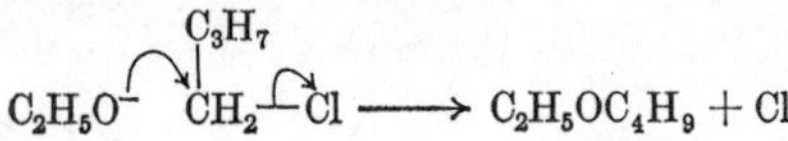

$$C_2H_5O^- \quad \overset{C_3H_7}{\underset{}{CH_2}} \quad Cl \longrightarrow C_2H_5OC_4H_9 + Cl^-$$

Nomenclature

The concept of a functional group is a cardinal principle in systematic nomenclature. Alcohols are given the name of the hydrocarbon from which they are derived, followed by the suffix '-ol'; e.g.

Methanol	CH_3OH
Ethanol	C_2H_5OH
Hexanol	$C_6H_{13}OH$

Cyclohexanol

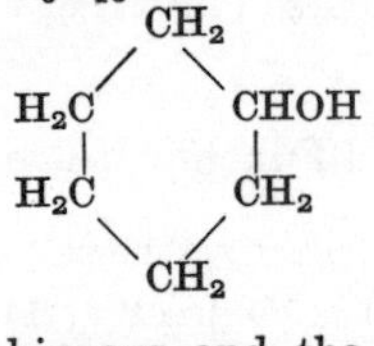

$$\begin{array}{ccc} & CH_2 & \\ H_2C & & CHOH \\ H_2C & & CH_2 \\ & CH_2 & \end{array}$$

The word hexanol is clearly ambiguous and the position of the hydroxyl group is indicated by an arabic number; e.g.

$CH_3CH_2CH_2OH$	Propan-1-ol
CH_3CHCH_3	Propan-2-ol
$\overset{\mid}{OH}$	

For alcohols with less than five carbon atoms, semi-systematic names are frequently used. In the following scheme the systematic name is given with the semi-systematic name in square brackets.

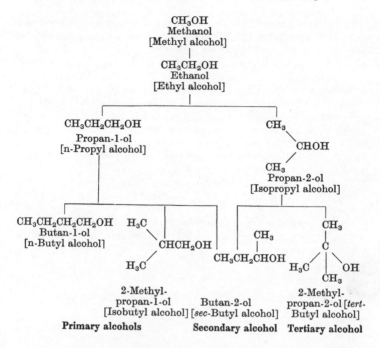

Alcohols are often classified as primary, secondary, or tertiary according to atoms attached to the carbon atom adjacent to the hydroxyl group (RCH_2OH, primary; R_2CHOH, secondary; R_3COH, tertiary; where R is any alkyl radical).

A halogen-substituted alcohol is numbered so that the lowest number is given to the principal function, e.g.

$$CH_3CHCH_2CH—CHCH_3$$
$$\quad\;\; | \qquad\quad | \quad |$$
$$\quad\;\; Cl \qquad\; CH_3\; OH$$

5-Chloro-3-methylhexan-2-ol

Ethers can be regarded as hydrocarbons in which one or more hydrogen atoms are replaced by alkoxy groups. Thus

$$CH_3OCH_3 = \text{Methoxymethane}$$

However, the older nomenclature by which the above compound is called dimethyl ether is still in general use, e.g.

$$CH_3CH_2OCH_3 = \text{Methoxyethane or Ethyl methyl ether}$$

The nomenclature of amines is somewhat exceptional. The correct systematic name for $CH_3CH_2NH_2$ would be ethanamine, but by long established custom radical names are attached to the ending amine, giving ethylamine for this compound. $(C_2H_5)_2NH$ is diethylamine and $(C_2H_5)_3N$ is triethylamine. Notice how nomenclature depends on the chemical properties. The principal reactions of alcohols involve breaking the oxygen–hydrogen bond and CH_3OH has quite different chemical properties to CH_3OCH_3 so that they receive quite different names (methanol for the former, and methoxymethane for the latter). On the other hand, the reactions of amines depend principally on the availability of a non-bonded pair of electrons on the nitrogen so that some kind of name is given to CH_3NH_2, $(CH_3)_2NH$, and $(CH_3)_3N$ (methylamine, dimethylamine, and trimethylamine). For compounds containing quinquevalent nitrogen the ending '-mine' is changed to 'mmonium', i.e. $(CH_3CH_2)_4N^+I^-$ = tetraethylammonium iodide. The name changes as the chemical properties change. A tertiary amine with different alkyl chains is named as a derivative of the longest or most complex chain.

$$CH_3(CH_2)_5N \overset{\displaystyle (CH_2)_3CH_3}{\underset{\displaystyle CH_2CH_3}{<}} \qquad N\text{-Butyl-}N\text{-ethylhexylamine}$$

The italic capital N indicates that the substituent radicals are attached to the nitrogen. A compound containing both a hydroxy group and an amino group is regarded as an amino alcohol rather than a hydroxy amine, e.g.

$$\underset{\displaystyle NH_2 \qquad\qquad OH}{CH_3CHCH_2CH_2CHCH_3} \qquad 5\text{-Aminohexan-2-ol}$$

Problems

1. What reaction, if any, would you expect between (1) ethanol and (2) ethylamine with the following reagents:

(a) HCl (b) Na (c) H_2O (d) $NaNH_2$ (e) C_2H_5Br

2. What reaction, if any, would you expect between diethyl ether, $C_2H_5OC_2H_5$, and the following reagents:

(a) HBr (b) Cl_2 (c) Na

CHAPTER 5

Elimination Reactions and the Formation of the Carbon–Carbon Double Bond

We have represented the attack of a nucleophile such as the ethoxide ion, $C_2H_5O^-$, on an alkyl halide as follows:

| Ethoxide anion | Methyl bromide | Methyl ethyl ether |

When the alkyl halide is a methyl halide this is the only reaction that can occur but with the ethyl halides and the majority of longer-chain alkyl halides another reaction can occur simultaneously; for example:

$$C_2H_5O^- + CH_3CH_2Br \nearrow C_2H_5OC_2H_5 + Br^- \quad \textbf{Nucleophilic substitution}$$
$$\searrow CH_2{=}CH_2 + C_2H_5OH + Br^- \quad \textbf{Elimination}$$

In the second of these reactions the elements of hydrogen bromide have been eliminated from ethyl bromide and this is therefore called an *elimination reaction* in contrast to the nucleophilic

43

substitution described previously. This reaction can be represented as follows:

Ethanol   **Ethylene**   Bromide
                          anion

Let us examine this reaction sequence very carefully. A pair of non-bonded electrons on the ethoxide anion is donated to one of the hydrogen atoms of the ethyl bromide, forming a new oxygen–hydrogen bond and ultimately a molecule of ethanol. The pair of electrons that originally formed the bond between the hydrogen atom and the carbon atom in the ethyl bromide are now transferred into the bond between the two carbon atoms. This means that the first carbon atom still retains eight electrons in its outer shell, and in order that the second carbon atom likewise only retains eight electrons in its outer shell the two electrons in the carbon–bromine bond must be transferred to the bromine atom to yield the bromine anion. We are thus left with a carbon–carbon bond in which four electrons are shared instead of two.

Before discussing the elimination any further, we must consider briefly the new type of molecule that has been formed in this reaction. All the chemical bonds between two atoms in the previous chapters have been formed by the sharing of two electrons. This type of bond can be called a **single bond**. In ethylene the bond between the two carbon atoms is formed by the sharing of four electrons and this type of bond may reasonably be called a **double bond**. We shall see that the double bond undergoes many interesting reactions, but for the moment we will only consider its geometry. An important feature of the single bond, emphasized previously, is that there is free rotation between atoms along the axis of the bond and thus there are no positional isomers of, e.g., 1,2-dichloroethane. The bonds in ethane subtend 109° 28′ to each other. In ethylene all the atoms lie in one plane, the bonds subtending exactly 120° to each other. While it is possible to rotate atoms around a single bond this is not possible in a double bond. Thus there are two 1,2-dichloroethylenes: *cis* and *trans*.

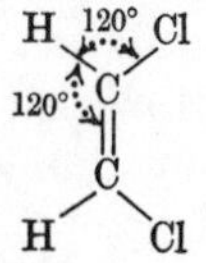

cis-Dichloroethylene 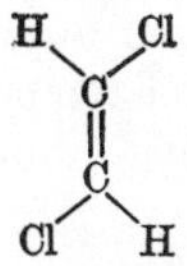   *trans*-Dichloroethylene

cis and *trans* isomers are distinct compounds. Their physical properties are often very different (e.g. boiling points, melting points, etc.) and although their chemical reactions are necessarily similar they differ fairly substantially in certain cases.

Ethylene is the simplest example of an *unsaturated compound* (i.e. one having a multiple bond). The reason for this name will be apparent in the next chapter when we come to consider the

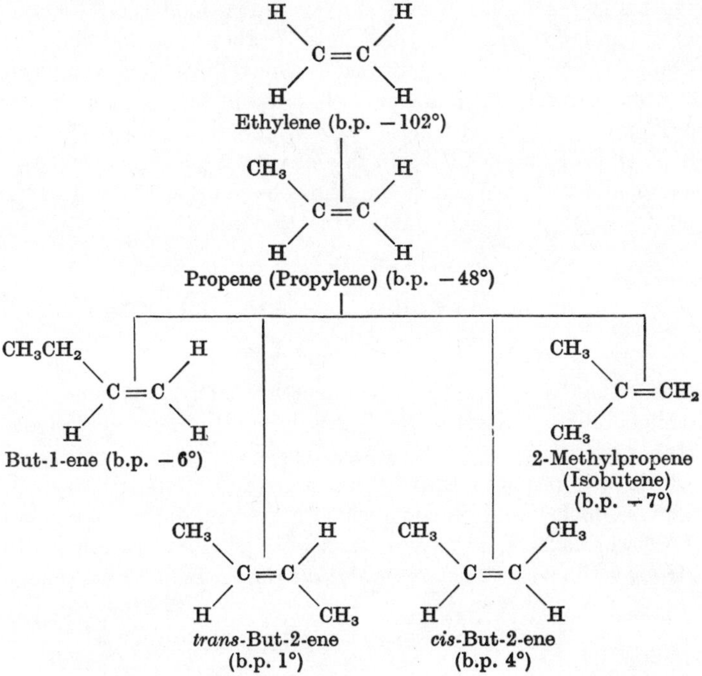

Ethylene (b.p. −102°)

Propene (Propylene) (b.p. −48°)

But-1-ene (b.p. −6°)

2-Methylpropene
(Isobutene)
(b.p. −7°)

trans-But-2-ene
(b.p. 1°)

cis-But-2-ene
(b.p. 4°)

reactions of these compounds. The generic name for the unsaturated hydrocarbons is **alkene** (cf. alkane for saturated hydrocarbons). We can build up from ethylene a series of alkenes by
replacing hydrogen atoms severally by methyl groups, exactly
as we built up the alkanes (see p. 45). How many hydrocarbons
can you draw with the formula C_5H_{10} (cf. Problem 1)?

We will return to the chemical reactions of the alkenes in the
next chapter but at present we must consider eliminations in
more detail. The first point to notice is that in Chapter 3 we said
that the reaction between sodium ethoxide and ethyl bromide led
to diethyl ether and now we have said that it may also lead to
ethylene. Great stress is usually laid on the percentage yield
obtained in an organic reaction. Students sometimes disparagingly
describe practical organic chemistry as cookery. When carrying
out a preparation you are given a very detailed 'recipe' describing
exactly how many grams of this and how many grams of that you
must mix together and how long you must heat them together,
very similar to the directions in a cookery book for making a
cake. The reasons why the directions have to be so explicit and why
you have to record your yield is because in the reaction of most
organic compounds with most reagents more than one reaction path
is possible. In order to obtain the maximum yield of any desired
compound, very particular conditions have to be adhered to. Let
us look again at the elimination reaction as we have described it:

Notice that this process is almost exactly analogous to bimolecular
nucleophilic substitution, the S_N2 reaction; we therefore designate
this elimination as an $E2$ reaction. There are various nucleophiles
which will promote the S_N2 reaction and similarly there are
various nucleophilic reagents which will promote the $E2$ reaction.
The two reactions usually occur side by side and in general the
stronger the base the more important the $E2$ reaction becomes.

Strong bases   Weak bases
$$NH_2^- > OC_2H_5^- > OH^- > OCOCH_3^-$$
    $E2$ S_N2

The structure of the alkyl halide also helps to determine which reaction predominates. The more branched the alkyl halide, the more likely the *E*2 reaction.

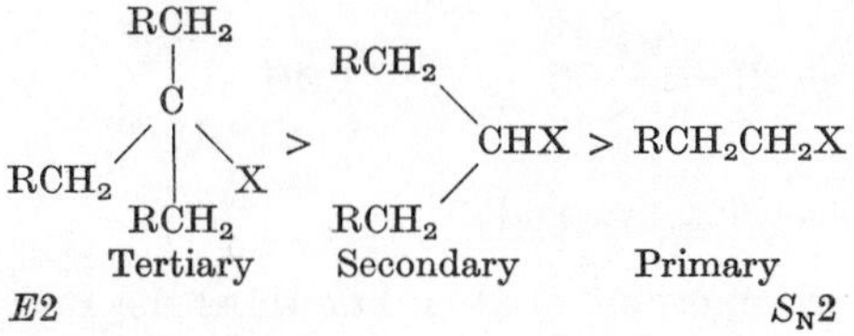

The R in the above diagram can be H or any alkyl group.

With the above information we can now consider the best way in which to prepare methyl isopropyl ether, $CH_3OCH(CH_3)_2$ Suppose that 2-iodopropane was treated with sodium methoxide in methanol solution; from the above discussion we would expect the main products to be methanol, propene, and sodium iodide:

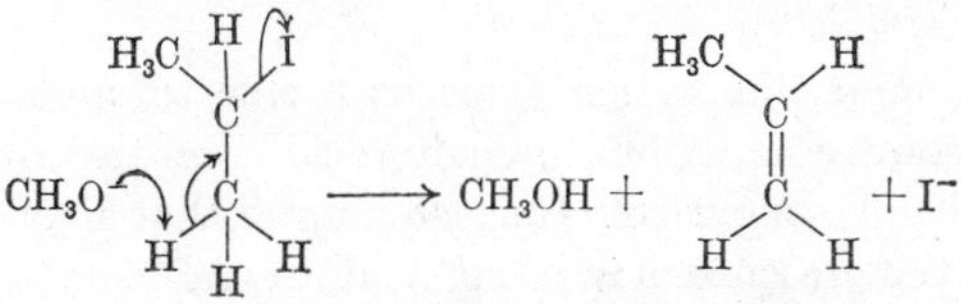

If instead methyl iodide was treated with sodium isopropoxide the principal product would be the desired ether:

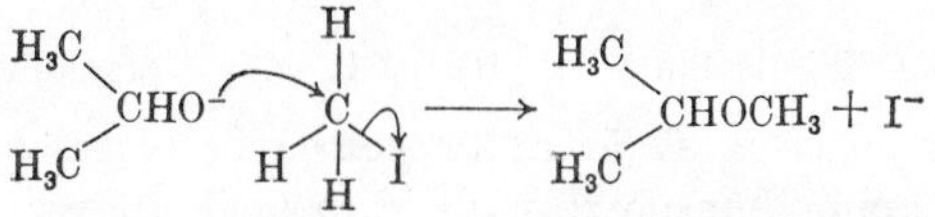

Methyl isopropyl
ether

In the eliminations described so far, the halide ions are called the *leaving group*. A good leaving group, i.e. a leaving group that facilitates elimination, is one which on elimination either yields a very stable ion (e.g. the halide ions already described), or else yields a stable molecule. Examination of the quaternary ammonium salts discussed in the previous two chapters shows that it is possible to eliminate a tertiary amine molecule from the quaternary salt:

$$HO \overset{\curvearrowleft}{\;} \overset{H}{\underset{H}{R-C}} \overset{\curvearrowright}{-CH_2-} \overset{+}{N} \overset{CH_3}{\underset{CH_3}{-CH_3}} \xrightarrow[\text{Aq. soln.}]{\text{Heat}} HOH + \overset{R}{\underset{H}{\diagup}} C=CH_2 + N(CH_3)_3$$

Quaternary ammonium hydroxide

This is a very important reaction known as the **Hofmann elimination**. It is a quite general reaction and cycloheptyltrimethylammonium hydroxide can be decomposed to yield cycloheptene, trimethylamine, and water:

Cycloheptyltrimethylammonium   Cycloheptene
              hydroxide

The Hofmann elimination gives us a clue to another type of very important elimination, namely, acid-catalysed dehydration of an alcohol. We know from the last chapter that alcohols behave as bases in the presence of a strong acid, to yield an oxonium ion:

$$\overset{R}{\underset{H}{\diagup}} \overset{H}{\underset{H}{\diagdown}} H-C-C-O \quad + HA \longrightarrow H-C-C-O^+ \quad + A^-$$

RCH$_2$CH$_2$OH   Alcohol   RCH$_2$CH$_2\overset{+}{O}$H$_2$ Oxonium ion

The oxonium ion is structurally very closely related to the quaternary ammonium hydroxide discussed above and elimination is therefore to be expected:

This dehydration of alcohols by strong acids is both common and important. Sometimes the reaction can be facilitated by making the acid derivative of the alcohol, i.e. the ester, and heating this. For example, ethanol can be dehydrated directly by sulphuric acid or alternatively ethyl hydrogen sulphate can be prepared at low temperatures, and this on heating yields ethylene and regenerates sulphuric acid.

$$CH_3CH_2OH + H_2SO_4 \underset{}{\overset{0°C}{\rightleftharpoons}} CH_3CH_2OSO_3H + H_2O$$
Ethyl hydrogen
sulphate
(Ester)

$$CH_3CH_2OSO_3H \xrightarrow{\text{Heat}} CH_2{=}CH_2 + H_2SO_4$$

The esters of acetic acid can be pyrolysed at 400°C to yield olefins:

$$RCH_2CH_2OH + HOCOCH_3 \rightleftharpoons RCH_2CH_2OCOCH_3 + H_2O$$
Acetic acid   Acetate (Ester)

$$RCH_2CH_2OCOCH_3 \xrightarrow[400°C]{\text{Pyrolysis}} RCH{=}CH_2 + HOCOCH_3$$

At 400° other kinds of decomposition are likely to set in and for this reason a more useful reaction is the **Tschugaev** reaction in which **xanthate** esters are pyrolysed.

$$RCH_2CH_2OH + CS_2 \xrightarrow{\text{NaOH}} RCH_2CH_2OCS_2{}^- + Na^+$$
Sodium xanthate
ester

$$RCH_2CH_2OCS_2{}^- \overset{\frown}{} CH_3{-}I \longrightarrow RCH_2CH_2OCS_2CH_3 + I^-$$
Methyl xanthate
ester

$$RCH_2CH_2OCS_2CH_3 \xrightarrow[200°C]{\text{Pyrolysis}} RCH{=}CH_2 + COS + CH_3SH$$

The Tschugaev reaction, and possibly the ester decompositions, are reactions which probably involve the molecule 'biting its own tail', e.g.:

In the eliminations we have discussed so far the reaction has been initiated by the attack of an anion (or by a nucleophilic 'tail' of the same molecule). These reactions therefore correspond to S_N2 substitutions and we call them *E*2 reactions. Just as there are substitution reactions initiated by the ionization of the reacting molecule so there are elimination reactions initiated in the same way; i.e. the rate-determining step of the process involves the departure of the leaving group, and not the attack by a nucleophile as in the *E*2 reactions. Tertiary butyl halides undergo S_N1 rather than S_N2 displacements; analogously they undergo *E*1 elimination rather than *E*2 elimination:

The rate of both these reactions depends only on the concentration of the tertiary butyl chloride

Alkenes are also formed from vicinal dihaloalkanes by a variety of reactions. If, for example, 2,3-dibromobutane is treated with sodium iodide in acetone, instead of getting the expected 2,3-diiodobutane, but-2-ene is formed:

$$IBr + I^- \longrightarrow I_2 + Br^-$$

This reaction is usually represented as shown, i.e. as an $E2$ reaction in which the iodide anion abstracts Br^+ from the dibromide. Two adjacent halogen atoms can also be removed by treatment with metals such as zinc:

This reaction undoubtedly goes by exactly the same process as an $E2$ reaction.

Nomenclature

Unsaturated, unbranched acyclic hydrocarbons having one double bond are named by replacing the ending '-ane' of the corresponding saturated hydrocarbon by the ending '-ene'. If there are two or more double bonds, the ending will be '-adiene', '-atriene', etc. The chain is so numbered to give the lowest possible numbers to the double bonds; e.g.

$$CH_3CH_2CH_2CH_2CH{=}CH_2 \quad \text{Hex-1-ene}$$
$$CH_3CH_2CH_2CH{=}CHCH_3 \quad \text{Hex-2-ene}$$
$$CH_3CH{=}CHCH_2CH{=}CH_2 \quad \text{Hexa-1,4-diene}$$
$$CH_2{=}CHCH{=}CHCH{=}CH_2 \quad \text{Hexa-1,3,5-triene}$$

The generic name of these hydrocarbons is **alkene** (alkadiene, alkatriene, etc.).

Monocyclic compounds are named in the same way, e.g.

Cyclopentene   Cyclohexa-1,3-diene

Problems

1. How many alkenes with molecular formula C_5H_{10} can you draw ? (Include *cis* and *trans* isomers.)

5

2. Suggest reaction sequences for the following transformations:

(a) $CH_3CH_2Br \longrightarrow CH_2{=}CH_2$

(b)

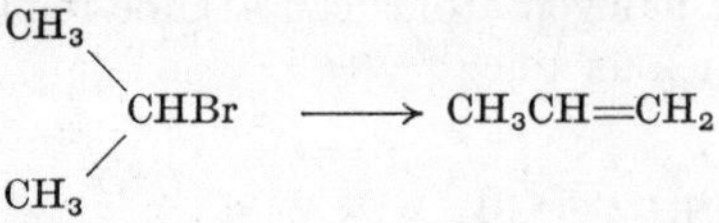

$$\begin{array}{c} CH_3 \\ \diagdown \\ CHBr \\ \diagup \\ CH_3 \end{array} \longrightarrow CH_3CH{=}CH_2$$

(c)

$$\begin{array}{c} CH_3 \\ \diagdown \\ CHBr \\ \diagup \\ CH_3 \end{array} \longrightarrow \begin{array}{c} CH_3 \\ \diagdown \\ CHOCH_3 \\ \diagup \\ CH_3 \end{array}$$

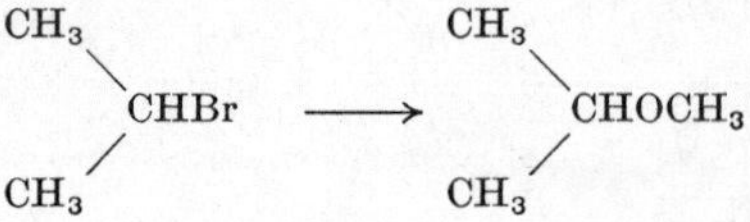

Addition Reactions:
to the Carbon–Carbon Double Bond

The energy required to break a carbon–carbon single bond is about 83 kcal mole^{-1}:

$$\overset{|}{\underset{/}{C}}\diagdown\underset{|}{\underset{/}{C}}\diagup \longrightarrow \overset{|}{\underset{/}{C}}\cdot + \cdot\underset{|}{\underset{/}{C}} \qquad \Delta H \approx +83 \text{ kcal mole}^{-1}$$

The uncoupling of one of the pairs of electrons in a double bond, however, only requires about 63 kcal:

$$\diagdown_{/}C{=}C\diagdown^{/} \longrightarrow -\underset{\bullet}{C}-\underset{\bullet}{C}- \qquad \Delta H \approx +63 \text{ kcal mole}^{-1}$$

It follows that 'addition reactions' are very exothermic processes.

$$CH_2{=}CH_2 + Br_2 \longrightarrow CH_2BrCH_2Br \quad \Delta H \approx -26 \text{ kcal mole}^{-1}$$
$$CH_2{=}CH_2 + H_2 \longrightarrow CH_3CH_3 \qquad \Delta H \approx -30 \text{ kcal mole}^{-1}$$

The above equations indicate that the addition of bromine or of hydrogen to ethylene is an exothermic process, i.e. it is downhill energetically. This does not mean, however, that either of these reactions will occur in the fashion described in the above equations. A mixture of gaseous ethylene and gaseous hydrogen in a flask would remain unchanged indefinitely, and even a mixture of gaseous bromine and gaseous ethylene in a completely clean flask in the dark would remain unchanged for considerable time. In Chapter 2 we saw that, although the chlorination of methane was an exothermic process, methane and chlorine do not react until light is shone on the gaseous mixture. All we learn from knowing that a reaction is very exothermic is that if we can find a way of initiating it, it is likely to continue readily.

Addition reactions to double bonds, i.e.:

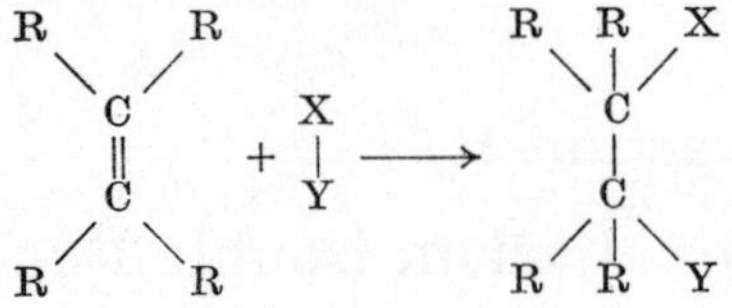

can go by four different mechanisms.

1. Electrophilic addition (very common and important for hydrocarbon olefins):

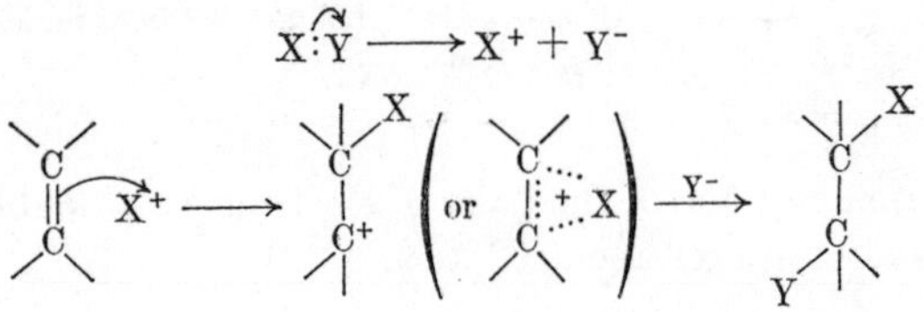

$$X = H, Br, NO_2, \text{etc.}$$

X^+ is called an *electrophile* because it carries a positive charge and is seeking electrons. Compare this with the definition of a nucleophile in Chapter 3, p. 28. An electrophile need not necessarily carry a positive charge but it must be a species which seeks electrons (e.g. BF_3). In a similar way not all nucleophiles possess a negative charge (e.g. $R_3N:$). In the above reaction sequence one of the pairs of electrons in the carbon–carbon double bond is donated to the electrophile. If X^+ is a proton, a new carbon–hydrogen bond is formed, but for other electrophiles we have a triangular structure with dotted lines from the two carbon atoms to X. This is to represent that the electrophile is not attached specifically to one carbon atom but is bonded to some extent to both. There is good evidence that in electrophilic additions to carbon–carbon double bonds a bridged intermediate complex is formed. The same is not true for other types of additions.

2. Nucleophilic addition (uncommon for hydrocarbon olefins):

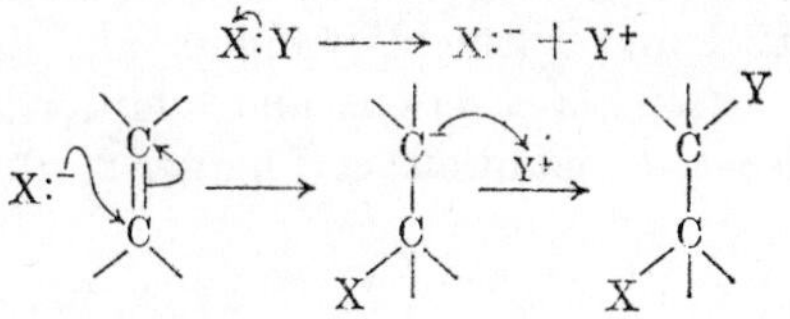

Nucleophilic addition does not normally occur with hydrocarbon olefins and we shall, therefore, not be discussing this kind of addition further in this chapter; but in subsequent chapters we shall show that for carbon–oxygen double bonds it is a very important reaction.

3. Free-radical addition:

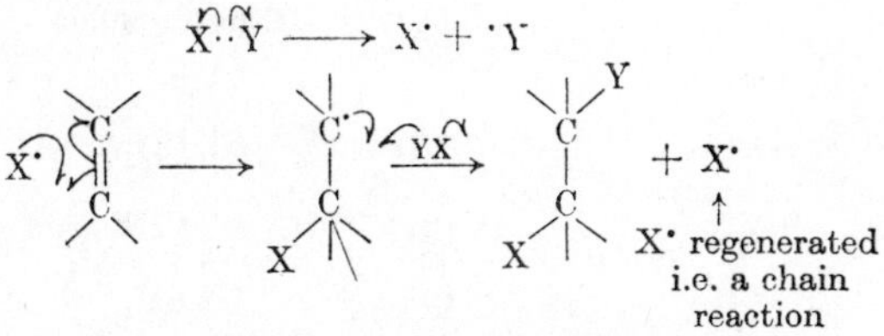

(X = Cl, Br, RO, etc.)

In the above scheme, we have introduced a new symbolism. In Chapter 3 we introduced the use of a curved arrow with a full head to represent the transfer of a pair of electrons from one nucleus to another (⌢). We now introduce a curved arrow with only half a head (⌢). This half-headed arrow is used to represent the *transfer of a single electron*, from one nucleus to another.

4. Four-centre reaction:

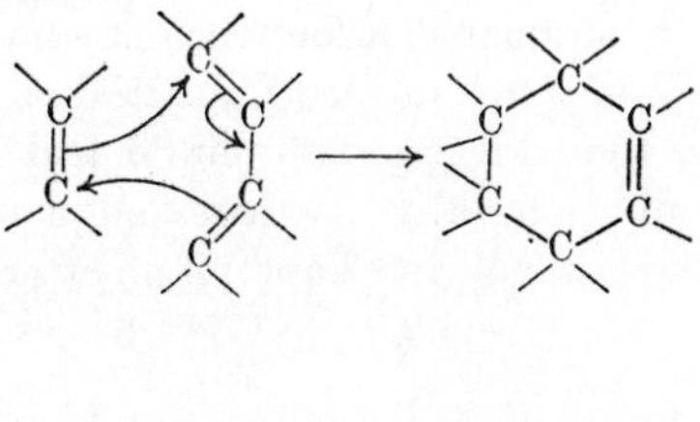

The term 'four-centre reaction' refers to a reaction in which four nuclei undergo valency changes more or less simultaneously.

The additions 1 and 2 (the electrophilic and the nucleophilic additions) are *heterolytic* reactions and addition 3 (free-radical addition) is a *homolytic* addition (cf. Chapter 2, p. 18).

Electrophilic Additions

a. *Mineral acids*

Mineral acids add across carbon–carbon double bonds in the hydrocarbon olefins:

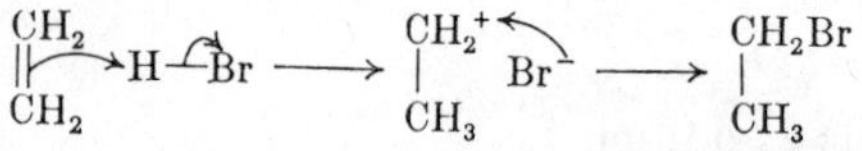

$$\begin{array}{c} CH_2 \\ \| \\ CH_2 \end{array} H\!-\!Br \longrightarrow \begin{array}{c} CH_2^+ \\ | \\ CH_3 \end{array} Br^- \longrightarrow \begin{array}{c} CH_2Br \\ | \\ CH_3 \end{array}$$

Ethyl bromide

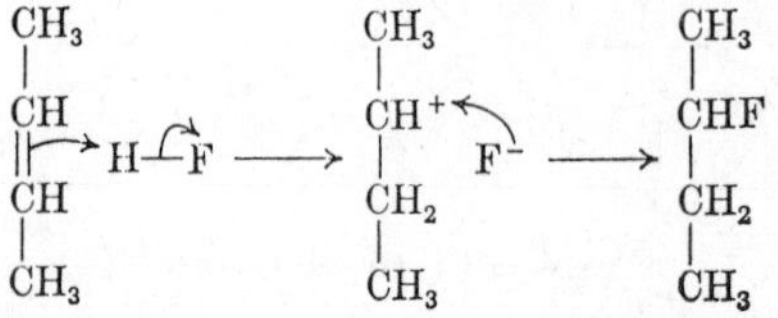

$$\begin{array}{c} CH_3 \\ | \\ CH \\ \| \\ CH \\ | \\ CH_3 \end{array} H\!-\!F \longrightarrow \begin{array}{c} CH_3 \\ | \\ CH^+ \\ | \\ CH_2 \\ | \\ CH_3 \end{array} F^- \longrightarrow \begin{array}{c} CH_3 \\ | \\ CHF \\ | \\ CH_2 \\ | \\ CH_3 \end{array}$$

2-Fluorobutane

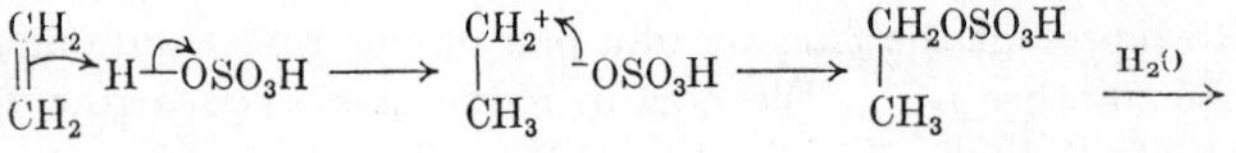

$$\begin{array}{c} CH_2 \\ \| \\ CH_2 \end{array} H\!-\!OSO_3H \longrightarrow \begin{array}{c} CH_2^+ \\ | \\ CH_3 \end{array} OSO_3H \longrightarrow \begin{array}{c} CH_2OSO_3H \\ | \\ CH_3 \end{array} \xrightarrow{H_2O}$$

Ethyl hydrogen sulphate
(Ester)

$$CH_3CH_2OH + H_2SO_4$$

The last of the above reactions, that of ethylene with sulphuric acid, is a very important industrial process. Ethanol used to be prepared solely by fermentation but the demand now far exceeds the possible supply by this means. Industrial alcohol is therefore also prepared by the addition of sulphuric acid to ethylene. The product of this addition, ethyl hydrogen sulphate, is an ester of sulphuric acid and ethanol. In Chapter 4 an ester was defined as a molecule of an acid from which the elements of water had been replaced by the elements of ethanol; this reaction is, in general, reversible, so that if ethyl hydrogen sulphate is treated with an excess of water, sulphuric acid and ethanol will be formed.

b. *Addition of halogens*

Bromine and chlorine add in a heterolytic fashion if the reaction is carried out in the liquid phase in the dark.

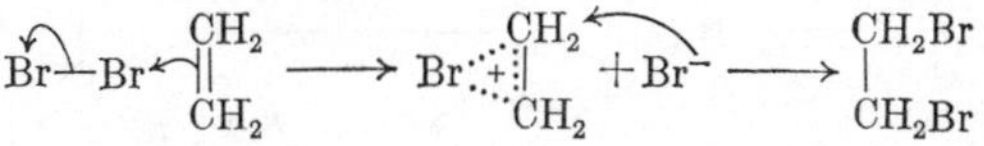

1,2-Dibromoethane

We shall see below that bromine and chlorine can also add by a homolytic process and fluorine adds only by a homolytic reaction.

c. *Addition of 'hypohalous acids'*

When bromine or chlorine is dissolved in water, a solution called bromine water or chlorine water is obtained and this solution contains some hypohalous acid:

$$Br_2 + H_2O \rightleftharpoons BrOH + HBr$$

The experimental fact is that a hydrocarbon olefin, treated with the solution, adds the elements of the hypohalous acid. However, there is very good experimental evidence to show that the reaction does not involve addition of the hypohalous acid itself but involves the following mechanism:

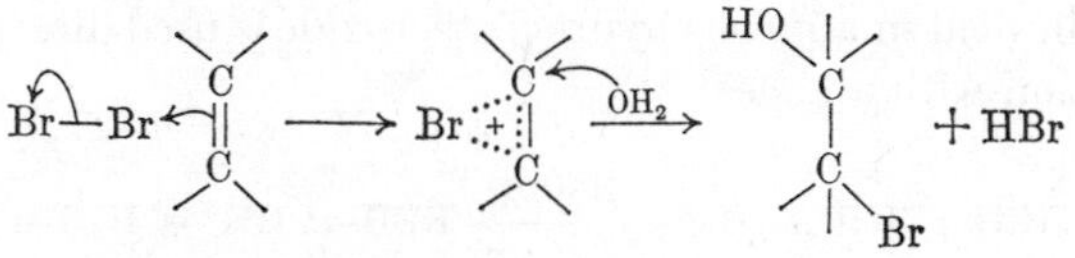

If the olefin is treated with a solution of bromine in ethanol, the products of the reaction are the 2-bromo ether, or if the reaction is carried out in an aqueous solution containing another anion then the product contains the other anion, as shown in the following equations:

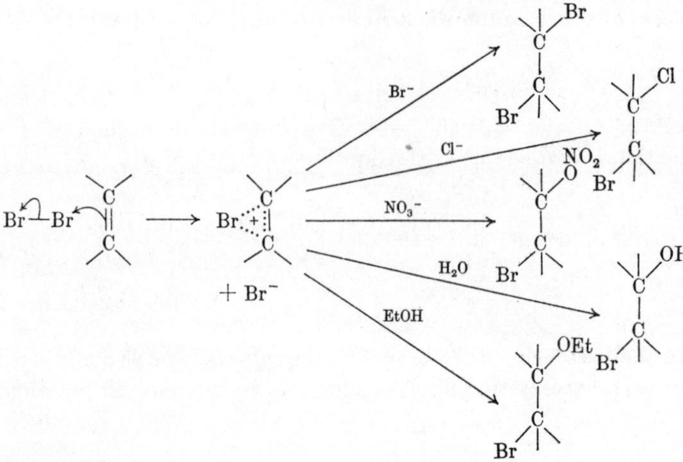

d. Addition of peroxy acids

When a carboxylic acid is treated with a solution of hydrogen peroxide the —OH group is replaced by an —OOH group. The product of this reaction is called a peroxy acid.

$$CH_3CO\text{—}OH + H_2O_2 \rightleftharpoons CH_3CO\text{—}O_2H + H_2O$$

Acetic acid   Peracetic acid

$$HCO\text{—}OH + H_2O_2 \rightleftharpoons HCO\text{—}O_2H + H_2O$$

Formic acid   Performic acid

In practice the peroxy acid is not isolated. The solution of the carboxylic acid in aqueous hydrogen peroxide is used directly, e.g. for reaction with alkenes:

$$RCH\text{=}CHR' + H_2O_2 \xrightarrow{\text{HCOOH}} RCH\text{—}CHR' + H_2O$$

$$\underset{\text{Epoxide}}{\overset{\diagdown\!O\!\diagup}{}}$$

The product of this reaction is a cyclic ether, called an *epox-*

ide. The mechanism of the addition is of an electrophilic character:

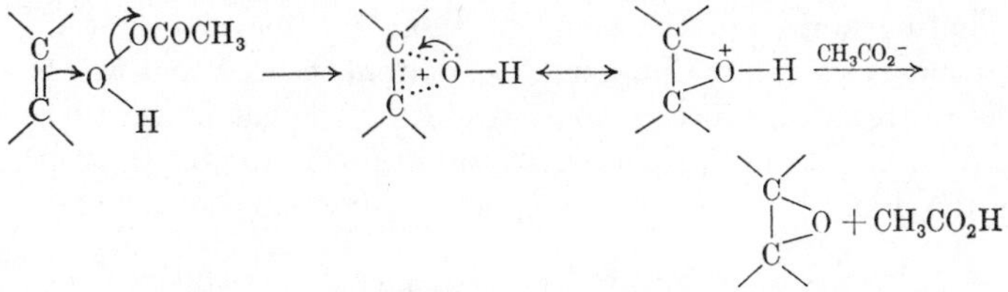

The initial stages of this reaction are probably identical with all the electrophilic additions so far discussed. The reaction is initiated by the electrons in the oxygen–oxygen bond separating and leaving the OH group of the peroxy acid with a positive charge. This positive charge is neutralized by a pair of electrons from the double bond to give us the same type of addition complex as we had above. What is different about this addition complex is that the oxygen atom has two non-bonded pairs of electrons, one of which can be used to form a bond with the carbon atoms, so that the positive charge is no longer distributed over the two carbon atoms and the oxygen but is now located on the oxygen atom, thus giving two normal bonds between the oxygen atom and the two carbon atoms. We represent the transition from one form of the addend complex to the other by a double-headed arrow to indicate that this reaction only involves the movement of electrons and not the movement of nuclei. The use of a double-headed arrow to represent structures which differ only in the position of electrons will be discussed in much greater detail later on.

Homolytic Additions

We have seen that in the liquid phase in the dark, chlorine and bromine add by a heterolytic or ionic process to the olefins. However, in the gas phase in the presence of light the reaction occurs by a different route:

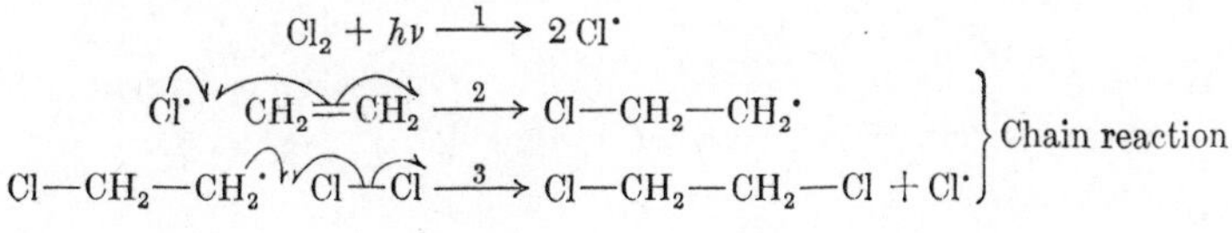

$$Cl_2 + h\nu \xrightarrow{1} 2\ Cl^\cdot$$

This is another example of a chain reaction (see Chapter 2, p. 12). Reactions 2 and 3 are the chain propagating steps. The chain terminating steps are the same as those for the chlorination of methane as given in Chapter 2. Apart from the fact that this free-radical reaction proceeds most readily in the gas phase there is another important difference. The addition of bromine to propene in the liquid phase in the dark yields only a single product:

$$Br_2 + CH_3CH{=}CH_2 \xrightarrow[\text{in the dark}]{\text{Liquid phase}} CH_3CHBrCH_2Br$$

1,2-Dibromopropane
(**only product**)

This is because Br^+ will not attack a carbon–hydrogen bond (see Chapter 2). On the other hand, a bromine atom will abstract a hydrogen atom from a carbon–hydrogen bond.

$$Br \cdot \curvearrowright H \frown CH_2CH{=}CH_2 \longrightarrow Br{-}H + \dot{C}H_2CH{=}CH_2$$
$$CH_2{=}CH\dot{C}H_2 \curvearrowright Br \frown Br \longrightarrow CH_2{=}CHCH_2Br + Br \cdot$$

Thus bromine and propene react together in the gas phase in the presence of light to yield three products: 1,2-dibromopropane (as before), 3-bromoprop-1-ene, and 1,2,3-tribromopropane. The tribromo compound comes from the addition of the bromine to the bromopropene formed by the abstraction reaction. Homolytic additions are not restricted to halogen atoms, and it is possible to add such apparently ionic molecules as hydrogen bromide homolytically, although reactions of this kind require an initiator:

$$R{-}O\frown O{-}R \xrightarrow{\text{Heat}} 2\,RO \cdot \left.\right\} \text{Initiation}$$
$$RO \cdot \curvearrowright H \frown Br \longrightarrow ROH + Br \cdot$$

$$Br \cdot \curvearrowright CH_2{=}CH_2 \longrightarrow BrCH_2CH_2 \cdot \left.\right\} \text{Chain propagation}$$
$$BrCH_2CH_2 \cdot \curvearrowright H \frown Br \longrightarrow BrCH_2CH_3 + Br \cdot$$

In this reaction the initiator is a peroxide in which the oxygen–oxygen bond is broken homolytically by heat.

Oxidation Reactions (Four-centre Reactions)

Carbon–carbon double bonds react with powerful oxidizing agents such as potassium permanganate, osmium tetroxide, or ozone to yield addition products. The mechanism of these reactions is very complex and numerous side reactions occur. Nonetheless the basic reaction in each case is probably essentially the same.

a. Potassium permanganate

$$RCH{=}CHR' \xrightarrow[\text{Aq. soln.}]{\text{KMnO}_4} \underset{\underset{\text{OH \quad OH}}{|\quad\;\; |}}{RCH{-}CHR'}$$

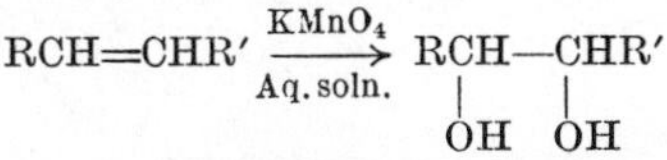

A glycol

This reaction is probably initiated by a four-centre reaction between two of the oxygen atoms of the permanganate ion and the olefin*:

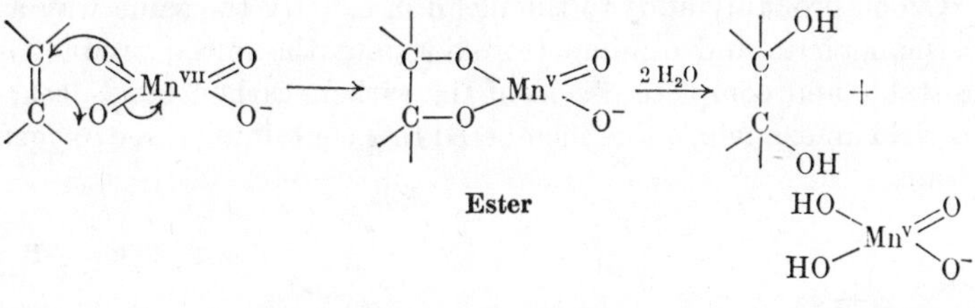

The roman numerals represent the valency state of manganese; in the same way we can write Fe^{III} to represent an iron atom in the ferric state and Fe^{II} to represent an iron atom in the ferrous

---

* In this particular reaction it clearly does not matter which way round the curved arrows are drawn; reversing the directions of the arrows would be just as satisfactory.

state. Mn^V is an unstable state and the hypothetical acid $H_2MnO_4{}^-$ will react with a permanganate ion as follows:

$$H_2Mn^VO_4{}^- + Mn^{VII}O_4{}^- \longrightarrow 2\ HMn^{VI}O_4{}^-$$
Manganate
anion

b. Osmium tetroxide

An olefin reacts with osmium tetroxide to produce an osmate ester which will hydrolyse to yield a glycol in a way analogous to the reaction of an olefin with permanganate. In this case the mechanism of the reaction is far more certainly known and the intermediate osmate ester can be isolated.

Cyclohexene   Osmate ester   Cyclohexane-1,2-diol

c. Ozone

Ozone probably adds to the olefin in exactly the same way as permanganate and osmium tetroxide, but the initial product is unstable and complete fission of the carbon–carbon bond occurs to yield an ozonide, a five-membered ring containing three oxygen atoms:

Unstable   **Ozonide**

The ozonides are very reactive substances and can be hydrolysed by water:

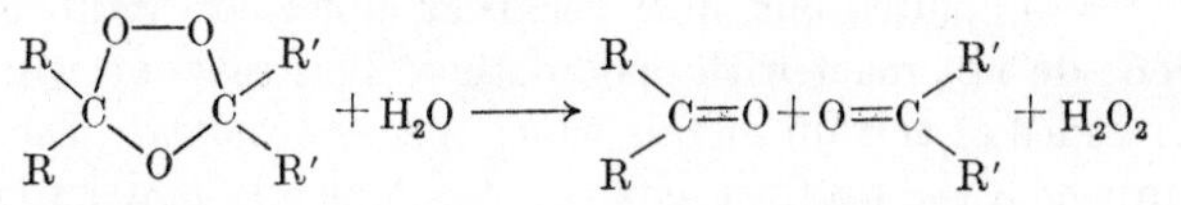

Ozonide   Ketones

Because the product of the reaction with water yields hydrogen peroxide which may cause further oxidation, hydrolysis is usually carried out with zinc and acetic acid, so that the overall reaction with the alkene $RCH{=}CHR'$ can be written as:

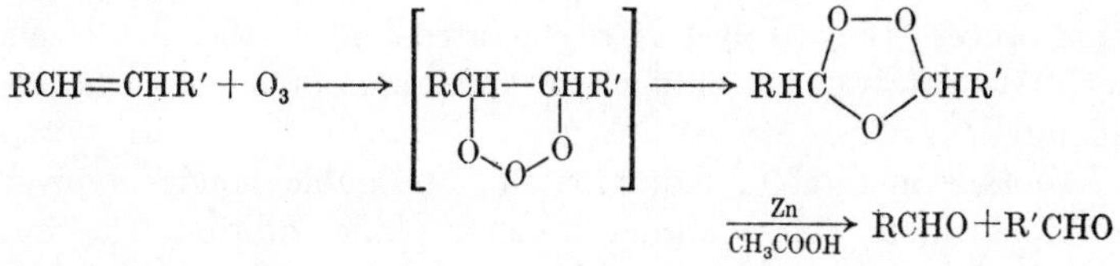

Hydrogenation Reactions

At the beginning of this chapter we set out an equation for the reaction of hydrogen with ethylene to yield ethane and showed that this reaction was exothermic to approximately 30 kcal

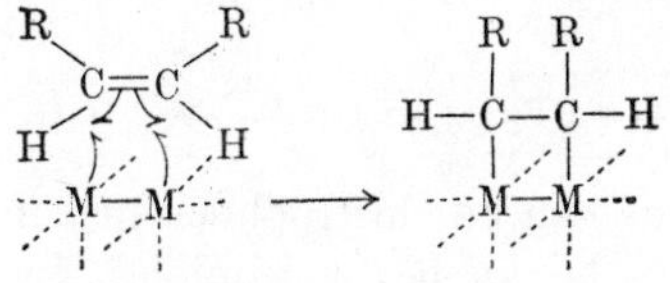

Surface of metal

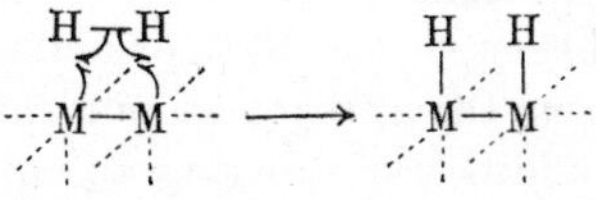

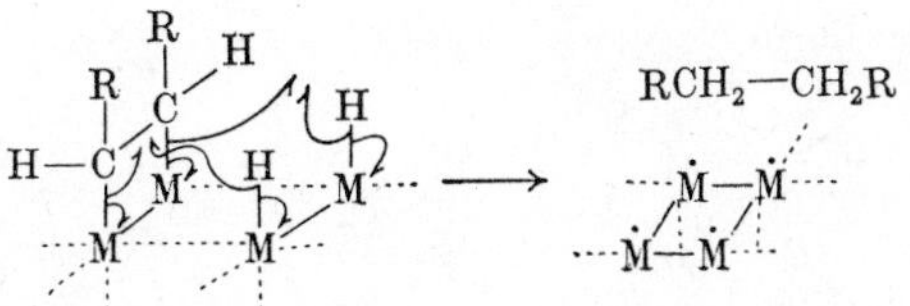

mole^{-1}. We pointed out, however, that molecular hydrogen and
ethylene do not react with one another. This reaction will go in
the presence of certain metals which act as catalysts. The exact
way in which the catalyst acts is not completely understood but
we do know that olefins are absorbed quite strongly on the metal
surface. Presumably the surface of the metal contains unsatis-
fied valencies which form bonds with the olefin. Molecular hydrogen is also absorbed on metal surfaces although the metal–
hydrogen bond is considerably weaker. It seems probable that the
actual hydrogenation occurs by reaction between absorbed olefin
and absorbed hydrogen (see equations on p. 63). Notice that in
this process the catalyst is regenerated and so the metal acts
as a true catalyst, i.e. only a very small area of metal surface is
required.

Another method of reduction of the double bonds involves
hydroboration. This is a kind of electrophilic addition. The first
step is the addition of diborane to an olefin:

$$6 \text{ CH}_2{=}\text{CH}_2 + \text{B}_2\text{H}_6 \xrightarrow{\;0°\;} 2 \text{ (CH}_3\text{CH}_2)_3\text{B}$$

Diborane is spontaneously inflammable in air and in practice it is
formed in solution by treating sodium borohydride with boron
trifluoride:

$$3 \text{ Na}^+\text{BH}_4^- + 4 \text{ BF}_3 \text{ (in Et}_2\text{O)} \xrightarrow{\;0°\;} 2 \text{ B}_2\text{H}_6 + 3 \text{ Na}^+\text{BF}_4^-$$

Boron compounds can be electrophiles just in the same way as
nitrogen compounds can be nucleophiles. In a trivalent boron
compound the boron atom has only six electrons in its outer shell.
Boron trifluoride and ammonia react to form a complex which has
a very strong bond between the nitrogen and the boron. Two non-
bonded electrons from the nitrogen atom complete the outer shell
of the boron. The addition of diborane to an olefin starts by the
donation of a pair of electrons from the carbon–carbon double
bond to the boron:

The alkylborane can then be decomposed by aqueous acid to yield the hydrocarbon or with hydrogen peroxide and alkali to yield an alcohol.

$$(CH_3CH_2)_3B + 3 H_2O \xrightarrow{H^+} 3 CH_3CH_3 + B(OH)_3$$
$$(CH_3CH_2)_3B + 3 H_2O_2 \longrightarrow 3 CH_3CH_2OH + B(OH)_3$$

Polymerization

At the beginning of this chapter we considered the types of addition that could occur at a double bond and the first three that we listed were (i) electrophilic, (ii) nucleophilic, and (iii) free-radical. The initial addend in an electrophilic addition must itself be an electrophile, so it would be reasonable to expect it to add to another olefin molecule, the probability of such a reaction depending on the concentration of the olefin.

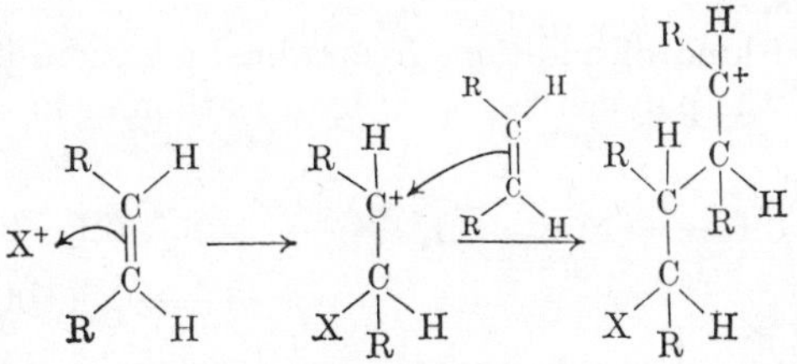

If we treat isobutene with sulphuric acid, for example, we obtain two dimers by this process:

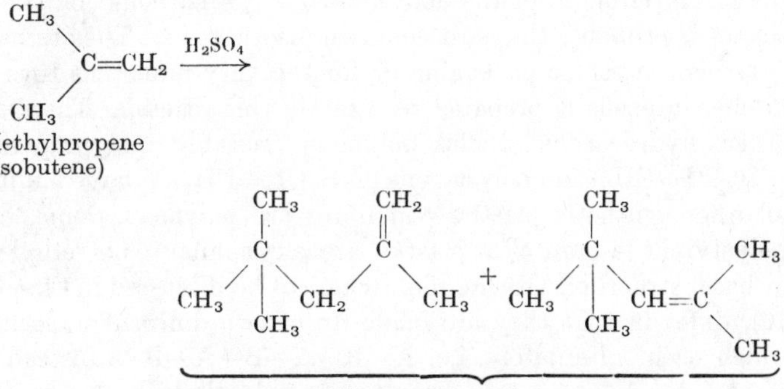

2-Methylpropene
(Isobutene)

Dimers of 2-methylpropene

If instead we use BF_3 as the electrophile there is no anion to halt the reaction and a long-chain polymer is obtained:

$$\underset{H_3C}{\overset{H_3C}{>}}C{=}CH_2 \xrightarrow{BF_3/H_2O} \underset{H_3C}{\overset{CH_3}{\underset{CH_3}{\overset{|}{C}}}} \left(CH_2 \underset{CH_3}{\overset{CH_3}{\overset{|}{C}}} \right)_n$$

Polymer

This kind of polymerization initiated by an electrophile is called *cationic polymerization*.

The fact that nucleophilic addition to hydrocarbon olefins is rare has been discussed and thus *anionic polymerization* in which the polymerization process is initiated by an anion and the growing chain is a carbanion is likewise not important for hydrocarbon olefins, though anionic polymerization can occur with other types of molecules.

The third kind of addition, free-radical addition, is very important for the polymerization of hydrocarbon olefins:

$$X^{\cdot} \quad CH_2{=}CH_2 \longrightarrow XCH_2{-}\dot{C}H_2 \xrightarrow{CH_2{=}CH_2} XCH_2{-}CH_2{-}CH_2{-}\dot{C}H_2$$
$$\xrightarrow{CH_2{=}CH_2} X{-}(CH_2{-}CH_2)_n\,Y$$

It can be seen that this reaction and ionic polymerization are chain reactions and in order for the chains to be long to give a long polymer we must have a high concentration of ethylene relative to the initiator. Polyethylene, known as 'Alkathene' or 'Polythene' is probably the most common plastic today. The ordinary polythene used for packaging or for the very numerous toys or kitchen utensils is prepared by exactly this reaction. There are other hydrocarbon olefin polymers, notably polypropylene ($CH_3CH{=}CH_2$) and polystyrene ($C_6H_5CH{=}CH_2$). A large number of other synthetic plastics and fibres are polymers. Some, like polystyrene (a hard clear plastic), are very similar to polyethylene in basic structure. Others, like nylon (to be discussed in Chapter 16), differ in that they are made up of two different molecules which occur alternately, i.e. A—B—A—B—A—B—, instead of the A—A—A—A— arrangement as in polyethylene.

Unsaturation

In the previous chapter we stated that ethylene is the simplest example of an unsaturated compound. Olefins are given this name because they undergo addition reactions, and the whole of this chapter has been devoted to describing the principal types of addition reaction. The alkanes, the reactions of which were discussed in Chapter 2, are called saturated hydrocarbons and you will remember that the saturated bonds in a hydrocarbon do not undergo ionic reactions. Hydrocarbon olefins, on the other hand, undergo a wide variety of ionic and homolytic reactions. The next few chapters will be concerned with further examples of addition reactions; not to carbon–carbon double bonds, but to carbon–oxygen double bonds. The term unsaturation is somewhat loosely used but according to many authors it only refers to carbon–carbon bonds; carbon–oxygen bonds would not be regarded as unsaturated by these authors. We think this is an unfortunate distinction and it is one that we will endeavour to avoid using.

Problems

1. Starting from ethylene, how would you prepare the following compounds:

(a) C_2H_5OH (b) CH_2BrCH_2OH (c) $CH_2(OH)CH_2OH$
(d) CH_3CH_2Br (e) $-(CH_2CH_2)_n-$ (polyethylene)

2. Distinguish between homolytic and heterolytic addition. Show how bromine can add either heterolytically or homolytically to but-2-ene. Under what conditions would you expect heterolytic addition and under what conditions would you expect homolytic addition? What additional products might you expect from the homolytic reaction?

CHAPTER 7

Addition Reactions:
to the Carbon–Oxygen Double Bond

The previous two chapters have been concerned with bonds between carbon atoms in which four electrons are shared, giving a double bond. Clearly we can equally well form double bonds between carbon and nitrogen or carbon and oxygen.

$$\diagdown C = N - \qquad\qquad \diagdown C = O$$

Imine group   **Carbonyl group**

This chapter will not be concerned with the carbon–nitrogen double bond (as occurring in the imine group) but with the carbon–oxygen double bond (as in the carbonyl group) which is one of the most important groups in organic chemistry. The simplest molecule containing a carbonyl group is formaldehyde and it is possible to build up a series of compounds containing the carbonyl group by successively replacing hydrogen atoms by methyl groups in just the same way as we built up the alkanes and the alkenes (see next page). Notice that so long as a hydrogen atom is still attached directly to the carbon atom of the carbonyl group, the compound is called an aldehyde. The addition reactions of aldehydes and ketones with which we are concerned at present are the same.

In Chapter 3 we considered the single bond between carbon and halogen in an alkyl halide and came to the conclusion that the pair of electrons would not be equally shared between the carbon

$$\begin{array}{c} H \\ \diagdown \\ C{=}O \\ \diagup \\ H \end{array}$$

Formaldehyde (b.p. −21°)

$$\begin{array}{c} CH_3 \\ \diagdown \; | \\ C{=}O \\ \diagup \\ H \end{array}$$

Acetaldehyde (Ethanal)
(b.p. 20°)

$$\begin{array}{c} CH_3CH_2 \\ \diagdown \\ C{=}O \\ \diagup \\ H \end{array}$$

Propionaldehyde (Propanal)
(b.p. 49°)

$$\begin{array}{c} CH_3 \\ \diagdown \\ C{=}O \\ \diagup \\ CH_3 \end{array}$$

Acetone (Propan-2-one)
(b.p. 57°)

$$\begin{array}{c} CH_3CH_2CH_2 \\ \diagdown \\ C{=}O \\ \diagup \\ H \end{array}$$

Butyraldehyde
(Butanal)
(b.p. 76°)

$$\begin{array}{c} CH_3 \\ | \\ CH \\ \diagdown \\ CH_3 \quad C{=}O \\ \diagup \\ H \end{array}$$

2-Methylpropanal
(b.p. 62°)

$$\begin{array}{c} CH_3CH_2 \\ \diagdown \\ C{=}O \\ \diagup \\ CH_3 \end{array}$$

Ethyl methyl ketone
(Butan-2-one)
(b.p. 80°)

$$\begin{array}{c} R \\ \diagdown \\ C{=}O \quad \textbf{Aldehydes} \\ \diagup \\ H \end{array} \qquad \begin{array}{c} R \\ \diagdown \\ C{=}O \quad \textbf{Ketones} \\ \diagup \\ R' \end{array}$$

and the halogen and the bond would therefore be slightly polarized in the direction $C{+}{\rightarrow}Cl$:

$$\begin{array}{c} | \;\; {}^{\delta +} \\ C \\ \diagup \; | \; \diagdown \\ {}^{\delta -} \\ Cl \end{array}$$

We thus distinguished between the completely non-polar carbon–carbon single bond and the slightly polarized carbon–halogen single bond. In exactly the same way the carbon–carbon bond in ethylene is completely non-polar, the four electrons being equally shared between the two carbon atoms. In a carbon–oxygen double bond we may expect the more electronegative oxygen atom to have slightly the greater share of the electrons and the double bond will therefore be polarized:

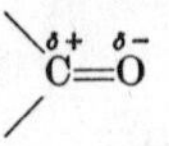

$$\overset{\delta+\ \delta-}{C=O}$$

If we now compare the carbon–oxygen double bond with the carbon–carbon double bond we should expect the polarization of the former to make ionic addition occur more readily. In the previous chapter we considered the addition of both electrophiles and nucleophiles to the carbon–carbon double bond but we found that nucleophiles do not in general add to hydrocarbon olefins. Clearly in a polarized double bond as in the carbonyl bond, the situation is very different and we would expect nucleophiles to add to the carbon atom and electrophiles to add to the oxygen atom. This is exactly what does occur. We will begin by discussing the addition of nucleophiles, first, because this is a new kind of reaction and second, because nucleophilic addition is, in general, more important than electrophilic addition to the carbonyl double bond.

Nucleophilic Addition to the Carbonyl Bond

The commonest nucleophile is, of course, the hydroxyl anion and it will add to the carbonyl bond as shown:

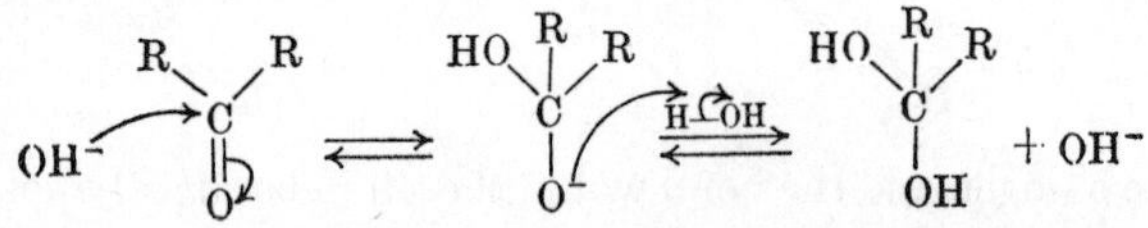

Notice that this addition amounts to the addition of water to the carbonyl bond and that the products of the reaction contain two hydroxyl groups on the same carbon atom. This is not a stable molecule in most cases, and notice that the reaction has been drawn as being reversible. In some special cases the hydrate, as the reaction product is called, can be quite stable. For instance, trichloroacetaldehyde, called chloral, forms an exceedingly stable hydrate, called chloral hydrate.

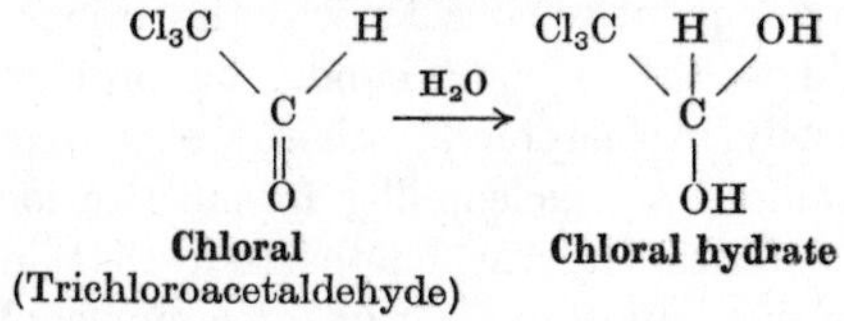

Chloral   **Chloral hydrate**
(Trichloroacetaldehyde)

In general, however, the aldehyde and ketone hydrates are unstable substances and exist only in solution.

In the substitution reactions of alkyl halides, an important nucleophile was the cyanide anion. The cyanide anion will add nucleophilically to the carbonyl bond:

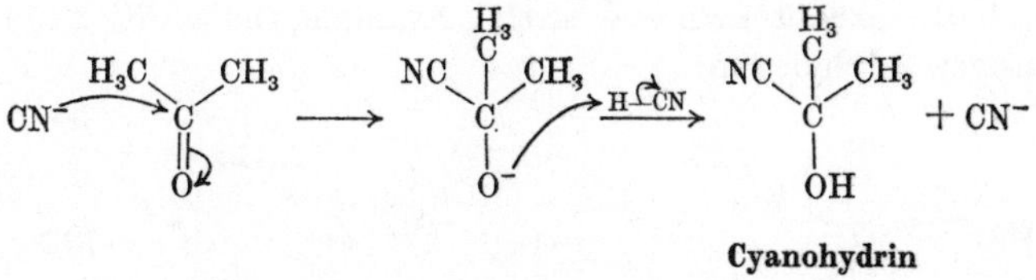

Cyanohydrin

This reaction is carried out in an aqueous solution containing an excess of sodium cyanide to which one mole of acid has been added. The reaction is effectively the addition of hydrogen cyanide across the carbon–oxygen double bond. Another example of the anion of a weak acid adding to the carbonyl bond is the bisulphite anion:

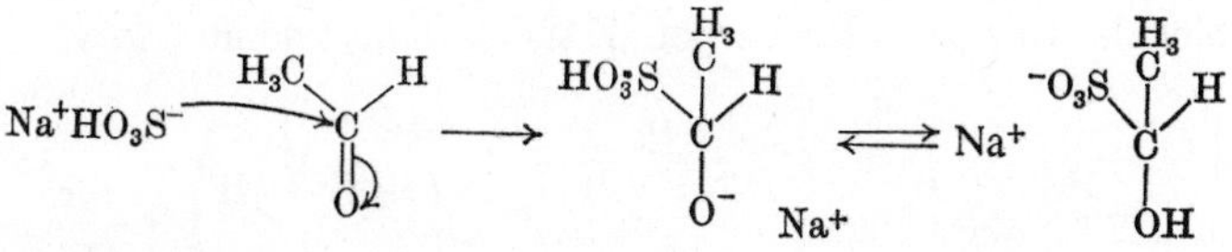

Sodium bisulphite

This reaction occurs much more readily with aldehydes than with ketones and will only take place with ketones when there is a CH_3 group attached to the carbonyl group. The product of the

reaction, the bisulphite compound, is crystalline and, if an aldehyde is shaken with a saturated solution of sodium bisulphite,
the bisulphite compound crystallizes.

It is useful at this point to consider why the anions of a strong
acid will not add to the carbonyl bond. This problem has been
discussed previously in Chapter 3, when we were considering
the reaction of anions as nucleophiles in substitution reactions
with the alkyl halides. It was emphasized that in the substitution reaction an important feature of a nucleophilic anion
was that it donated a pair of electrons to the carbon atom.
The same applies to a nucleophilic addition. The only anions that
will add to the carbon of the carbonyl group are those which are
ready to give up their non-bonded pair of electrons. The stronger
the acid, the more firmly the anion holds on to the electron pair,
so that only the anions of weak acids add to the carbonyl bond.
We shall consider here one further example, the addition of the
hydrogen sulphide ion:

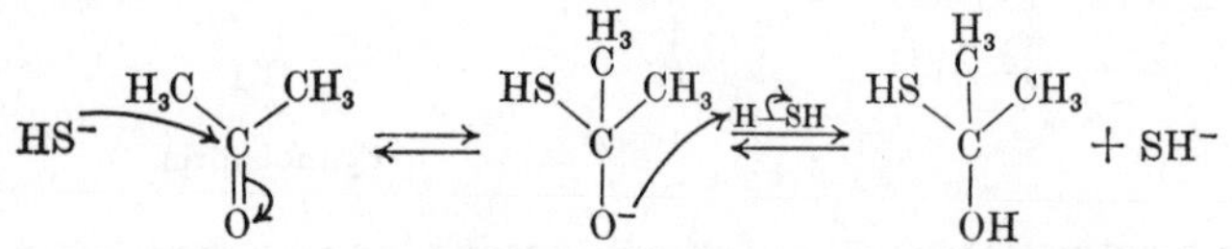

In Chapter 3 it was emphasized that the electron pair of the anion
was important in initiating the displacement reaction. The discussion then turned to molecules such as ammonia which have a
pair of non-bonded electrons and are capable of behaving as
nucleophiles. The same situation applies for nucleophilic addition
to the carbonyl bond. Therefore, we expect ammonia and similar
molecules to add to the carbon of the carbonyl bond, e.g.:

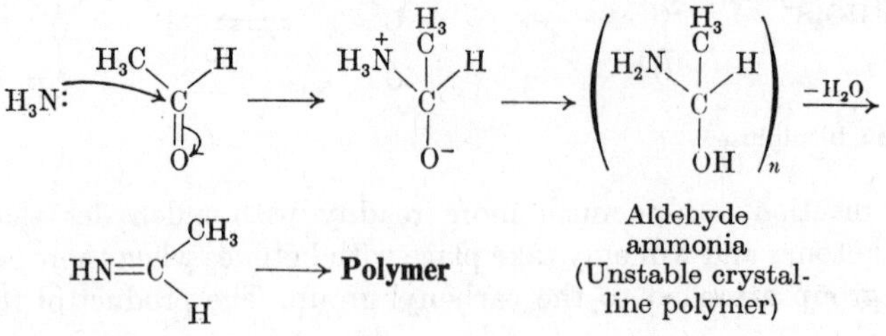

Aldehyde
ammonia
(Unstable crystal-
line polymer)

Under carefully controlled conditions ammonia adds directly to acetaldehyde to yield the unstable solid 'aldehyde ammonia'; but in general the aldehyde ammonia is too unstable to be isolated and the products from the reaction between an aldehyde and ammonia are polymeric.

In some cases the structure of the polymer is known. For example, the product formed from ammonia and formaldehyde is known as hexamethylenetetramine:

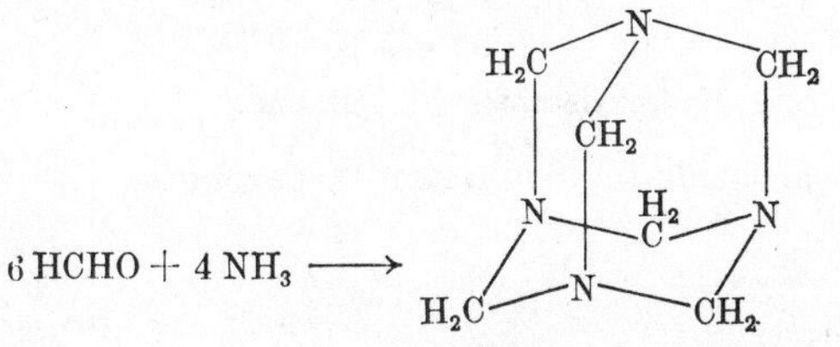

$$6\ HCHO + 4\ NH_3 \longrightarrow$$

Hexamethylenetetramine

Although the reaction between carbonyl compounds and ammonia is often very complex, the reaction between carbonyl compounds and primary amines is usually more straightforward and yields an imine or Schiff base:

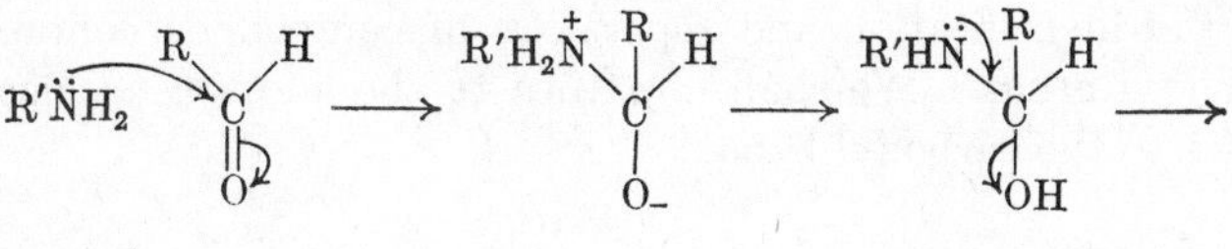

Primary amine

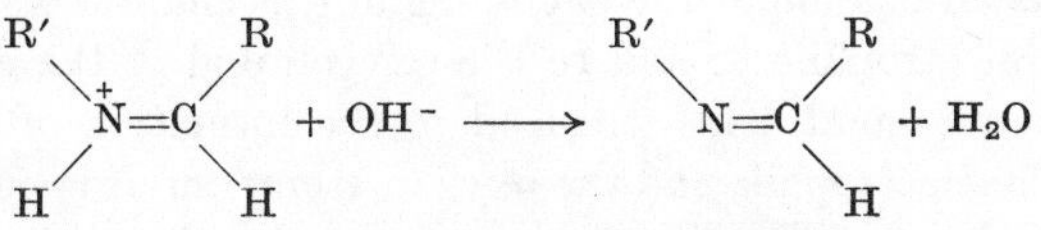

Imine
(Schiff base)

Reactions of this kind between a carbonyl compound and compounds containing nitrogen are both common and extremely important. Other examples include the reaction with hydrazine to yield a hydrazone:

$$\begin{matrix} CH_3 \\ \diagdown \\ \quad \quad C{=}O \\ \diagup \\ CH_3 \end{matrix} + NH_2NH_2 \xrightarrow{\ -H_2O\ } \begin{matrix} CH_3 \\ \diagdown \\ \quad \quad C{=}NNH_2 \\ \diagup \\ CH_3 \end{matrix}$$

Hydrazine   **Hydrazone**

with hydroxylamine to yield an oxime:

$$\begin{matrix} C_2H_5 \\ \diagdown \\ \quad \quad C{=}O \\ \diagup \\ C_2H_5 \end{matrix} + NH_2OH \dashrightarrow \begin{matrix} C_2H_5 \quad \quad OH \\ \diagdown \quad \diagup \\ \quad \quad C{=}N \\ \diagup \\ C_2H_5 \end{matrix} + H_2O$$

Hydroxylamine   **Oxime**

or with semicarbazide to yield a semicarbazone:

Cyclohexanone   **Semicarbazide**   **Cyclohexanone
semicarbazone**

These last three reactions are important because they are used for the identification and separation of compounds containing carbonyl groups. We shall now turn to the addition of electrophiles to the carbonyl bond.

Electrophilic Addition

From our discussion at the beginning of this chapter we should expect an electrophile to add to the oxygen end of the carbon–oxygen double bond. This will lead to the formation of a bond between the electrophile and the oxygen atom, and it is pertinent to consider briefly the characteristics of such a bond because it will differ considerably from a bond to carbon. Great stress was laid in the early chapters on the fact that the carbon–hydrogen bonds were completely non-polar; on the other hand we know very well that the oxygen–hydrogen bond, as in water, is very polar—water ionizes readily. We have also discussed the fact that the oxygen–hydrogen bond in alcohols will also ionize. This

easy heterolysis of bonds between electrophiles and oxygen means
that the only important electrophile we need consider as adding
to the carbonyl bond is the proton, because other bonds are likely
to yield unstable products.

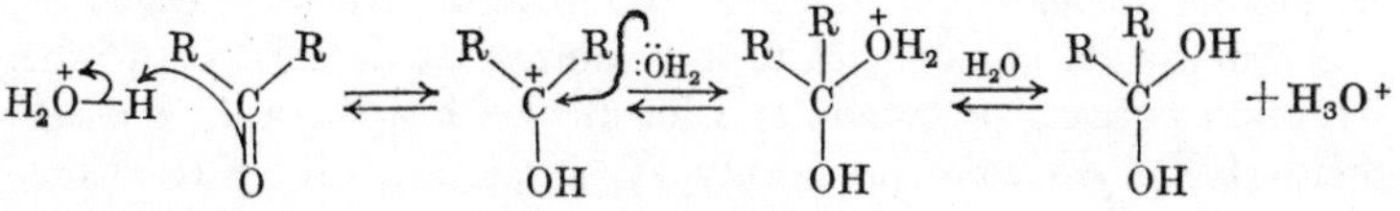

The above equation simply illustrates that the hydration of an
aldehyde or ketone can be acid-catalysed in the same way as it
can be base-catalysed. The fact that the hydrates are normally

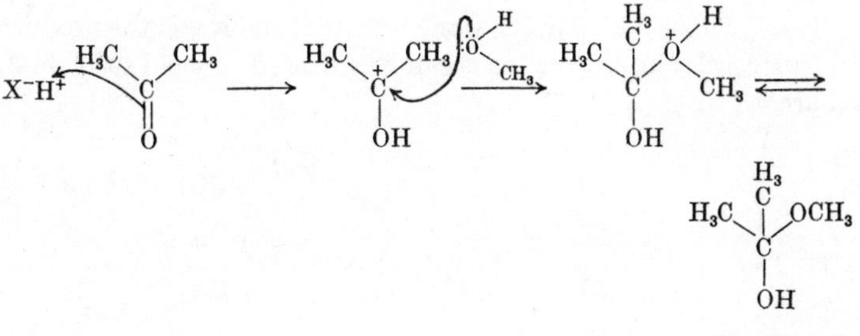

Hemiacetal

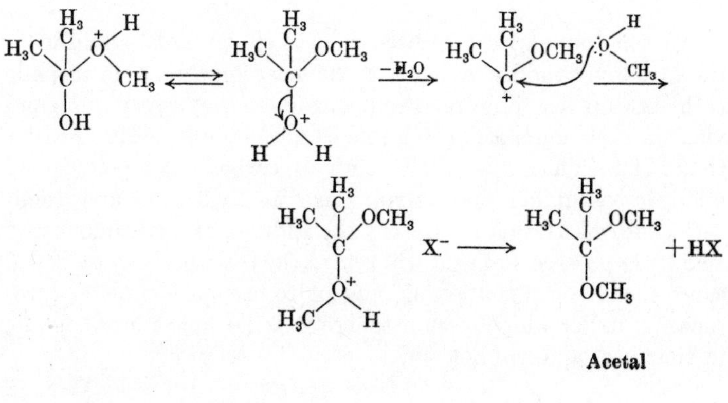

Acetal

unstable substances existing only in solution has already been discussed. The important feature of the above equations, however, is that the first product from the addition of a proton to a carbonyl compound yields a carbonium ion and this species will be a much more powerful electrophile than the carbonyl bond itself, so that it will add nucleophiles which are too weak to attack the carbonyl bond in the absence of acid. As an example, we depict on p. 75 the reaction between a ketone and an alcohol in the presence of an acid (HX). We have used only reversible arrows for reactions involving migrations of a proton because these transformations are extremely rapid, but it is important to realize that all the steps in the above sequence are reversible. A significant feature of the above sequence is the fact that the addition of the proton makes the carbonyl group sufficiently electrophilic to add an alcohol molecule.

Thiols can be added in the same way as alcohols and the product in this case is interesting as it can be oxidized to yield sulphonal, a narcotic drug:

$$
\begin{array}{l}
CH_3 \\
\quad \diagdown \\
\quad\quad C{=}O + 2\ C_2H_5SH \xrightarrow[CH_3OH]{As\ for}
\end{array}
\quad
\begin{array}{l}
CH_3 \qquad SC_2H_5 \\
\quad\diagdown\quad\diagup \\
\quad\quad\quad C \xrightarrow{KMnO_4} \\
\quad\diagup\quad\diagdown \\
CH_3 \qquad SC_2H_5
\end{array}
$$

$$
\begin{array}{l}
CH_3 \qquad SO_2C_2H_5 \\
\quad\diagdown\quad\diagup \\
\quad\quad\quad C \\
\quad\diagup\quad\diagdown \\
CH_3 \qquad SO_2C_2H_5 \\
\quad\quad\textbf{Sulphonal}
\end{array}
$$

We can summarize our discussion of electrophilic addition to the carbonyl bond by saying that the most important electrophile is the proton. The proton, of course, adds to the oxygen atom and yields a carbonium ion which makes nucleophilic addition easier than before. Thus, the reaction between carbonyl compounds and nitrogen-containing derivatives, such as hydrazine and semi-carbazide, may be accelerated by the addition of small amounts of acid. A large excess of acid will retard the reaction because it will cause the nitrogen-containing reagent to become completely pro-tonated, under which circumstances it is no longer nucleophilic in character and will not add.

Hydrogenations

The carbonyl double bond in aldehydes and ketones can be catalytically hydrogenated in exactly the same manner as the carbon–carbon double bond in olefins. The mechanism of the reaction is similar and for this reason we will not discuss it in detail again here.

$$
\underset{R}{\overset{R}{\diagdown}} C{=}O + H_2 \xrightarrow[\text{Pt or Pd}]{\text{Ni}} \underset{R}{\overset{R}{\diagdown}} CHOH
$$

The reaction is less exothermic than the hydrogenation of olefins and thus somewhat more sluggish:

$$
\overset{\diagdown}{\underset{\diagup}{C}}{=}\overset{\diagup}{\underset{\diagdown}{C}} + H_2 \longrightarrow \quad \Delta H = -30 \text{ kcal mole}^{-1}
$$

$$
\overset{\diagdown}{\underset{\diagup}{C}}{=}O + H_2 \longrightarrow \quad \Delta H = -12 \text{ kcal mole}^{-1}
$$

Aldehydes and ketones can also be reduced to alcohols by sodium amalgam in an acid solution. In this case the function of the metal is to provide two electrons in the reduction process:

$$
H^+ \; \overset{R}{\underset{O}{\diagup}}C \rightleftharpoons \overset{R}{\underset{OH}{\overset{R}{\diagup}}}C^+ \xrightarrow[+ 2e^-]{M} \overset{R}{\underset{OH}{\overset{R}{\diagup}}}C^- \; (M^{2+}) \xrightarrow{H-OH} \overset{R}{\underset{OH}{\overset{R}{\diagup}}}\overset{H}{C} + OH^-
$$

The next three reactions involve 'hydride transfer'. We are well acquainted with reactions of hydrogen atoms in which the hydrogen atom nucleus, a proton, takes part in the reaction. H^+ is something learned about at the very beginning of any study of chemistry. H^-, the hydride anion, is very much less common although it is met in compounds such as sodium hydride. Though the free existence of a hydride anion is not very common in normal systems, reactions in which a hydrogen atom transfers with two electrons are quite common, and we have already discussed one such reaction. In the previous chapter the hydroboration of olefins was discussed and we said this reaction began by the two electrons from the carbon–carbon double bond being donated to the incomplete outer shell of the boron atom, i.e. an electrophilic addition to the double bond. We then said that a hydrogen atom on the boron migrated with two electrons to complete the addition process. This reaction is an example of hydride transfer.

Returning now to consider the reduction reactions of aldehydes and ketones, we come to the Meerwein–Ponndorf reaction. In this reaction the aldehyde or ketone to be reduced reacts with aluminium isopropoxide, prepared from aluminium and isopropyl alcohol. When the ketone and aluminium isopropoxide are mixed an equilibrium is set up forming acetone and the aluminate of the alcohol derived from the reduced form of the carbonyl compound.

$$3 \quad \begin{array}{c} R \\ \diagdown \\ R \end{array} C{=}O + Al\left(OCH\begin{array}{c} CH_3 \\ \diagup \\ \diagdown \\ CH_3 \end{array}\right)_3 \rightleftharpoons \left(\begin{array}{c} R \\ \diagdown \\ R \end{array} CHO\right)_3 Al + 3 \begin{array}{c} CH_3 \\ \diagup \\ \diagdown \\ CH_3 \end{array} C{=}O$$

So long as the aldehyde or ketone being reduced is reasonably high boiling the acetone can be distilled out from the reaction mixture, thus pushing the reaction to the right-hand side. The resulting aluminate can then be treated with dilute acid to yield the alcohol:

$$\left(\begin{array}{c} R \\ \diagdown \\ R \end{array} CHO\right)_3 Al \xrightarrow[\;H_2O\;]{\;H_2SO_4\;} \begin{array}{c} R \\ \diagdown \\ R \end{array} CHOH$$

The mechanism of this reaction is very similar to the hydroboration reaction described in the last chapter. The reaction is initiated by the donation of a pair of electrons from the carbonyl double bond to the incomplete outer shell of the aluminium. Subsequent steps of the reaction follow as in hydroboration:

Another method of reducing aldehydes and ketones to the corresponding alcohols is to treat them with lithium aluminium hydride, $Li^+AlH_4{}^-$, in ether in which the lithium aluminium hydride is soluble. This reaction also involves hydride transfer:

$$Li^+(AlH_3\!-\!H)^- \overset{R}{\underset{O}{\searrow}}C\!\!\diagup^R \longrightarrow \underset{O^-Li^+}{\overset{H}{\underset{}{\overset{R}{\underset{}{C}}}}}R + AlH_3 \xrightarrow[H_2SO_4]{H_2O} \underset{OH}{\overset{H}{\overset{R}{C}}}R$$

Sodium borohydride, $NaBH_4$, behaves in a very similar fashion to lithium aluminium hydride, but is a somewhat milder reagent. The mechanism of this reduction is the same as that of lithium aluminium hydride and likewise involves a hydride shift.

Another reaction, restricted to aldehydes which do not contain a CH_2 group adjacent to the carbonyl group, known as the Cannizzaro reaction, also involves hydride transfer. When such aldehydes are treated with alkali an equimolar mixture of the corresponding carboxylic acid salt and primary alcohol is formed:

$$2\,RC\!\!\overset{H}{\underset{O}{\diagup}} \xrightarrow{NaOH} RC\!\!\overset{O}{\underset{O}{\diagup}}{}^-\ Na^+ + RCH_2OH$$

This reaction occurs with formaldehyde, HCHO, or with 2,2-dimethylpropanal, $(CH_3)_3CCHO$, but not with acetaldehyde where the reactions are much more complex and involve the methyl group. The mechanism of the reaction involves addition of a hydroxyl anion to the carbonyl group, followed by hydride transfer from the hydrated anion to another molecule of aldehyde:

We next consider reactions in which the oxygen is completely eliminated from the organic compound to be replaced by two hydrogen atoms. The first of these, called the Wolff–Kishner reaction, involves treating the hydrazone of the aldehyde or ketone with alkali at a fairly high temperature:

$$\underset{C_3H_7}{\overset{C_3H_7}{\diagdown}}C{=}O + NH_2NH_2 \xrightarrow{-H_2O} \underset{C_3H_7}{\overset{C_3H_7}{\diagdown}}C{=}NNH_2 \underset{(CH_2OH)_2}{\overset{NaOH}{\rightleftharpoons}}$$

Heptan-4-one   **Hydrazine**   **Hydrazone**

$$\left(\underset{C_3H_7}{\overset{C_3H_7}{\diagdown}}C{=}N\bar{N}H \longleftrightarrow \underset{C_3H_7}{\overset{C_3H_7}{\diagdown}}\bar{C}{-}N{=}NH \right) \rightleftharpoons \underset{C_3H_7}{\overset{C_3H_7}{\diagdown}}CH{-}N{=}N{-}H \longrightarrow$$

$$\underset{C_3H_7}{\overset{C_3H_7}{\diagdown}}CH_2 + N_2 \uparrow$$

The first step in the reduction is the reversible removal of a proton from the hydrazone. This yields an anion, and we have written two structures for the anion, one with the negative charge on the nitrogen atom and the other with the negative charge on the carbon atom. We have again used the symbol of the double-headed arrow between these two structures which differ only in the positions of electrons (see Chapter 6). The implications of this symbolism will be discussed in detail in the next chapter.

Another method of replacing the oxygen in the carbonyl bond by two hydrogen atoms involves the reaction of the aldehyde or ketone with a thiol, as described above, and the treatment of the thioacetal with hydrogen and nickel:

$$\underset{R'}{\overset{R}{\diagdown}}C{=}O \xrightarrow{2\,C_2H_5SH} \underset{R'}{\overset{R}{\diagdown}}\underset{SC_2H_5}{\overset{SC_2H_5}{\diagup}}C \xrightarrow[Ni]{H_2} \underset{R'}{\overset{R}{\diagdown}}CH_2 + NiS \downarrow + C_2H_6$$

This removal of divalent sulphur from aliphatic compounds by treatment with nickel and hydrogen is a general reaction and is known as desulphurization.

A final method for directly removing oxygen from a carbonyl group and replacing it by two hydrogen atoms is by Clemmensen reduction, in which the aldehyde or ketone is treated with amalgamated zinc and hydrochloric acid. The mechanism of the Clemmensen reduction is not well understood. Probably bonding of the organic molecule to the metal surface is involved. Certainly alcohols are not intermediates as they are unaffected by amalgamated zinc and hydrochloric acid.

$$
\begin{array}{c}
C_3H_7 \\
\diagdown \\
C{=}O \xrightarrow[\text{HCl}]{\text{Zn(Hg)}} C_5H_{12} \\
\diagup \\
CH_3
\end{array}
$$

Oxidation of Aldehydes

Aldehydes can be readily oxidized to the corresponding carboxylic acids. Ketones, on the other hand, can only be oxidized by breaking the carbon–carbon chain. The latter does not occur particularly readily and will not be discussed in the present chapter. Aldehydes can be oxidized to the corresponding carboxylic acids by a wide variety of oxidizing agents; for example, acid, alkaline, or neutral permanganate. The mechanism of this reaction depends slightly on the acidity of the medium but the reaction involves, as we should expect, nucleophilic addition to the carbonyl double bond:

$$
C_2H_5C{=}O + H^+ + MnO_3^-
$$

$$
(2\,MnO_3^- + H_2O \longrightarrow HMnO_4^- + MnO_2 + OH^-)
$$

Some aldehydes can also be oxidized by a large variety of other reagents and in some cases even by the air. Oxidation by the air involves a free-radical process for which an initiator, usually a peroxide, is required. For this reason aldehydes stored in reagent bottles are often decomposed and open bottles of benzaldehyde slowly develop crystals of benzoic acid inside them.

Nomenclature

Aldehydes are given the name of the hydrocarbon from which they are derived, followed by the suffix '-al'. Thus:

$$CH_3CHO \quad \text{Ethanal}$$
$$CH_3(CH_2)_4CHO \quad \text{Hexanal}$$

(The semi-systematic nomenclature, by which aldehydes are named as derivatives of the corresponding carboxylic acid, e.g. CH_3CHO (derived from CH_3CO_2H) is called acetaldehyde, is still in general use.)

Ketones receive the suffix '-one'.

$$CH_3COCH_3 \quad \text{Propan-2-one}$$
$$CH_3CH_2CH_2CH_2COCH_3 \quad \text{Hexan-2-one}$$
$$CH_3CH_2CH_2COCH_2CH_3 \quad \text{Hexan-3-one}$$

(The semi-systematic name in this case uses the word 'ketone'; thus hexan-2-one becomes butyl methyl ketone and hexan-3-one becomes ethyl propyl ketone.)

Problems

1. What addition reaction, if any, would you predict between (a) ethylene and (b) formaldehyde with the following reagents:

(1) a solution of sodium cyanide to which a trace of acid has been added;

(2) an aqueous solution of sodium chloride;

(3) hydrogen chloride;

(4) an aqueous solution of hydroxylamine;

(5) an aqueous solution of ammonia.

2. What reaction, if any, would you expect between the following reagents and (a) ethyl bromide; (b) acetone:

(1) NH_3 (2) Na^+CN^-
(3) $Na^+OC_2H_5^-$ (4) H^+Cl^- in CH_3OH

CHAPTER 8

Reactions of the OH and C=O Bonds of the Carboxyl Group

So far we have only considered the reactions of one bond at a time. We now wish to consider the carboxyl group where not only are there two 'functional groups' but they are both attached to the same carbon atom, forming what we might call a 'composite functional group'. Although the carboxyl group is apparently made up of a carbonyl and a hydroxyl function, they so modify each other that their reactions are markedly different from those of the carbonyl group in ketones or the hydroxyl group in alcohols. Compounds containing the carboxyl group are called carboxylic acids. The simplest carboxylic acid is formic acid and we can formally build up a series of straight-chain and branched-chain carboxylic acids as before (see next page).

The straight-chain carboxylic acids with eight carbon atoms or less are liquids but with chains longer than this they become low-melting solids. The lower members of this series are completely soluble in water. As with alcohols (Chapter 4), hydrogen bonding is very important in the liquid state. Carboxylic acids form dimers which persist in dilute solution in non-hydroxylic solvents (e.g. carbon tetrachloride) and in some cases even in the gas phase.

Just as ethers have lower boiling points than alcohols of considerably lower molecular weight, so methyl and ethyl esters in

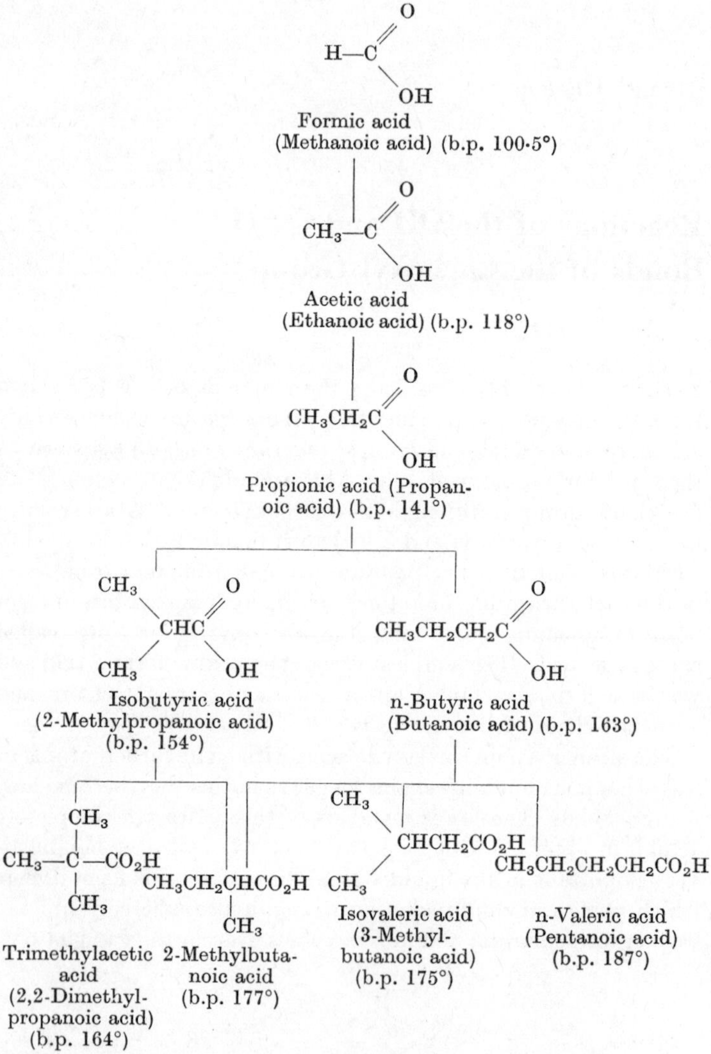

$$H-C\overset{\displaystyle O}{\underset{\displaystyle OH}{=}}$$

Formic acid
(Methanoic acid) (b.p. 100·5°)

$$CH_3-C\overset{\displaystyle O}{\underset{\displaystyle OH}{=}}$$

Acetic acid
(Ethanoic acid) (b.p. 118°)

$$CH_3CH_2C\overset{\displaystyle O}{\underset{\displaystyle OH}{=}}$$

Propionic acid (Propan-
oic acid) (b.p. 141°)

$$\overset{\displaystyle CH_3}{\underset{\displaystyle CH_3}{>}}CHC\overset{\displaystyle O}{\underset{\displaystyle OH}{=}}$$

Isobutyric acid
(2-Methylpropanoic acid)
(b.p. 154°)

$$CH_3CH_2CH_2C\overset{\displaystyle O}{\underset{\displaystyle OH}{=}}$$

n-Butyric acid
(Butanoic acid) (b.p. 163°)

$$CH_3-\overset{\displaystyle CH_3}{\underset{\displaystyle CH_3}{\overset{\displaystyle |}{\underset{\displaystyle |}{C}}}}-CO_2H$$

Trimethylacetic
acid
(2,2-Dimethyl-
propanoic acid)
(b.p. 164°)

$$CH_3CH_2\overset{\displaystyle CHCO_2H}{\underset{\displaystyle CH_3}{|}}$$

2-Methylbuta-
noic acid
(b.p. 177°)

$$\overset{\displaystyle CH_3}{\underset{\displaystyle CH_3}{>}}CHCH_2CO_2H$$

Isovaleric acid
(3-Methyl-
butanoic acid)
(b.p. 175°)

$$CH_3CH_2CH_2CH_2CO_2H$$

n-Valeric acid
(Pentanoic acid)
(b.p. 187°)

which hydrogen bonding is much less important than in the free acid boil much lower than the carboxylic acids from which they are derived (see Table 8.1).

Table 8.1. Boiling points of methyl and ethyl esters of some carboxylic acids

Acid	B.p. (°c)	Methyl ester	B.p. (°c)	Ethyl ester	B.p. (°c)
Formic					
HCO_2H	100·5	HCO_2CH_3	32	$HCO_2C_2H_5$	54
Acetic					
CH_3CO_2H	118	$CH_3CO_2CH_3$	57	$CH_3CO_2C_2H_5$	77
Propionic					
$CH_3CH_2CO_2H$	141	$CH_3CH_2CO_2CH_3$	80	$CH_3CH_2CO_2C_2H_5$	99

The Acidity of the O—H Bond

When discussing alcohols, we described how they could behave as very weak acids. Ethanol, with an acid dissociation constant of 10^{-18}, is a very much weaker acid than water, the dissociation constant of which is 2×10^{-16}. The dissociation constant of acetic acid in water is $1·8 \times 10^{-5}$.

$$K_a = \frac{[H_3O^+][CH_3CO_2^-]}{[CH_3CO_2H]}$$

$$= 1·8 \times 10^{-5} \text{ at } 25°$$

This means that the molecule CH_3CO_2H is a more favourable state (of lower free energy) in water than

On the other hand, since acetic acid is so very much stronger an acid than water or ethanol, the acetate ion in water must be of lower energy (free energy) than OH^- or $C_2H_5O^-$ in the same solvent. In both these molecules the negative charge is situated exclusively on the oxygen atom. In the acetate anion there are two oxygen atoms to choose from and there is no means of distinguishing them. In fact the negative charge is distributed equally between the two oxygen atoms. We can either represent this as we have done in the equations above, by drawing a dotted line between the two oxygen atoms and a negative charge somewhere in between them; or we can draw two 'classical structures' with a double-headed arrow between them:

$$CH_3-C\underset{O^-}{\overset{O}{\Big\langle}} \quad \longleftrightarrow \quad CH_3-C\underset{O}{\overset{O^-}{\Big\langle}}$$

The objection to the latter method of representing the acetate anion is that it suggests that the negative charge is oscillating backwards and forwards between the two oxygen atoms. This is not so. In acetic acid the two carbon–oxygen bonds are of different lengths, approximately 1·24 Å for the carbonyl oxygen bond and 1·43 Å for the carbon–hydroxyl bond. But in the acetate anion the two carbon–oxygen bonds are of identical length. Although the classical structure is misleading in this respect, it is useful in that it tells us, for example, that the negative charge is situated on the oxygen atoms and not on the carbon atom as might appear from the picture we have drawn with a dotted line between the two oxygen atoms and a negative charge somewhere between. We shall find as we consider further classes of organic compounds more and more molecules that cannot be represented by a single structure.

Esterification and Hydrolysis

In Chapter 4 we considered esters as being built up formally by the elimination of water from alcohol and an organic acid. We took the reaction between ethanol and acetic acid to form ethyl acetate and water as a specific example.

$$C_2H_5OH + CH_3C\underset{OH}{\overset{O}{\Big\langle}} \rightleftharpoons CH_3C\underset{O}{\overset{OC_2H_5}{\Big\langle}} + H_2O$$

It was emphasized that this was a reversible reaction. The numerical value of the equilibrium constant, K, is approximately 4 at room temperature.

$$K = \frac{[CH_3CO_2C_2H_5][H_2O]}{[CH_3CO_2H][C_2H_5OH]}$$
$$= 4 \text{ at } 25°$$

This equilibrium is established very slowly indeed and it is important to distinguish between this equilibrium and the dissociation equilibrium we discussed above. The reaction between acetic acid and water to form the hydroxonium ion and the acetate ion only involves proton transfer and is extremely rapid—too rapid indeed to be measured by any normal method. On the other hand, the reaction between acetic acid and ethanol is a complex bimolecular process and in the absence of a catalyst occurs very, very slowly. Ethanol is too weak a nucleophile to add readily to the carbonyl double bond in acetic acid. However, if we have a strong acid present as a catalyst it may protonate the acetic acid to yield a carbonium ion which is sufficiently electrophilic to attack the ethanol molecule:

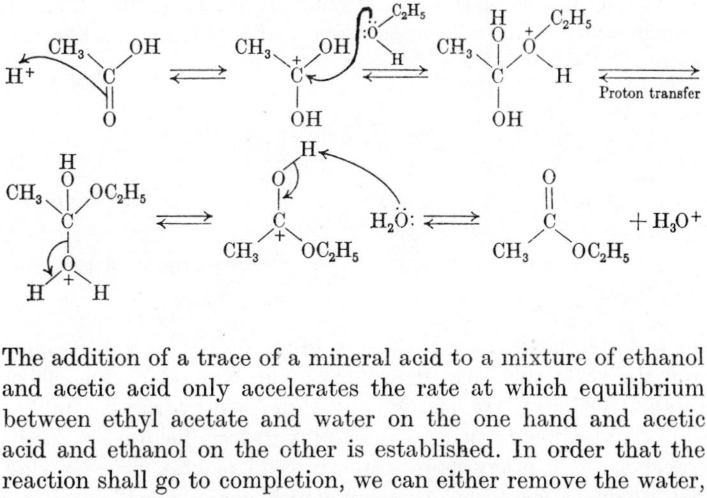

The addition of a trace of a mineral acid to a mixture of ethanol and acetic acid only accelerates the rate at which equilibrium between ethyl acetate and water on the one hand and acetic acid and ethanol on the other is established. In order that the reaction shall go to completion, we can either remove the water, keeping the other concentrations unchanged, or add a considerable excess of ethanol. An example of the latter method is sometimes known as the Fischer–Speier method of esterification. The carboxylic acid is treated with a vast excess of an alcohol which must be low boiling, and dry hydrogen chloride is added as catalyst. The excess of alcohol ensures that almost all the acid is converted into the ester. The alternative way of pushing the reaction over to the ester side of the equation is to remove the water. This can be done by using concentrated sulphuric acid. You will see that the sulphuric acid serves two functions. First and most important, as a catalyst it makes the reaction go at a reasonable speed and second, as a dehydrating agent to remove the water. Another method of removing the water is by azeotropic distillation, in which a solvent is added to the reaction mixture and then distilled out again. During this distillation the solvent carries with it the water formed in the esterification.

Acid-catalysed esterification is a reversible reaction; so, to hydrolyse an ester, besides a mineral acid, all we require is an excess of water. This will clearly push the reaction over to the free acid and alcohol. Ethyl acetate, for example, is hydrolysed by heating it with dilute mineral acid. However, it is often more convenient to hydrolyse esters by base catalysis. We should expect a base such as the hydroxyl anion to add to the carbonyl bond in an ester just as it adds to the carbonyl bond of a ketone:

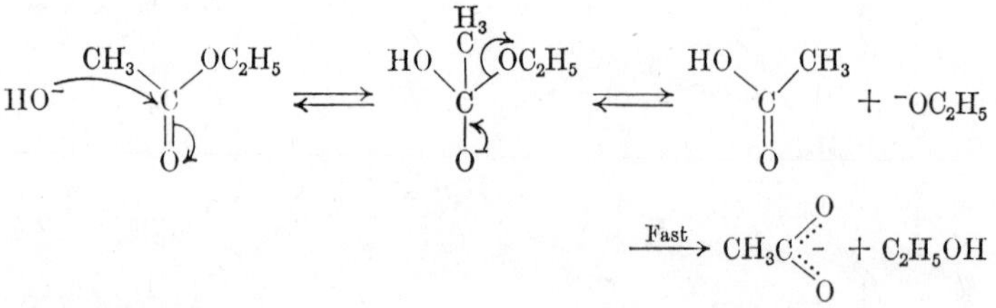

The last step in the base hydrolysis of an ester is proton transfer from the carboxylic acid molecule to the alkoxide anion. This reaction is almost irreversible, and thus base hydrolysis, unlike acid hydrolysis, of an ester is a virtually irreversible process. Base hydrolysis is in many ways a more useful reaction because the acid is now in the form of its salt which is non-volatile and insoluble in organic solvents whereas the alcohol is volatile and soluble in organic solvents, so that the two components of the ester can be separated. It is worthwhile considering why ethyl acetate can be made by taking acetic acid, an excess of ethanol, and a trace of a mineral acid but cannot be made by taking acetic acid, an excess of ethanol and a trace of sodium hydroxide.

The similarity of the acid-catalysed esterification, and the acid-

and the base-catalysed hydrolysis of esters, with the electrophilic and nucleophilic addition reactions of the carbonyl bond in aldehydes and ketones (cf. Chapter 7) should be noted.

The Reaction of Other Nucleophiles with Esters; the Formation of Amides

As the hydroxyl anion will add to the carbonyl double bond in an ester (as in ester hydrolysis), we should expect other nucleophiles to add in the same fashion. A particularly important example is the addition of ammonia:

Ethyl propionate

Propionamide

The product of this reaction is an amide, a class of compounds we briefly mentioned in Chapter 4, in which we considered the amides as compounds in which the OH group in a hydroxy acid had been replaced by NH_2 or RNH group. We have illustrated the reaction with ammonia itself but the same reaction will occur with primary and secondary amines to yield N-substituted or N,N-disubstituted amides. Aldehydes and ketones, besides adding ammonia, also add a variety of similar derivatives, notably hydrazine and its derivatives, or hydroxylamine and its derivatives. Esters behave in the same fashion and, just as the addition of ammonia to an ester results eventually in the elimination of a molecule of alcohol, so the addition of hydrazine or of hydroxylamine also results in the elimination of a molecule of alcohol (see next page). Although esters undergo these nucleophilic additions, note that carboxylic acids do not. In the presence of a nucleophile, a carboxylic acid simply loses a proton to give the carboxylate anion and the protonated nucleophile, e.g. ammonia and acetic acid

$$
\begin{array}{ccc}
\underset{\text{Ethyl butyrate}}{\underset{\parallel}{\overset{\text{C}_3\text{H}_7}{\diagdown}\text{C}\overset{\text{OC}_2\text{H}_5}{\diagup}}} + \underset{\text{Hydrazine}}{\text{NH}_2\text{NH}_2} & \longrightarrow & \underset{\text{Butyryl hydrazide}}{\underset{\parallel}{\overset{\text{C}_3\text{H}_7}{\diagdown}\text{C}\overset{\text{NHNH}_2}{\diagup}}} + \text{C}_2\text{H}_5\text{OH}
\end{array}
$$

$$
\begin{array}{ccc}
\underset{\text{Ethyl acetate}}{\underset{\parallel}{\overset{\text{CH}_3}{\diagdown}\text{C}\overset{\text{OC}_2\text{H}_5}{\diagup}}} + \underset{\text{Hydroxylamine}}{\text{NH}_2\text{OH}} & \longrightarrow & \underset{\substack{\textit{N}\text{-Acetylhydroxamic}\\ \text{acid}}}{\underset{\parallel}{\overset{\text{CH}_3}{\diagdown}\text{C}\overset{\text{NHOH}}{\diagup}}} + \text{C}_2\text{H}_5\text{OH}
\end{array}
$$

gives ammonium acetate. Reactions of esters with nucleophiles, although taking the same course as the reaction of aldehydes and ketones with nucleophiles, are in general much slower. This is because the alkoxyl oxygen atom to some extent diminishes the electron-withdrawing effect of the carbonyl oxygen atom. Al-

$$
\underset{(1)}{\text{CH}_3-\text{C}\overset{\text{O}}{\underset{\text{OEt}}{\diagup}}} \longleftrightarrow \underset{(2)}{\text{CH}_3-\text{C}\overset{\text{O}^-}{\underset{\text{OEt}^+}{\diagup}}}
$$

though no complete electron transfer, as depicted in **2**, actually occurs, the carbon atom of the carboxylate group is less electropositive than it is in an aldehyde or ketone group. Thus esters react more slowly with ammonia, amines, and hydrazine and will not react at all with weaker nucleophiles such as the bisulphite anion. In amides this effect is even stronger, and **4** makes a bigger contribution to the ground state of the amide molecule.

$$
\underset{(3)}{\text{CH}_3-\text{C}\overset{\text{O}}{\underset{\text{NH}_2}{\diagdown}}} \longleftrightarrow \underset{(4)}{\text{CH}_3-\text{C}\overset{\text{O}^-}{\underset{\overset{+}{\text{NH}_2}}{\diagup}}}
$$

Amides do not react readily with nucleophilic reagents, though they can be hydrolysed with aqueous alkali like the esters discussed above. They can also be hydrolysed by using acid catalysts; again the mechanism is similar to that for ester hydrolysis. If the ionic structure of the amide is important we should expect amides to show some acidic properties and this is, in fact, found. Thus amides are amphoteric substances and under special an-hydrous conditions form salts both with mineral acids and with alkali metals.

Acetamide as a base   Acetamide as an acid

Resonance Theory and Canonical Forms*

At the beginning of this chapter we found it was impossible to write a classical structure for the acetate anion and we suggested that one way of representing it was to draw two classical struc-tures separated by a double-headed arrow. The two classical structures are called *canonical forms*. The term 'canonical' meaning that, in the structures drawn, the classical theories of valency are obeyed. We were very careful to emphasize that the double-headed arrow does not mean that the negative charge is rapidly oscillating from one oxygen atom to another. The double-headed arrow is intended to indicate that the ground state of the acetate anion cannot be represented by either single structure but is somewhere between the two of them, i.e. with half a negative charge on each oxygen atom. In the last section of this chapter we have introduced canonical forms for ethyl acetate and aceta-mide. These differ very substantially from the acetate ion case because whereas the two structures of the acetate ion are of equal energy the two structures for ethyl acetate (**1** and **2**) or for aceta-mide (**3** and **4**) are of very different energy. The electronic distri-bution in ethyl acetate is fairly accurately represented by struc-ture **1** but there is a very slight migration of charge from the alkoxyl oxygen atom to the carbonyl oxygen atom. Complete transfer of charge is represented in structure **2**. We therefore say that structure **2** makes a very small contribution to the ground state of ethyl acetate which is more accurately represented by

* This section can be omitted in a first reading. It deals with more ad-vanced theory which is not essential to the present discussion.

structure 1. When we come to the amides the transfer of charge is much more important and structure 4 makes a much bigger contribution to the ground state of acetamide. This is to be expected because we know oxonium ions are, in general, much less stable than ammonium ions. Let us now consider the three examples: ethyl acetate, acetamide, and the acetate anion. The electronic distribution in ethyl acetate is fairly accurately represented by structure 1 although if we want to give a slightly more accurate picture we can say that structure 2 also contributes very slightly to the ground state of the molecule. With acetamide structure 3 does not give a very accurate picture of the electronic distribution in the ground state of the molecule although it is closer to it than structure 4. We can in this case say that 3 is still the predominant form but that 4 makes an appreciable contribution to the ground state. Finally, we come to the acetate anion. In this case a single canonical structure is definitely incorrect and the true electronic distribution in the acetate anion can best be depicted by saying that the two canonical forms make equal contributions to the ground state of the molecule.

This way of depicting organic structures is called 'resonance theory'. This is a most unfortunate name because it once again implies that the electrons are jumping backwards and forwards between the two structures. We can only emphasize for the third time that this is *not* the case. The term 'resonance' is derived from the quantum-mechanical theory from which resonance theory is derived. According to resonance theory, the acetate anion is not represented by either of the two canonical forms but as we have indicated is a combination of the two of them which is called 'the resonance hybrid'. Resonance theory further postulates that if a molecule can be represented as a hybrid of a number of canonical forms then the hybrid will be of lower energy than any of the constituent structures. We argued at the beginning of this chapter that acetic acid was a stronger acid than water or ethanol because in the acetate anion the negative charge is spread over two oxygen atoms and not isolated on one oxygen atom as it is in the hydroxyl anion or the ethanolate anion. This situation is described in resonance theory by saying that the acetate anion is a resonance hybrid of the two canonical structures and is therefore of lower energy than either canonical structure with the negative charge isolated on the oxygen atom. Resonance theory is an extremely valuable qualitative tool but it must be used with great caution. Particular attention must be paid to stability and to the number of canonical structures. All resonance theory says is that a resonance hybrid will be of lower energy than any single canonical form. Resonance theory tells us nothing about the absolute stability of a species relative to other species. This is a very common mistake. As we continue we shall use resonance theory more and more as a means of depicting electron distribution in organic molecules but it must always be remembered that it is only a crude picture and suffers from all the disadvantages associated with very simple theories if we attempt to carry it too far.

Nomenclature

Acids are named by adding the suffix '-oic acid' to the hydrocarbon from which they are derived ($CO_2H = 1$), e.g.

$$CH_3(CH_2)_3CH_2CO_2H \quad \text{Hexanoic acid}$$
$$CH_3CH_2CH_2\underset{\underset{CO_2H}{|}}{C}HCH_3 \quad \text{2-Methylpentanoic acid}$$

Esters are named by putting the radical derived from the alcohol as a first word and forming a second word by adding the suffix '-oate' to the name of the hydrocarbon from which the acid is derived, e.g.

$$CH_3(CH_2)_3CH_2CO_2CH_3 \quad \text{Methyl hexanoate}$$
$$CH_3CH_2\underset{\underset{CO_2C_2H_5}{|}}{C}HCH_2CH_3 \quad \text{Ethyl 2-ethylbutanoate}$$

Amides are named simply by adding the suffix 'amide' to the name of the corresponding hydrocarbon, e.g.

$$CH_3CH_2CH_2CONH_2 \quad \text{Butanamide}$$
$$CH_3CH_2CH_2CH(CH_2CH_3)CONHCH_3 \quad \text{\textit{N}-Methyl-2-ethylpentanamide}$$

Note elision of 'e' (hexane → hexanamide) before a vowel.

CHAPTER 9

Further Reactions of the Carboxyl Group

When considering the reactions of alcohols in Chapter 4, we discussed the reaction of an alcohol with phosphorus pentachloride to produce the alkyl chloride, phosphorus oxychloride, and hydrogen chloride:

$$\text{ROH} + \text{PCl}_5 \longrightarrow \text{RCl} + \text{POCl}_3 + \text{HCl}$$

Does the same reaction occur with the OH portion of the carboxyl group? The answer is 'yes'. These reactions probably involve electrophilic addition to the carbonyl oxygen. Thionyl chloride, $SOCl_2$, is usually a better reagent than phosphorus pentachloride because the inorganic products from the reaction—sulphur dioxide and hydrogen chloride—are both gases:

Electrophilic addition of $SOCl_2$ to the C=O bond followed by the elimination of HCl

An unsymmetric anhydride. Nucleophilic addition of Cl to C=O followed by the elimination of SO_2

**Acetyl
chloride**

Acetyl chloride is the first member of a general series of compounds called *acid chlorides* in which the hydroxyl group of the carboxyl composite group has been replaced by a chlorine atom. In Chapter 3 we considered how nucleophiles reacted with alkyl halides to give a substitution reaction, e.g.

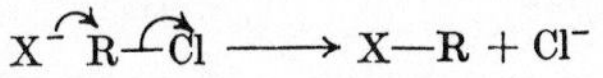

$$X^{\frown}R\frown Cl \longrightarrow X-R + Cl^-$$

and in Chapter 7 we considered how nucleophiles add to the carbonyl double bond, e.g.

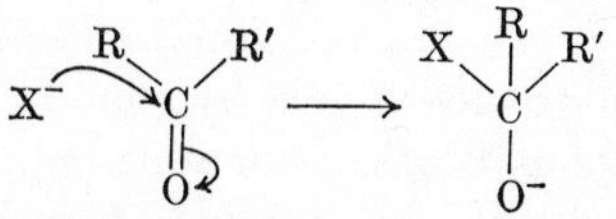

We therefore expect acid chlorides to react extremely rapidly with nucleophiles. Thus, even such an unreactive nucleophile as ethanol reacts rapidly with propionyl chloride:

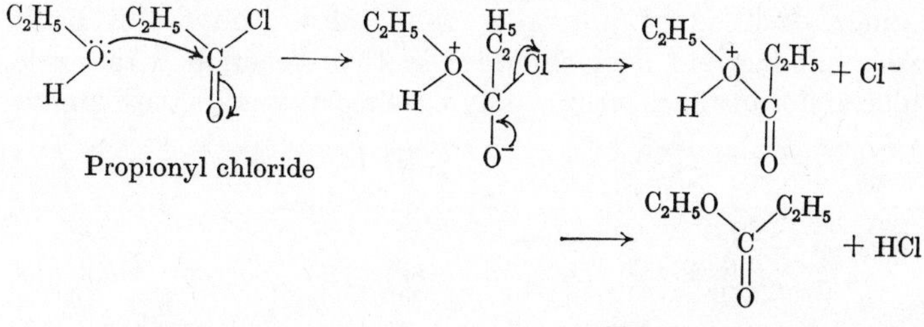

Propionyl chloride

Ethyl propionate

In a similar way acid chlorides react with water to regenerate the starting acid and hydrogen chloride. Amides can be prepared by the reaction of amines with acid chlorides:

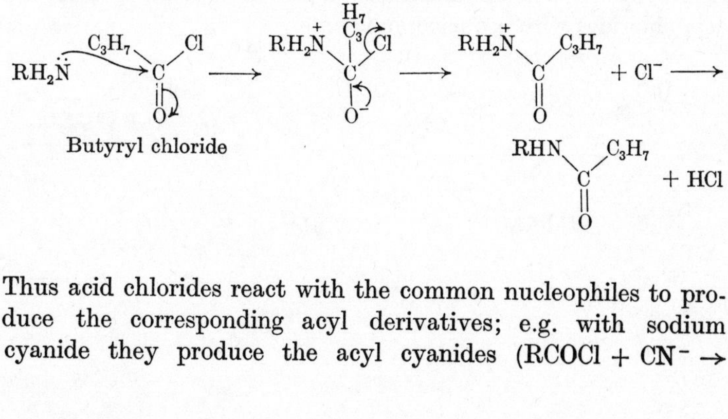

Butyryl chloride

Thus acid chlorides react with the common nucleophiles to produce the corresponding acyl derivatives; e.g. with sodium cyanide they produce the acyl cyanides ($RCOCl + CN^- \rightarrow$

RCOCN + Cl$^-$). A particularly interesting reaction is that in which the acetate anion is a nucleophile:

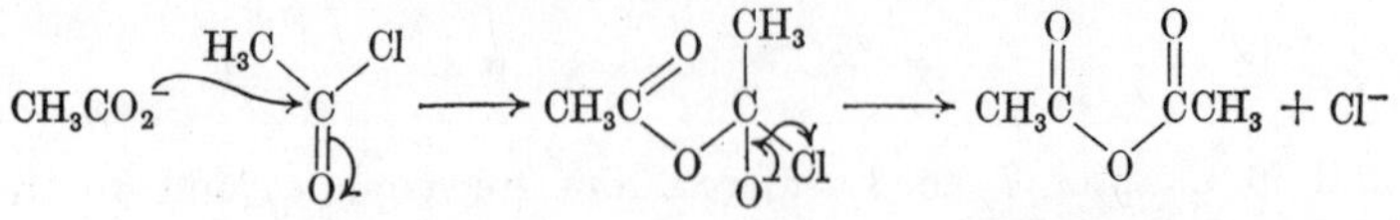

Acetic anhydride

Acid anhydrides, so called because they correspond to the combination of two molecules of acid by elimination of one molecule of water, are compounds of considerable importance in their own right. Acetic anhydride, for instance, is a commercial product used, among other things, in the manufacture of acetate rayon, a synthetic fibre. It is not made by the reaction of acetyl chloride and sodium acetate industrially, although this is a perfectly general method of preparing anhydrides. Anhydrides behave very similarly to acid chlorides in their reaction with nucleophiles. For instance, acetic anhydride reacts readily with amines:

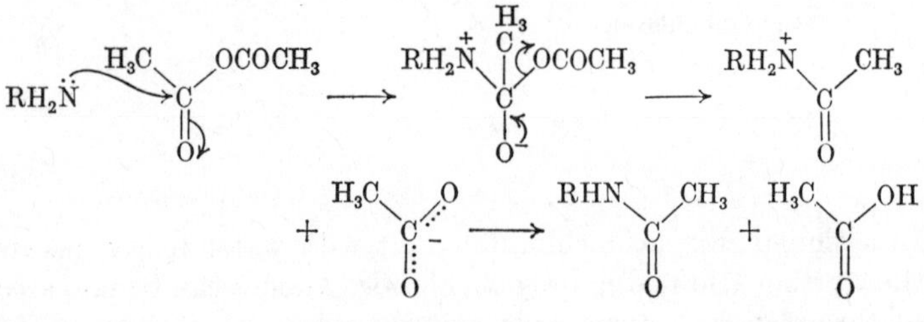

It is instructive to compare the reactions of esters, anhydrides, and acid chlorides with a nucleophilic anion:

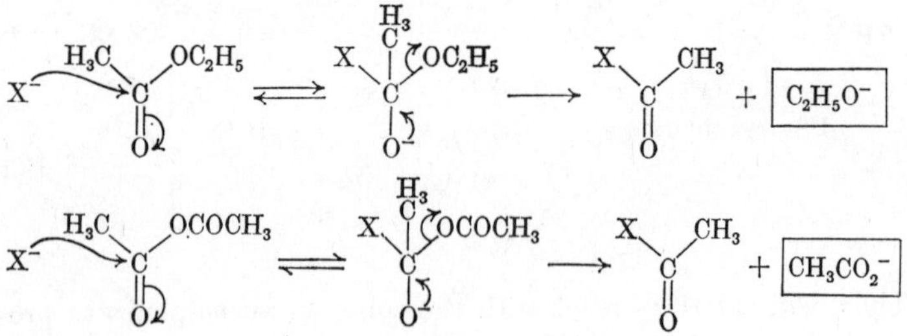

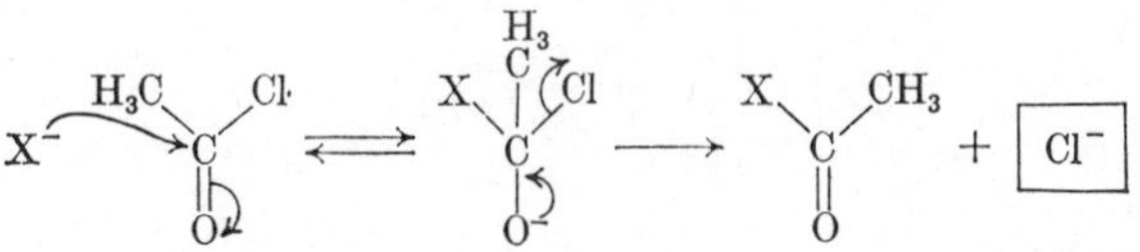

We need not consider the reaction between the nucleophile and the free acid because this only involves proton transfer:

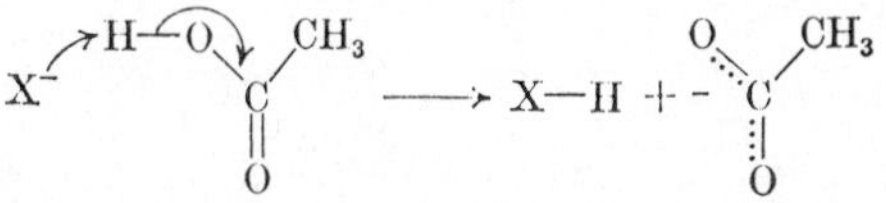

The other three reactions involve identical addition steps but in the subsequent elimination step they yield anions of increasing stability. The reaction with esters yields the ethanolate anion, the anion of an exceedingly weak acid, ethanol; the reaction with acetic anhydride yields the anion of an acid, but the weak acid, acetic acid; the reaction with acetyl chloride yields the chloride ion, the anion of a strong acid. Thus the reaction becomes faster down the series as the product anion becomes increasingly stable. The reaction of a secondary amine with ethyl acetate is extremely slow, with acetic anhydride it is quite rapid, but with acetyl chloride it can be violent and uncontrollable. Acid anhydrides and chlorides are used to prepare esters and amides. The acid-catalysed esterification of an acid is not always a practical proposition, particularly with unreactive alcohols such as tertiary alcohols, and the same argument applies to the synthesis of secondary amides.

Reduction Reactions

Esters, anhydrides, acid chlorides, and even free carboxylic acids can be reduced by lithium aluminium hydride. Like the reduction of aldehydes and ketones described in Chapter 7, this reaction involves 'hydride transfer' (see top of next page).

Notice that the first stage of the reaction yields the aldehyde which is then reduced further to the alcohol. In the reduction of esters and acids it is not practical to stop the reaction at the aldehyde stage, probably because hydride addition to the aldehyde

Ethyl butyrate   Butyraldehyde

Butanolate   Butan-1-ol
anion

goes more readily than hydride addition to the original ester. On
the other hand, with acid chlorides it is sometimes possible to
stop the reaction at the aldehyde stage. Amides can be reduced in
the same way to yield amines:

$$RCONHR' \xrightarrow[\text{Ether}]{\text{LiAlH}_4} RCH_2NHR'$$

Lithium aluminium hydride is a very expensive reagent; a cheaper
but sometimes less satisfactory reduction can be carried out by
using sodium in alcohol (the Bouveault–Blanc reaction).

$$RCO_2R' + 4\,Na + 4\,C_2H_5OH \longrightarrow$$
$$RCH_2OH + R'OH + 4\,C_2H_5O^- + 4\,Na^+$$

Catalytic hydrogenation of acids or esters is not normally a
practical laboratory reaction although it can be carried out on an
industrial scale with a copper chromite catalyst.

$$RCO_2R' + 2\,H_2 \xrightarrow[200°]{\text{Copper chromite catalyst}} RCH_2OH + R'OH$$

Although catalytic reduction of esters is a difficult reaction, catalytic reduction of acid chlorides to yield the aldehyde is a practical laboratory reaction (the Rosenmund reaction).

Though we have cited these reactions involving the reduction of carboxylic acid derivatives, none of them occur particularly readily and, in general, the reduction of the carboxyl group or its derivatives is not to be undertaken lightly.

Nomenclature

Carboxylic acid chlorides are named by adding the suffix '-oyl chloride' to the name of the hydrocarbon from which the acid is derived.

$$CH_3COCl \qquad \text{Ethanoyl chloride (Acetyl chloride)}$$

$$CH_3CH_2CH_2CHCOBr \quad \text{2-Methylpentanoyl bromide}$$
$$\underset{\displaystyle CH_3}{|}$$

Problem

1. Starting from acetic acid (ethanoic acid) how would you prepare the following compounds?

(a) ethyl acetate (ethyl ethanoate); (b) acetamide (ethanamide); (c) acetic anhydride (ethanoic anhydride); (d) N,N-dimethylacetamide (N,N-dimethylethanamide).

8

CHAPTER 10

Carbon Derivatives of the Inorganic Oxyacids

Derivatives of Sulphuric Acid

In a formal way we can replace the hydrogen atoms in sulphuric acid severally by methyl groups to yield methyl hydrogen sulphate and dimethyl sulphate. These are both esters of sulphuric acid. We can also replace a complete hydroxyl group by a methyl group and this gives us methanesulphonic acid; if both hydroxyl groups are replaced in this fashion we would obtain dimethyl sulphone.

| Sulphuric acid | Methyl hydrogen sulphate | Dimethyl sulphate | Methane-sulphonic acid | Dimethyl sulphone |

In Chapter 4 we considered esters of inorganic acids as being derived formally from the inorganic acid by replacing the OH group in the inorganic hydroxy acid by the alkoxy group of an alcohol. In Chapter 6 we showed how ethyl hydrogen sulphate can be prepared from ethylene and sulphuric acid. The sulphate esters can also be prepared directly from alcohols and sulphuric acid. We have discussed at some length how the esters of carboxylic acids usually react with nucleophiles in such a way that the carbon–oxygen bond of the alcohol remains intact.

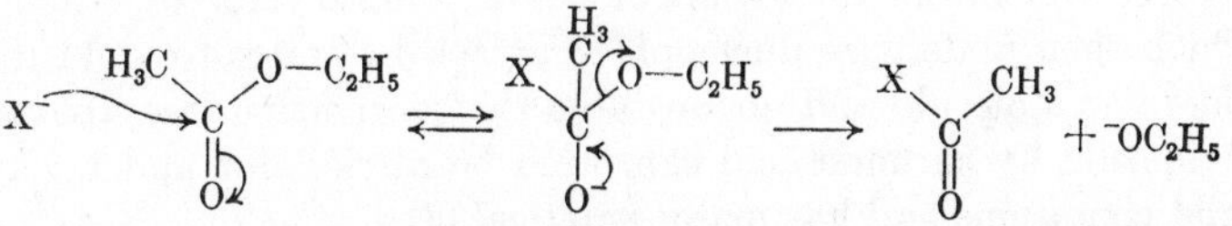

Esters of strong acids behave very differently. We could, for example, regard ethyl chloride as the ester of ethanol and hydrochloric acid. Ethyl chloride and a nucleophile undergo a displacement reaction. In a similar way esters of sulphuric acid undergo nucleophilic displacement at a carbon atom, rather than nucleophilic addition to the sulphur atom:

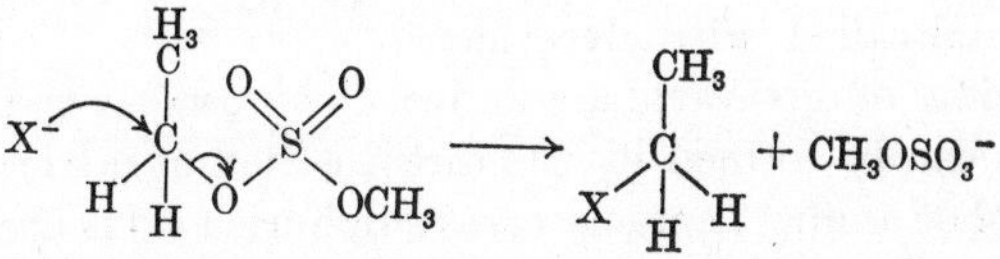

We see that if X is a hydroxyl anion and the product of the reaction is ethanol, the oxygen atom in the ethanol will be derived from the hydroxyl anion.

Organic amides of sulphuric acid are not particularly important but the amides of sulphonic acids are of great pharmaceutical interest as the so-called sulpha drugs or sulphonamides (extremely important antibiotic drugs) have the basic structure RSO_2NHR.

Derivatives of Chromic Acid

Although chromic acid esters are not readily isolated, they are believed to be intermediates in oxidation reactions involving chromic acid. Ethanol, for example, is converted into acetaldehyde when treated with chromic acid. This reaction is believed to

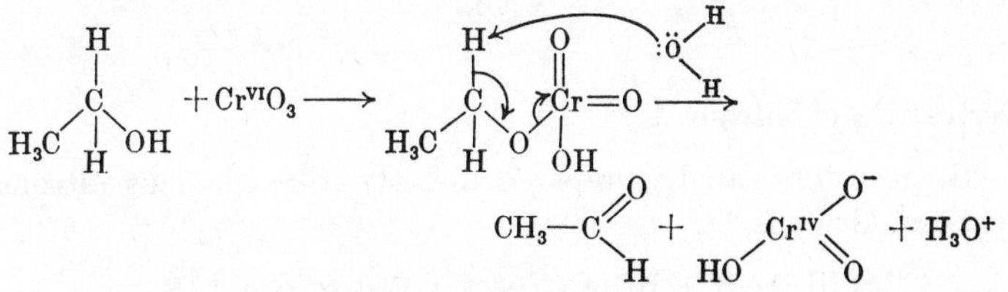

$$[3\ H_2Cr^{IV}O_3 + 6\ H^+ \longrightarrow Cr^{VI}O_3 + 2\ Cr^{3+} + 6\ H_2O]$$

involve the initial formation of the chromate ester of ethanol which then undergoes nucleophilic attack by water to yield the aldehyde molecule and an unstable Cr^{IV} derivative (see above). Oxidation by chromic acid can often be carried out under very mild conditions and has many practical uses.

Derivatives of Nitric Acid

In Chapter 4 we described how esters of nitric acid could be considered as being derived formally from the elimination of water between nitric acid and ethanol. We also discussed how the nitrate esters were explosive substances and glyceryl trinitrate is manufactured and called 'nitroglycerine'.

The amides of nitric acid are known as *nitramines* and they and the esters can be formed by the direct action of nitric acid with the alcohol or amine. In many cases sulphuric acid is used both as a catalyst and as a dehydrating agent.

$$RNH_2 + HO{-}NO_2 \longrightarrow RNH{-}NO_2 + H_2O$$
Nitramine

Nitramines, like nitrate esters, are explosive; the nitramine obtained by treating hexamethylenetetramine (see Chapter 7, p. 73) with nitric acid is known as RDX, and was one of the major explosives used by the allies during the Second World War.

RDX

Derivatives of Nitrous Acid

Nitrite esters can be prepared directly from aqueous nitrous acid and alcohols:

$$C_2H_5O{-}H + HO{-}NO \longrightarrow C_2H_5ONO + H_2O$$
Ethyl nitrite

The amides of nitrous acid are of considerable interest and importance. Tertiary aliphatic amines having no replaceable hydrogen do not react with aqueous nitrous acid. Secondary amines form the expected nitrosamines. These are yellow oils and, unlike the amine from which they are derived, are sparingly soluble in aqueous hydrochloric acid, so that an acid solution of a secondary amine treated with sodium nitrite yields the nitrosamine as a yellow oily precipitate:

$$
\begin{array}{c}
C_3H_7 \\
\diagdown \\
\hspace{1.5em} NH + HO{-}NO \longrightarrow \\
\diagup \\
C_3H_7 \\
\text{Dipropylamine}
\end{array}
\qquad
\begin{array}{c}
C_3H_7 \\
\diagdown \\
\hspace{1.5em} N{-}NO + H_2O \\
\diagup \\
C_3H_7 \\
\textbf{Nitrosamine}
\end{array}
$$

With primary aliphatic amines complications arise, for the initially formed nitrosamine undergoes rearrangement as shown in the following sequence:

$$
C_2H_5NH_2 + HO{-}NO \longrightarrow
\begin{array}{c}
C_2H_5 \\
\diagdown \\
\hspace{1em} N{-}N{=}O \\
\diagup \\
H
\end{array}
\longrightarrow C_2H_5{-}N{=}N{-}O^- + H^+
$$

$$
\longrightarrow C_2H_5{-}N{=}N{-}OH \longrightarrow
\left[
\begin{array}{c}
C_2H_5N{\equiv}N^+ \\
\updownarrow \\
C_2H_5\overset{+}{N}{\equiv}N
\end{array}
\right] + OH^-
$$

Diazonium cation

The product of these rearrangements is a diazonium hydroxide. Notice that one of the canonical forms drawn for the diazonium cation has a triple bond, i.e. six electrons shared between the two nitrogen atoms. This is the arrangement of electrons in the molecular nitrogen which we know is an extremely stable molecule. Aliphatic diazonium salts are unstable and decompose with the evolution of nitrogen, yielding a carbonium ion. In the particular case we have illustrated, the ethyl cation reacts with water to form ethanol but, contrary to what is said in many textbooks, this is not a general reaction and the carbonium ion may break down to yield a variety of other products.

$$C_2H_5 \overset{\curvearrowright}{\underset{}{-\overset{+}{N}}} \equiv N \longrightarrow C_2H_5^+ + N_2 \uparrow \xrightarrow{H_2O} C_2H_5OH + H^+$$

Ethyl diazonium salt Ethyl carbonium
(very unstable)   ion

One of the important features of these reactions is that it provides a method of distinguishing experimentally between aliphatic, primary, secondary, and tertiary amines. The amine may be dissolved in dilute hydrochloric acid to which sodium nitrite solution is then added: if the amine is primary, nitrogen will be evolved very rapidly; if it is secondary, a yellow oil will be precipitated; and if it is tertiary, no reaction will take place. Although the diazonium salt derived from primary aliphatic amines has only a transient existence it can be stabilized if the diazonium group is attached to an unsaturated carbon atom so that the positive charge on the nitrogen can be spread over more of the molecule. This is what happens with the amino derivatives of benzene, which we will have a great deal more to say about later on.

Aminobenzene (**Aniline**)   Benzene diazonium chloride
                               (moderately stable)

Finally, in certain cases instead of losing nitrogen the diazonium salt may lose a proton and this is what happens when glycine ethyl ester is treated with nitrous acid, and the product of the reaction is then called a *diazo compound*.

$$NH_2CH_2CO_2Et \xrightarrow{HNO_2} (\overset{+}{N} \equiv NCH_2CO_2Et) \xrightarrow{-H^+} \overset{-}{N} = \overset{+}{N} = CHCO_2Et$$
Glycine ethyl ester   Diazoacetic ester

Derivatives of Phosphoric Acid

With phosphoric acid we can clearly have three classes of ester: those in which one hydrogen atom has been replaced, those in which two hydrogen atoms have been replaced, and finally the neutral triphosphate ester.

$$
\begin{array}{cccc}
\text{HO}\diagdown\quad\diagup\text{OH} & \text{C}_2\text{H}_5\text{O}\diagdown\quad\diagup\text{OH} & \text{C}_2\text{H}_5\text{O}\diagdown\quad\diagup\text{OH} & \text{C}_2\text{H}_5\text{O}\diagdown\quad\diagup\text{OC}_2\text{H}_5 \\
\text{P} & \text{P} & \text{P} & \text{P} \\
\text{HO}\diagup\quad\diagdown\text{O} & \text{HO}\diagup\quad\diagdown\text{O} & \text{C}_2\text{H}_5\text{O}\diagup\quad\diagdown\text{O} & \text{C}_2\text{H}_5\text{O}\diagup\quad\diagdown\text{O} \\
\text{Phosphoric} & \text{Ethyl} & \text{Diethyl} & \text{Triethyl} \\
\text{acid} & \text{dihydrogen} & \text{hydrogen} & \text{phosphate} \\
 & \text{phosphate} & \text{phosphate} & \\
\end{array}
$$

We shall not discuss the reactions of phosphoric acid esters any further here, beyond briefly pointing out that the trialkyl esters can be prepared directly from phosphorus oxychloride, the acid chloride of phosphoric acid. The esters of phosphoric acid are of

$$3\ \text{C}_2\text{H}_5\text{OH} + \text{POCl}_3 \longrightarrow (\text{C}_2\text{H}_5\text{O})_3\text{PO} + 3\ \text{HCl}$$

interest because they occur very widely in biological systems. In living cells phosphoric acid residues are used in a manner somewhat similar to that in which an organic chemist might be considered to use the halogens. We use a halogen in an alkyl halide as a stepping stone to convert an alcohol, for example, into a carboxylic acid. We would convert the alcohol first into the alkyl halide and then treat that with sodium cyanide. Similarly, we would convert a carboxylic acid into an acid chloride before making an ester or an amide. In much the same way living cells convert compounds into phosphoric acid derivatives as stepping stones to converting them into some other product.

Problem

1. If you were given an unknown basic substance and were told that it was aliphatic, how would you distinguish as to whether it was a primary, secondary, or tertiary amine?

CHAPTER 11

The Carbon–Carbon Triple Bond
and the Carbon–Nitrogen Triple Bond

In Chapter 1 we considered a chemical bond as being formed by the sharing of two electrons between two atoms. In Chapter 5 the concept of a carbon–carbon double bond in which two atoms share four electrons or two pairs of electrons was introduced. We come now to consider a third type of bond in which two atoms share six electrons making up three pairs of electrons. This kind of bond is called a **triple bond**. We have already discussed two types of double bond: the carbon–carbon double bond occurring in ethylene, and the carbon–oxygen double bond occurring in aldehydes, ketones, and the derivatives of carboxylic acids. We shall similarly be concerned with two types of triple bond: the carbon–carbon triple bond occurring in acetylenes (alkynes), and the carbon–nitrogen triple bond occurring in nitriles (cyanides). It is worth noting that bonds between carbon atoms and other atoms involving four pairs of electrons are not possible.

We can consider acetylenes as built up in a formal manner from acetylene itself according to the scheme depicted opposite. Note that the acetylene molecule is linear.

Acetylenes undergo addition reactions similar to those described in Chapter 6 for the addition to the carbon–carbon double bond. Again, addition can occur by four different mechanisms: electrophilic addition, nucleophilic addition, free-radical addition, and a four-centre addition (re-read Chapter 6 carefully). With hydrocarbon acetylenes, the most important reaction is electrophilic addition. In spite of the fact that acetylenes appear to be more 'unsaturated' they undergo electrophilic addition less

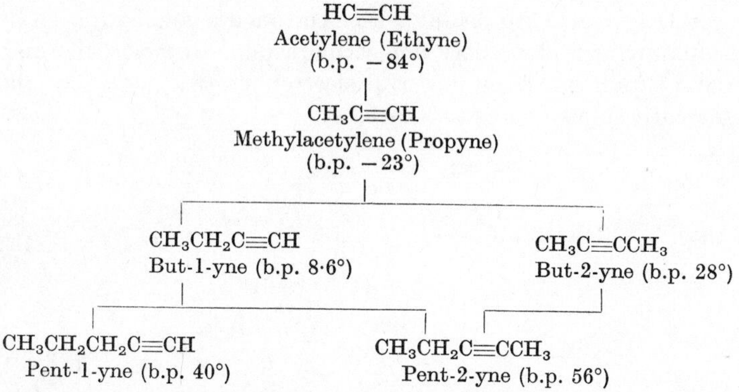

$$HC{\equiv}CH$$

Acetylene (Ethyne)
(b.p. $-84°$)

$$CH_3C{\equiv}CH$$

Methylacetylene (Propyne)
(b.p. $-23°$)

$$CH_3CH_2C{\equiv}CH$$
But-1-yne (b.p. $8\cdot6°$)

$$CH_3C{\equiv}CCH_3$$
But-2-yne (b.p. $28°$)

$$CH_3CH_2CH_2C{\equiv}CH$$
Pent-1-yne (b.p. $40°$)

$$CH_3CH_2C{\equiv}CCH_3$$
Pent-2-yne (b.p. $56°$)

readily than hydrocarbon olefins; for example, the reaction of vinylacetylene with one mole of bromine:

$$HC{\equiv}CCH{=}CH_2 \xrightarrow[\text{1 mole}]{Br_2} HC{\equiv}CCHBrCH_2Br$$

Apart from being slower, the electrophilic addition occurs by a similar mechanism to that previously described for olefins. For instance, the addition of hydrogen fluoride to but-2-yne can be formulated as follows:

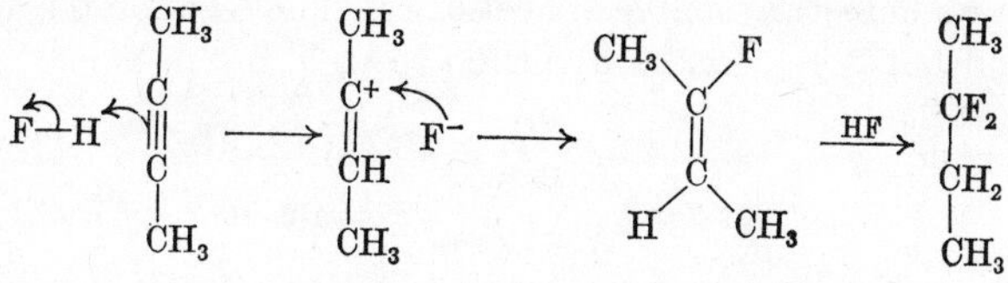

An extremely important reaction is the hydration of acetylenes. We recall·that the hydration of ethylene occurs by the addition of sulphuric acid to the ethylene molecule:

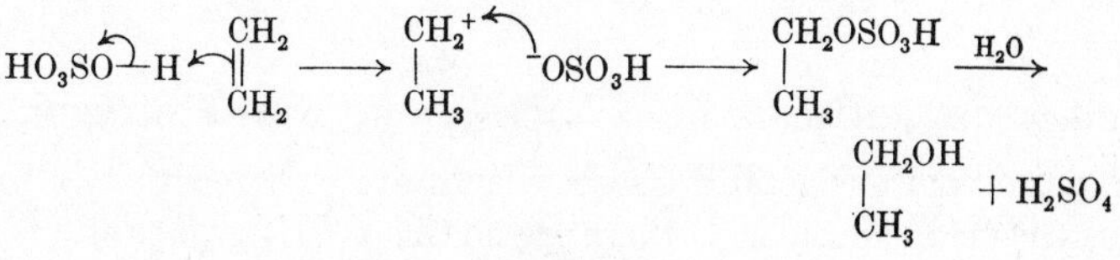

Acetylene reacts less readily with electrophiles, and hydration by sulphuric acid alone does not occur readily. However, the mercuric cation is a more powerful electrophile than a proton, and mercuric sulphate acts as a catalyst:

(Vinyl alcohol)   Acetaldehyde

The first product of this reaction, vinyl alcohol, cannot be isolated. The hydrogen atom migrates spontaneously from the oxygen atom to the carbon atom to yield acetaldehyde. The hydration of acetylene is an important industrial reaction. The acetaldehyde so formed may be oxidized to acetic acid. Acetylene is thus an industrial source of acetic acid. The reaction is a general one and but-2-yne can be hydrated to yield butan-2-one.

$$CH_3C{\equiv}CCH_3 \xrightarrow[\text{H}_2\text{SO}_4]{\text{Hg}^{2+}} CH_3CH_2COCH_3$$

But-2-yne   Butan-2-one

Acetylenes undergo nucleophilic addition more readily than alkenes and also undergo free-radical addition under certain circumstances, but both of these reactions are outside the scope of the present book.

The acetylenic triple bond can be oxidized but the reaction occurs much less readily than with an olefinic hydrocarbon. For example:

$$CH{\equiv}C(CH_2)_7CH{=}C(CH_3)_2 \xrightarrow{\text{CrO}_3} CH{\equiv}C(CH_2)_7CO_2H + O{=}C(CH_3)_2$$

In more vigorous conditions acetylenes are oxidized to two carboxylic acid molecules. If there are no CH or CH_2 groups adjacent to the triple bond, it is possible to stop the reaction at the α,β-diketone stage.

$$RC\equiv CR' \xrightarrow{\text{KMnO}_4} (RCOCOR') \longrightarrow RCO_2H + R'CO_2H$$

Hydrogenation of an acetylenic triple bond is an important reaction. Hydrogenation by means of gaseous hydrogen and the usual metal catalysts yields the saturated hydrocarbon. Partial hydrogenation over a special palladium catalyst yields the *cis*-olefin whereas hydrogenation by the chemical reaction of sodium and liquid ammonia yields the *trans*-olefin.

In Chapter 6 we discussed the mechanism of the catalytic reduction of olefins and it is easy to see how a similar mechanism applied to acetylenes will yield the *cis*-olefin. Chemical reduction, on the other hand, involves a two-step addition and yields the more stable *trans*-olefin.

We can regard the nitriles as being built up in a formal manner from hydrogen cyanide (see the scheme overleaf). Again the hydrogen cyanide molecule is linear.

It is instructive to compare the carbon–nitrogen triple bond in cyanides with the carbon–oxygen double bond in a carbonyl compound. As oxygen is more electronegative (i.e. attracts electrons more) than carbon we argued that two types of addition reaction were to be expected with a carbonyl compound: attack by a nucleophile at the carbon atom, or attack by an electrophile at the oxygen atom. We found that the most important electrophile was a proton. The same is true in the carbon–nitrogen triple bond. Nitrogen is more electronegative than carbon, and the cyanide triple bond can undergo nucleophilic addition by attack of the

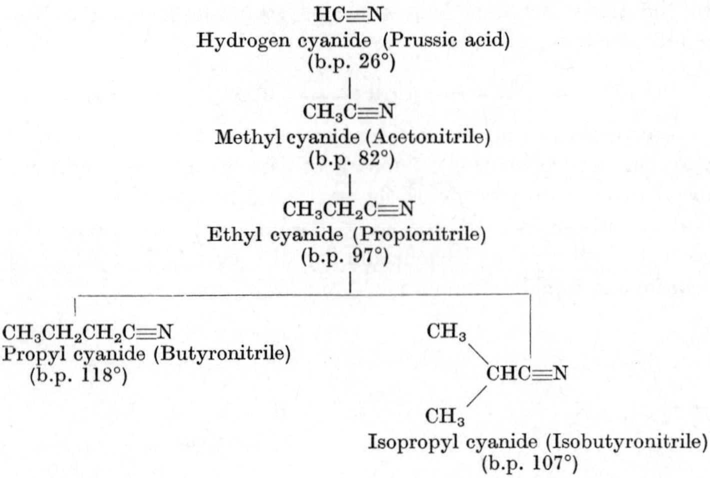
HC≡N
Hydrogen cyanide (Prussic acid)
(b.p. 26°)
CH3C≡N
Methyl cyanide (Acetonitrile)
(b.p. 82°)
CH3CH2C≡N
Ethyl cyanide (Propionitrile)
(b.p. 97°)
CH3CH2CH2C≡N
Propyl cyanide (Butyronitrile)
(b.p. 118°)
CH3
CHC≡N
CH3
Isopropyl cyanide (Isobutyronitrile)
(b.p. 107°)

nucleophile at the carbon atom or electrophilic addition as the result of an attack by the electrophile on the nitrogen atom. The most important reaction of a cyanide is hydrolysis to yield first the amide and then the carboxylic acid. This reaction can be either acid catalysed or base catalysed. We can write the base-catalysed hydrolysis as follows:

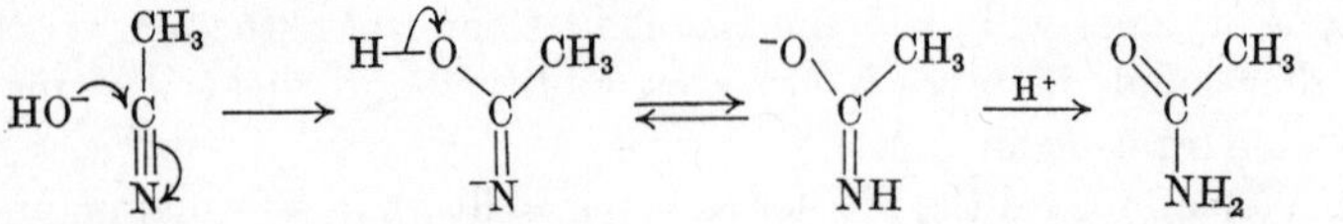
CH3
HO−
C
N
H
O
CH3
C
−N
−O
CH3
C
NH
H+
O
CH3
C
NH2

Nucleophilic addition to the carbon atom

The hydrogen atom migrates from the oxygen atom to the nitrogen, cf. vinyl alcohol above

The amide will then hydrolyse by the same mechanism as ethyl acetate (Chapter 8)

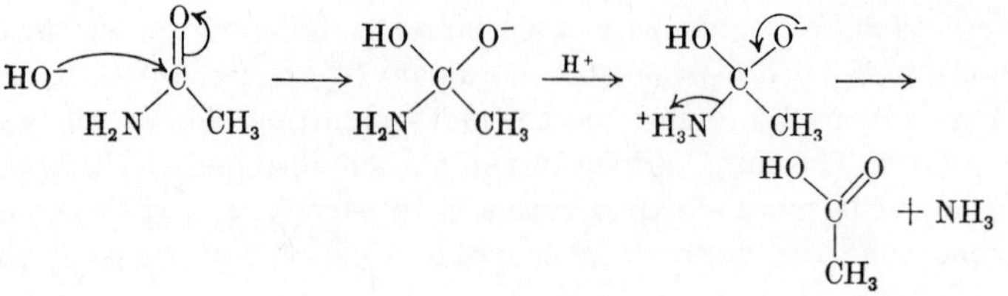
HO−
O
C
H2N
CH3
HO
O−
C
H2N
CH3
H+
HO
O−
C
+H3N
CH3
HO
O
C
+ NH3
CH3

In practice acid catalysis is a more useful reaction. In this case the proton adds to the nitrogen end of the triple bond:

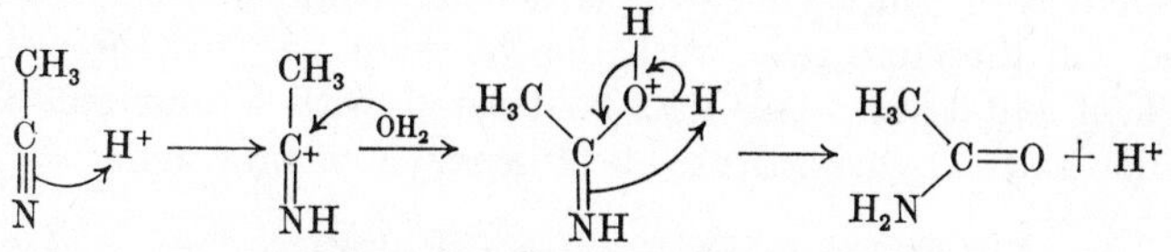

The hydrolysis of a cyanide to the corresponding carboxylic acid is of great synthetic importance. We have seen that it is possible to introduce the cyano group by replacement of a halogen. The cyano group can then be converted into the corresponding carboxylic acid. Thus we have lengthened the carbon chain.

For similar reasons the reduction of a cyano group is of synthetic importance. It can be achieved either catalytically or with lithium aluminium hydride:

$$R—C≡N \longrightarrow RCH_2NH_2$$

We are used to the idea that hydrogen cyanide is a weak acid ionizing to give a proton and a cyanide anion. It seems reasonable to ask whether acetylene might not also be an acid? The answer is 'yes', although it is an extremely weak one. The sodium salt of acetylene, sodium acetylide, can be prepared by direct interaction between acetylene and molten sodium. It is prepared more conveniently by the reaction of a solution of sodium in liquid ammonia. Alternatively, sodium acetylide can be made by displacing the anion of a still weaker acid from its sodium salt; e.g. acetylene and sodamide react together to yield sodium acetylide and ammonia:

$$HC≡CH + NaNH_2 \longrightarrow HC≡C^-Na^+ + NH_3$$

This reaction is also conveniently carried out in liquid ammonia solution. Now in Chapter 3 we considered the reaction of the cyanide anion with an alkyl halide resulting in a displacement reaction in which a carbon–carbon bond was formed and the halide ion expelled. We therefore expect that sodium acetylide would behave in the same fashion:

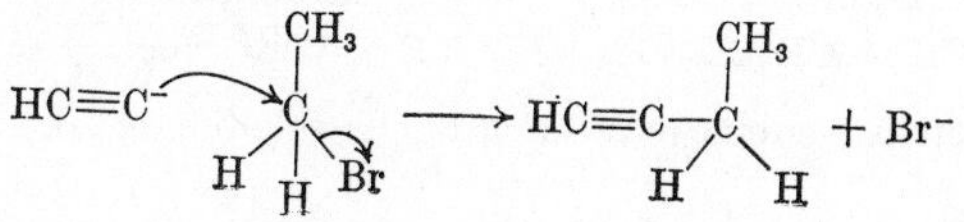

This is a general reaction and it is possible to build up a series of alkylacetylenes by this method. The compound so formed (in the present case, but-1-yne) still contains an acidic acetylenic group and will therefore react with the sodamide to yield the sodium salt of but-1-yne. This can be treated with a different alkyl halide and so a disubstituted acetylene will be prepared:

$$C_2H_5C{\equiv}CH + NaNH_2 \longrightarrow C_2H_5C{\equiv}C^-Na^+$$

$$C_2H_5C{\equiv}C^- \qquad \longrightarrow C_2H_5C{\equiv}CCH_3 + I^-$$
Pent-2-yne

Just as a cyanide anion will add to the carbonyl bond of a ketone forming a cyanohydrin, so, in a similar reaction, an acetylide anion will add to a ketone to produce an acetylenic alcohol:

The same reactions of the cyanide anions have been described in Chapter 3, p. 24 and Chapter 7, p. 71.

Nomenclature

Unbranched acyclic hydrocarbons having one triple bond are named by replacing the suffix '-ane' by '-yne' to the name of the corresponding saturated hydrocarbon; e.g.

$CH_3CH_2CH_2CH_2C{\equiv}CH$	Hex-1-yne
$CH_3CH_2CH_2C{\equiv}CCH_3$	Hex-2-yne
$CH{\equiv}CCH{=}CHCH{=}CH_2$	Hexa-1,3-dien-5-yne
$CH{\equiv}CCH_2CH_2CH{=}CH_2$	Hex-1-en-5-yne

(When there is a choice in numbering, double bonds take the lowest number.)

Problem

1. Starting from ethyl bromide how would you prepare the following compounds:

(i) propionic acid
(ii) hex-3-yne
(iii) hexan-2-one
(iv) n-propylamine

CHAPTER 12

Organometallic Compounds

In Chapter 3 the carbon–halogen bond was considered in the light of the first row of the periodic table. Lithium hydride is polarized in the form Li^+H^- while hydrogen fluoride is polarized in the direction H^+F^- and we argued that the carbon–chlorine bond would therefore be polarized in the direction C^+Cl^-. We should therefore predict that in methyllithium, the carbon–lithium bond would be strongly polarized in the direction $CH_3^-Li^+$. Hydrogen fluoride is a low-boiling liquid and hydrogen chloride is a gas. Lithium hydride and sodium hydride, on the other hand, are crystalline, and in the same way, methyl fluoride and methyl chloride are gases at room temperature whereas methyllithium and methylsodium are solids.

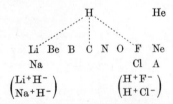

The organometallic compounds of the first two groups in the periodic table are most conveniently made by direct reaction of the metal with an alkyl halide in a solvent such as ether:

$$C_4H_9Br + 2\ Li \xrightarrow{(C_2H_5)_2O} C_4H_9Li + LiBr$$
$$\text{Butyllithium}$$

$$CH_3I + Mg \xrightarrow{(C_2H_5)_2O} CH_3MgI$$
$$\text{Methylmagnesium iodide}$$
$$\textbf{(Grignard reagent)}$$

Alkylsodiums are so reactive that ether is an unsatisfactory solvent because the alkylsodium attacks it. Even when a hydrocarbon solvent is used the alkylsodium is so reactive that further reactions can occur. Alkylsodiums behave, as we would expect, as powerful nucleophiles and react with unchanged alkyl halide either by a displacement reaction or by an elimination reaction:

$$C_2H_5Br + 2\ Na \longrightarrow C_2H_5^- Na^+ + Na^+Br^-$$

Unreacted   n-Butane
ethyl
bromide

Unreacted ethyl
bromide

The displacement reaction which leads to the coupling of two alkyl groups is often called the *Wurtz reaction*, but contrary to the impression given in many textbooks this is not a reaction of practical importance.

By far the most useful of the organometallic reagents are the Grignard reagents which can be prepared directly from an alkyl bromide or iodide and magnesium in dry ether. Unlike the sodium–carbon bond, the carbon–magnesium bond is only partially polarized and the Grignard reagents are soluble in ether and much more moderate in their reactions. In an alkyl halide the carbon atom attached to the halogen carries a partial positive charge. In a Grignard reagent the carbon atom attached to the metal has a partial negative charge so that, whereas the carbon atom attached to the halogen in an alkyl halide is susceptible to

9

attack by nucleophilic reagents, the carbon atom attached to the magnesium atom in a Grignard reagent is susceptible to attack by electrophilic reagents. The most common electrophile is a proton, and Grignard reagents will react rapidly with any source of a proton such as water or even an alcohol.

$$CH_3O\!-\!H \overset{\delta-}{C_2H_5}\!-\!\overset{\delta+}{MgBr} \longrightarrow C_2H_6 + CH_3OMgBr$$

$$HO\!-\!H \overset{\delta-}{C_4H_9}\!-\!\overset{\delta+}{MgI} \longrightarrow C_4H_{10} + MgIOH$$

Grignard reagents are a source of nucleophilic carbon and will react with any compound very susceptible to attack by a nucleophile, e.g. they will add to a carbonyl double bond:

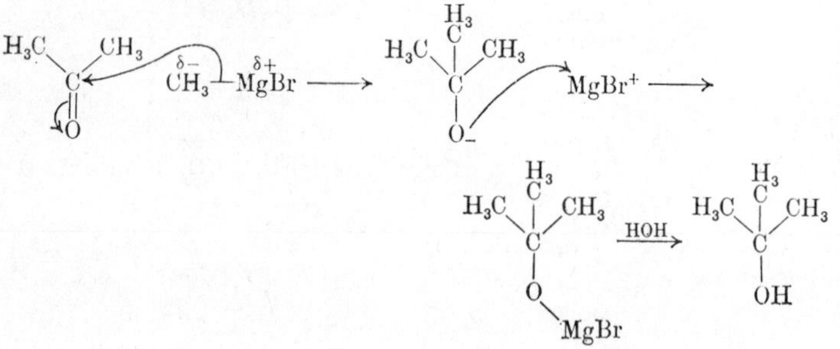

The initial addend formed in the ether solution is decomposed by water to yield the tertiary alcohol. In practice the mechanism of the reaction is slightly more complicated than this and two moles of the Grignard reagent may be involved.

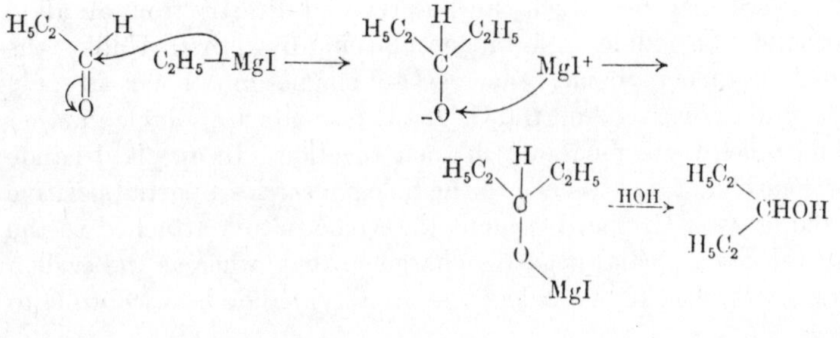

The reaction between a Grignard reagent and a ketone yields a tertiary alcohol. The reaction between a Grignard reagent and an aldehyde yields a secondary alcohol (see bottom of p. 116). Reaction with formaldehyde yields a primary alcohol, and this gives a method of ascending the homologous series:

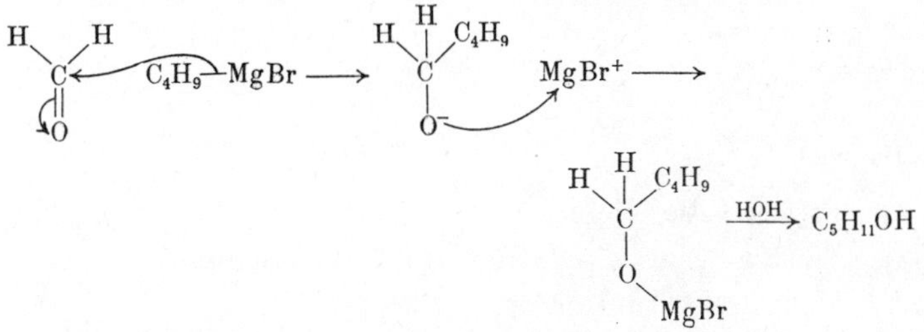

Just as nucleophiles add to aldehydes and ketones so they add to the derivatives of carboxylic acids. Grignard reagents react with carboxylic esters to yield initially ketones, which react further with more Grignard reagent so that the end product of the reaction of two moles of Grignard reagent with one of ester is a tertiary alcohol:

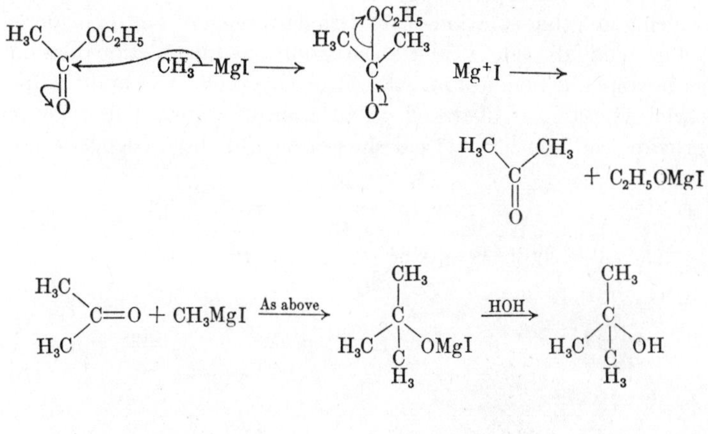

Acid chlorides behave in an analogous fashion:

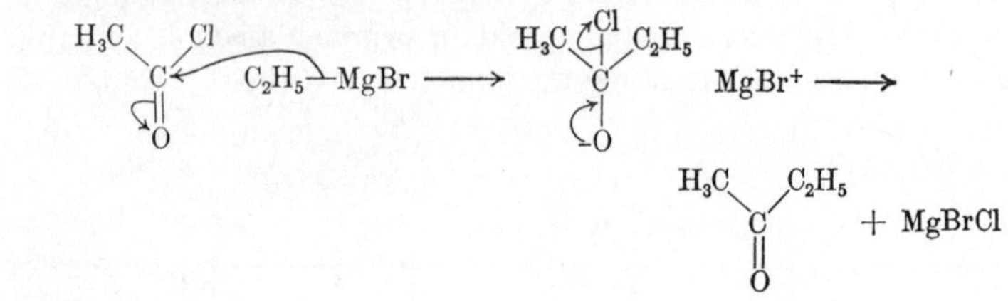

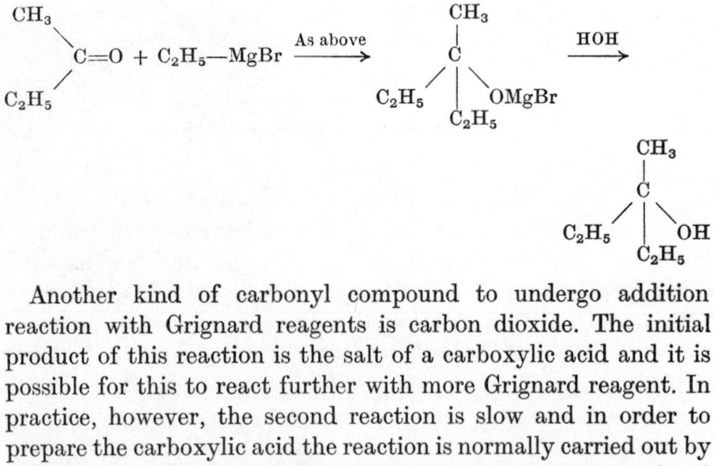

Another kind of carbonyl compound to undergo addition reaction with Grignard reagents is carbon dioxide. The initial product of this reaction is the salt of a carboxylic acid and it is possible for this to react further with more Grignard reagent. In practice, however, the second reaction is slow and in order to prepare the carboxylic acid the reaction is normally carried out by pouring an ether solution of the Grignard reagent on to powdered solid carbon dioxide. Under these conditions the reaction does not go beyond the magnesium salt of the carboxylic acid and the free carboxylic acid is liberated on addition of water. This reaction provides yet another method of ascending the homologous series.

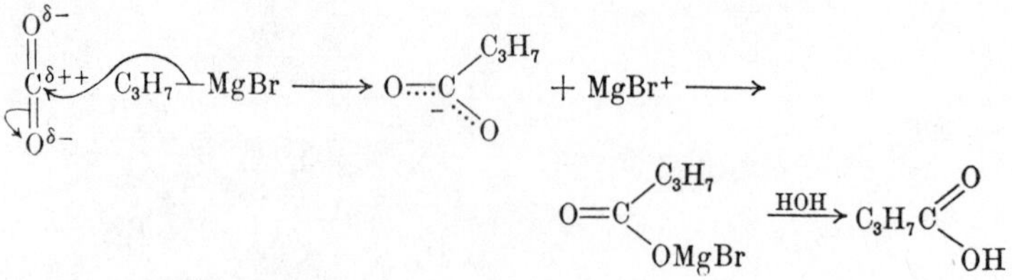

In the last chapter we discussed how nucleophiles would add to the carbon–nitrogen triple bond in a cyanide; therefore we should predict that Grignard reagents would add to the cyanide group in much the same way as they add to a carbonyl group. The initial products of the reaction, ketimines, are very unstable and rapidly hydrolyse to yield ketones:

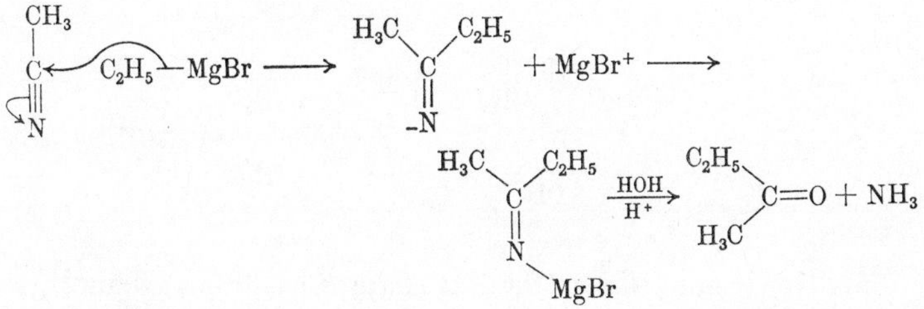

Grignard reagents can also be used for making other alkylmetal derivatives. For example, ethylmagnesium bromide reacts with lead chloride to yield tetraethyllead.

$$4 \ C_2H_5MgBr + 2 \ PbCl_2 \longrightarrow Pb(C_2H_5)_4 + 4 \ MgClBr + Pb$$

Tetraethyllead is the most important antiknock compound added to ordinary petroleum. Commercial preparation of tetraethyllead involves the reaction of ethyl chloride with a sodium–lead alloy at moderate temperatures and pressures.

$$4 \ PbNa + 4 \ C_2H_5Cl \longrightarrow Pb(C_2H_5)_4 + 4 \ NaCl + 3 \ Pb$$

Dialkylzincs, formed from the metal and an alkyl halide, are far too reactive for ordinary synthetic work; however, treatment of α-halo, preferably α-bromo, esters with metallic zinc dust, followed by addition of an aldehyde or ketone, results in a Grignard-type reaction. The product is a β-hydroxy ester, which can then be dehydrated to give an unsaturated ester (see top of page 120). This reaction is known as the *Reformatsky reaction* and is of considerable synthetic importance in the synthesis of a class of natural products known as the terpenes.

$$\text{BrCH}_2\text{CO}_2\text{Et} + \text{Zn} \longrightarrow \text{Br}\overset{\delta+}{\text{Zn}}\text{---}\overset{\delta-}{\text{CH}}_2\text{CO}_2\text{Et} \xrightarrow{\quad \overset{\overset{\displaystyle CH_3}{|}}{\underset{\underset{\displaystyle CH_3}{}}{O=C}} \quad}$$

$$\underset{\overset{|}{O^-}}{\overset{\overset{\displaystyle H_3C}{|}}{\underset{}{C}}}\!\!\!\overset{\displaystyle \text{H}_3\text{C}\quad\quad\text{CH}_2\text{CO}_2\text{Et}}{} + \text{Zn}^+\text{Br} \longrightarrow \underset{\overset{|}{O}\,\underset{\text{ZnBr}}{}}{\overset{\displaystyle \text{H}_3\text{C}\quad\quad\text{CH}_2\text{CO}_2\text{Et}}{C}} \xrightarrow{\text{H}_2\text{O}}$$

$$\underset{\overset{|}{OH}}{\overset{\overset{\displaystyle \text{H}_3\text{C}}{|}}{\text{H}_3\text{C}\quad C\quad\text{CH}_2\text{CO}_2\text{Et}}} \xrightarrow[\text{easily}]{\text{Loses H}_2\text{O}} \overset{\displaystyle \text{H}_3\text{C}}{\underset{\displaystyle \text{H}_3\text{C}}{}}C\!\!=\!\!CHCO_2Et$$

Finally, we note that in the last chapter we discussed another class of organometallic compound, namely, the alkali metal acetylides. Acetylenes are much more acidic than saturated or olefinic hydrocarbons and methylmagnesium iodide reacts with an acetylene to yield methane and the acetylenic Grignard reagent.

$$\text{C}_4\text{H}_9\text{C}\!\equiv\!\text{C}\!\!-\!\!\text{H} \quad \overset{\delta-}{\text{CH}}_3\!\!-\!\!\text{Mg}\overset{\delta+}{\text{I}} \longrightarrow \text{CH}_4 + \text{C}_4\text{H}_9\text{C}\!\equiv\!\overset{\delta-}{\text{C}}\!\!-\!\!\text{Mg}\overset{\delta+}{\text{I}}$$

Nomenclature

Organometallic compounds are designated by the names of the organic radicals united to the metal, followed by the name of the metal.

$$(\text{CH}_3)_2\text{Zn} \quad \text{Dimethylzinc}$$

For compounds in which an inorganic ion is also attached to the metal, the name of this ion follows the name of the metal as in any inorganic salt.

$$\text{C}_2\text{H}_5\text{MgBr} \quad \text{Ethylmagnesium bromide}$$

Problem

1. Starting from butyl bromide how would you synthesize the following compounds:

(a) n-$C_5H_{11}OH$

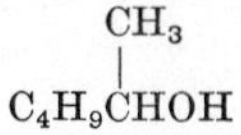

(b) $C_4H_9CO_2H$

(c)
$$C_4H_9\overset{\overset{\displaystyle CH_3}{|}}{C}HOH$$

(d)
$$\overset{\overset{\displaystyle CH_3}{|}}{\underset{\underset{\displaystyle CH_3}{|}}{C}}\diagup^{C_4H_3}\diagdown_{OH}$$

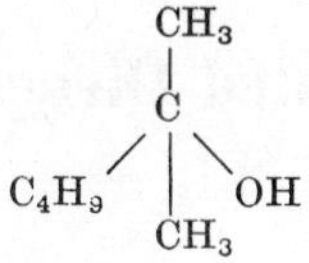

(e)
$$\overset{\overset{\displaystyle C_4H_9}{|}}{\underset{\underset{\displaystyle C_4H_9}{|}}{C}}\diagup^{CH_3}\diagdown_{OH}$$

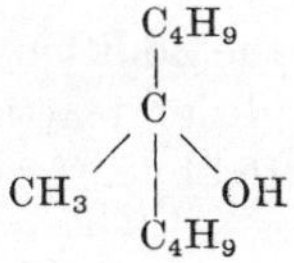

CHAPTER 13

Conjugated Dienes

In Chapter 6 we discussed the addition reactions of olefins. We come now to consider the addition reactions of diolefins in which two double bonds are separated by a single bond, as in butadiene:

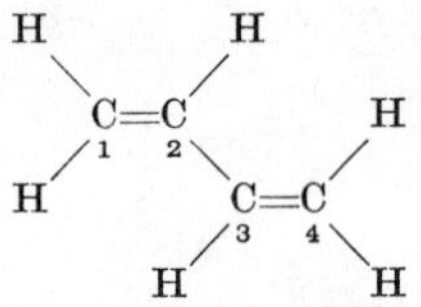

The reactions we particularly wish to consider are electrophilic additions to the double bond. As an example we choose the addition of bromine. The electrophilic addition of bromine to ethylene was described in Chapter 5 as a two-stage process:

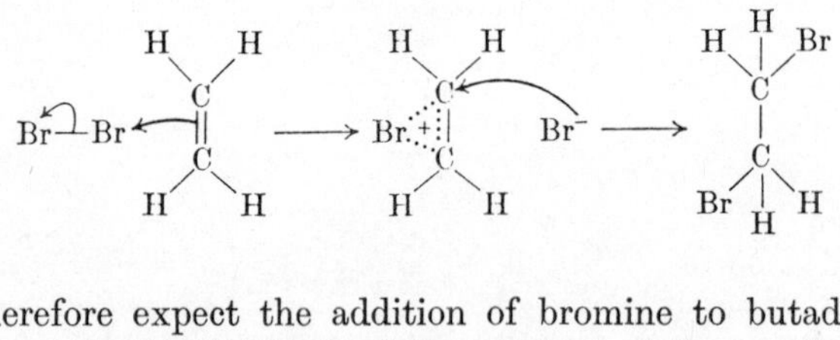

We therefore expect the addition of bromine to butadiene to occur in a similar fashion and the product of the reaction to be 1,2-dibromobut-3-ene. When we carry out the experiment we obtain two dibromobutenes. The 1,2-dibromobut-3-ene is usually present in the smaller amount while the predominant product is 1,4-dibromobut-2-ene.

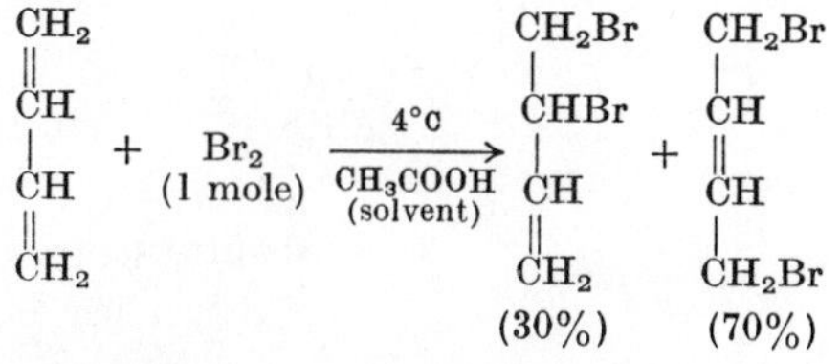

$$
\begin{array}{c}
CH_2 \\
\parallel \\
CH \\
\mid \\
CH \\
\parallel \\
CH_2
\end{array}
\;+\;
\begin{array}{c}
Br_2 \\
(1\ mole)
\end{array}
\;
\xrightarrow[\substack{CH_3COOH \\ (solvent)}]{4^\circ C}
\;
\begin{array}{c}
CH_2Br \\
\mid \\
CHBr \\
\mid \\
CH \\
\parallel \\
CH_2 \\
(30\%)
\end{array}
\;+\;
\begin{array}{c}
CH_2Br \\
\mid \\
CH \\
\parallel \\
CH \\
\mid \\
CH_2Br \\
(70\%)
\end{array}
$$

If we look at this reaction more carefully we see that we might have expected two isomers:

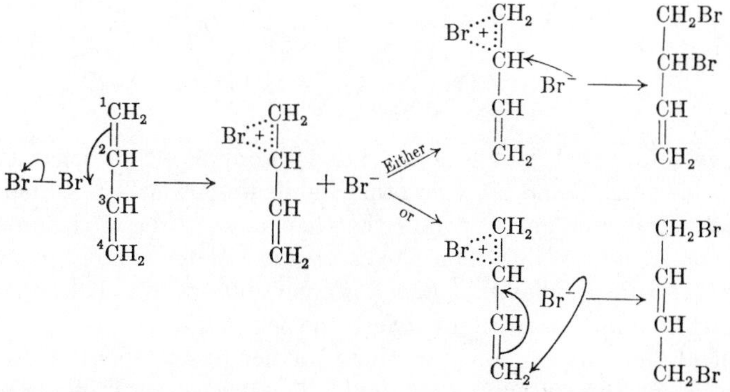

The first stage of the reaction proceeds exactly as with ethylene, but there are two positions at which the bromide anion can attack. It can either attack carbon atom 2 to yield 1,2-dibromobut-3-ene or the bromide anion can attack carbon atom 4. Such an attack will force one of the pairs of the electrons in the double bond between carbon atoms 3 and 4 to rearrange to form a double bond between carbon atoms 3 and 2, leaving one of the original pairs of electrons in the double bond between carbon atoms 1 and 2 to form the new carbon–bromine bond at carbon atom 1.

The next question we ask is, will the same reaction occur with longer chains of alternate single and double bonds? The answer is 'yes'. If, for example, we take hexa-1,3,5-triene and treat it with bromine two products are obtained: 1,2-dibromohexa-3,5-diene and 1,6-dibromohexa-2,4-diene (see top of next page). The one feature we should note about this reaction is that the 1,2- and the 1,6-dibromo compounds are formed, both of which

$$CH_2 \cdots CH - CH = CH_2 - CH = CH_2 \rightarrow$$

Br⁻

$$CH_2BrCHBrCH = CH - CH = CH_2$$
5,6-Dibromohexa-1,3-diene

$$CH_2 = CH - CH = CH - CH = CH_2$$
Br⌒Br

Either

to

$$CH_2 \cdots CH - CH = CH - CH = CH_2 \rightarrow$$

Br⁻

$$CH_2BrCH = CH - CH = CHCHBr$$
1,6-Dibromohexa-2,4-diene

have conjugated double bonds, i.e. with double bonds separated by one single bond. On the other hand, we get no 3,4-dibromo-hexa-1,5-diene. This suggests that a pair of conjugated double bonds is more stable than a pair of two isolated double bonds. This in turn implies that in the ground state of butadiene there must be some interaction between the two double bonds. We will not at the moment have anything further to say about electro-philic addition to conjugated double bonds. We simply note that the reactions we have described for bromine are quite general for all electrophilic additions, e.g. for the addition of HCl, although the reaction can be complicated in this case in that it may be a reversible reaction. Not only does electrophilic addition occur in a 1,4-fashion, but also free-radical and, when applicable, nucleo-philic addition can also occur in a 1,4-fashion. Conjugated double bonds will undergo all the same reactions that we described for ethylenic double bonds; for example, hydrogenation is usually by 1,4-addition.

There is one class of addition reaction which is peculiar to con-jugated dienes and this is the way they react with ethylenic double bonds to which a carbonyl or some similar grouping is attached. In this reaction, known as the Diels–Alder reaction, a conjugated diene reacts with a suitable ethylene called a *dienophile*. A classic example of this reaction would be that between butadiene and maleic anhydride:

Butadiene   Maleic
                 anhydride

The diene can be any hydrocarbon conjugated diene but the ethylene (the dienophile) must have an adjacent carbonyl or cyano group. Acrylonitrile, for example, will react with cyclohexadiene:

Cyclohexadiene   Acrylonitrile

The 1,4-addition and the Diels–Alder reaction are restricted to systems of alternate double and single bonds. Thus hexa-1,3-diene and hexa-2,4-diene both undergo 1,4-addition and will take part in Diels–Alder additions. Hexa-1,5-diene, on the other hand, shows none of these reactions, the two double bonds behaving like normal completely isolated ethylenic bonds. We may also note in passing that in hexa-1,2-diene (this type of compound is called an allene) the two double bonds do not interact in the same fashion as they do in a conjugated diene. Only in a conjugated diene is it possible to rearrange the electron pairs down the carbon chain when a reaction occurs.

$$CH_2=CH—CH=CH—CH_2CH_3$$
Hexa-1,3-diene

$$CH_3CH=CH—CH=CHCH_3$$
Hexa-2,4-diene

Conjugated double bonds

$$CH_2=CH—CH_2—CH_2—CH=CH_2$$
Hexa-1,5-diene   Isolated double bonds

$$CH_2=C=CH—CH_2—CH_2—CH_3$$
Hexa-1,2-diene   Cumulative double bonds

The Cyclohexatriene Problem

Let us now consider the possibility of a cyclic compound made up of alternate single and double bonds. In Chapter 5 we described how the bonds in ethylene all lie in one plane subtending exactly 120° to each other. We must now add the fact that the double bond in ethylene is slightly shorter (1·34 Å) than the single bond in ethane (1·54 Å). Cyclobutadiene, therefore, would not be perfectly square; nonetheless the carbon–carbon bonds would have to subtend an angle of 90° to each other. This would require substantial distortion of the ethylenic bond angles and as we discussed in the first chapter deforming bond angles introduces strain, making the molecule much less stable—so much so in this case that cyclobutadiene has not yet been isolated although many attempts have been made to make it.

Let us now turn to cyclohexatriene. We note at once that the internal angle of a regular hexagon is 120°, i.e. exactly the same as the bond angles in ethylene, so we come to the important conclusion that if cyclohexatriene exists it will be a completely planar molecule. We now have two possible structures for cyclohexatriene.

Two structures for 'cyclohexatriene'

These structures would only be distinguishable if we could distinguish between carbon atoms 1, 2, and 6. If, for example, carbon atoms 1 and 2 were carbon- 13 (^{13}C), while all the others were ^{12}C, then we could distinguish (a) which had a single bond between the two isotopic carbon atoms and (b) which had a double bond between the isotopic atoms.

Let us now compare these two structures with the structures we considered for the acetate anion in Chapter 8, page 86.

We found that whereas in acetic acid the two carbon–oxygen bonds are of different lengths, in the acetate anion they are of identical lengths and intermediate between the lengths of the two carbon–oxygen bonds in acetic acid. If we slightly distort our cyclohexatriene molecule, making all the bond lengths equal and retaining the 120° angle, we obtain a molecule in the shape of a regular hexagon. We now have a situation where it is no longer possible to distinguish between the 1,2-carbon–carbon bond and the 1,6-carbon–carbon bond. We can either write our molecule as the resonance hybrid of two canonical forms or we can do as we did with the acetate ion, write a dotted line as well as a single bond.

Now according to resonance theory (see Chapter 8), the resonance hybrid of our two structures will be of lower energy than either single structure. That is, 'cyclohexatriene' will be more stable than a normal conjugated diene, just as the acetate anion is more stable than an ethoxide anion.

Experiments show that the molecule C_6H_6, called **benzene**, is extremely stable. It shows none of the reactions of a polyene. It will not react immediately with bromine. It is only hydrogenated with considerable difficulty and it is not attacked by ordinary oxidizing agents. Very powerful electrophiles do add to benzene but instead of then adding an anion to yield a disubstituted cyclohexadiene the initial addend eliminates a proton, thus retaining the highly conjugated benzene ring. For example, although bromine itself will not add to benzene, in the presence of a catalyst such as aluminium bromide, reaction can occur. The product of this reaction is neither, 1,2- nor 1,4-dibromocyclohexadiene but bromobenzene.

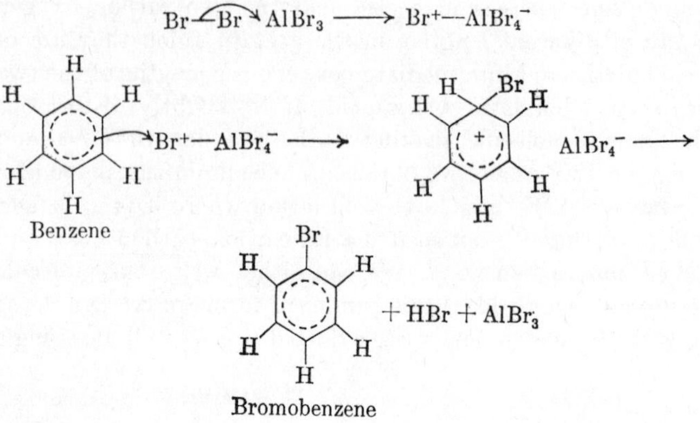

$$Br \overset{\frown}{-} Br \overset{\curvearrowleft}{} AlBr_3 \longrightarrow Br^+ \!\!-\!\! AlBr_4^-$$

Benzene

$\xrightarrow{Br^+ \!-\! AlBr_4^-}$

$AlBr_4^- \longrightarrow$

$+ \ HBr + AlBr_3$

Bromobenzene

It is commonly said that benzene undergoes not addition but substitution reactions. In some ways this is a somewhat unfortunate terminology because we see in the above equations that the first step of the reaction is identical with the electrophilic addition

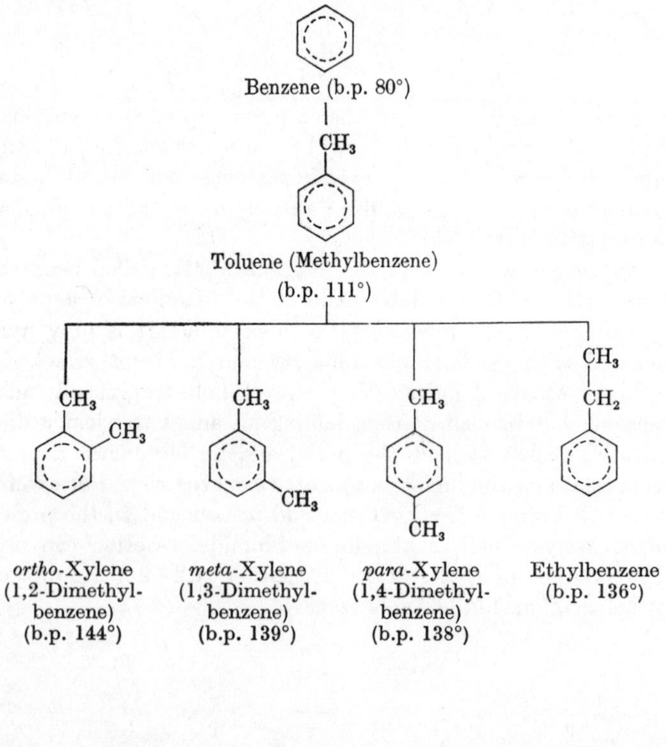

Benzene (b.p. 80°)

CH$_3$

Toluene (Methylbenzene)
(b.p. 111°)

ortho-Xylene	meta-Xylene	para-Xylene	Ethylbenzene

ortho-Xylene
(1,2-Dimethyl-
benzene)
(b.p. 144°)

meta-Xylene
(1,3-Dimethyl-
benzene)
(b.p. 139°)

para-Xylene
(1,4-Dimethyl-
benzene)
(b.p. 138°)

Ethylbenzene
(b.p. 136°)

we are familiar with in the reactions of ethylene. It is because of the great stability of the benzene ring that the initial addend prefers to eject the proton ultimately to form hydrogen bromide, rather than to add the bromine anion. This addition-with-elimination reaction of benzene, resulting in substitution, is very characteristic and benzene is considered to be the archetype of a group of cyclic molecules called *aromatic compounds* which undergo the same type of reaction.

The simpler derivatives of benzene have names as depicted above.

Polycyclic Aromatic Compounds

Phenylethylene ($C_6H_5CH=CH_2$), called *styrene*, behaves like a normal substituted ethylene and undergoes the usual electrophilic addition reactions; it can be readily oxidized and reduced. All these reactions occur at the side-chain double bond, the benzene nucleus remaining unaffected. Similarly 1,4-diphenyl-buta-1,3-diene ($C_6H_5CH=CHCH=CHC_6H_5$) undergoes the normal reactions of a conjugated diene. However, we can visualize a compound in which four carbon atoms are attached to a benzene

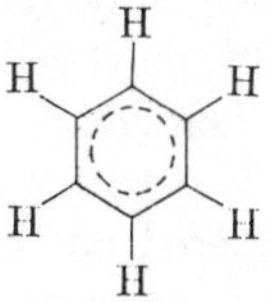

Benzene
(Colourless
liquid,
b.p. 80°)

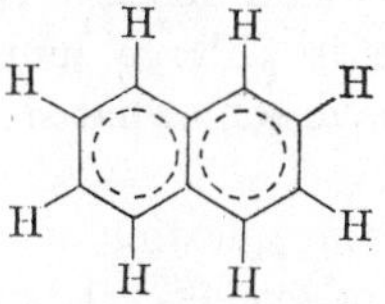

Naphthalene
(White solid,
m.p. 80°)

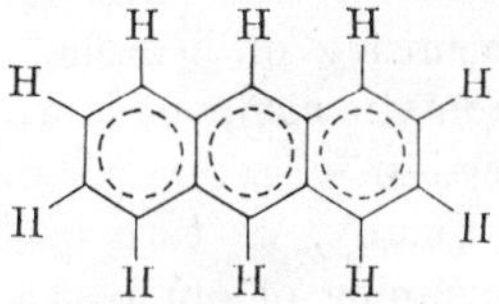

Anthracene
(Blue fluorescent
solid, m.p. 216°)

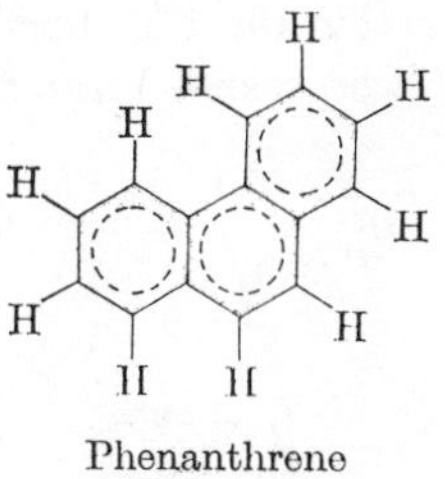

Phenanthrene
(White solid,
m.p. 101°)

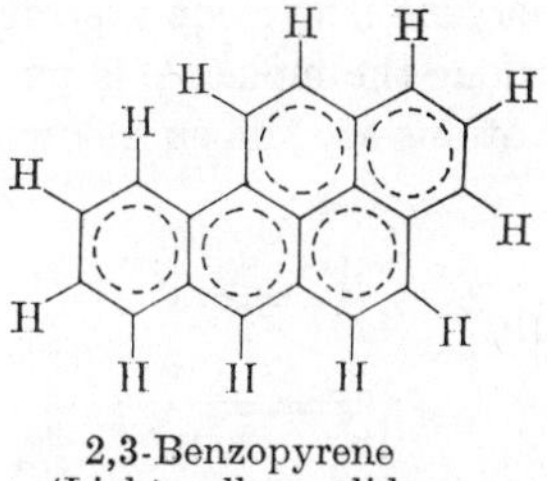

2,3-Benzopyrene
(Light yellow solid,
m.p. 179°)

ring so as to form a second benzene ring fused to the first. This compound is called *naphthalene* and it possesses most of the chemical properties of benzene.

It is possible to build up a series of condensed ring systems. We have drawn two compounds containing three benzene rings: anthracene, the linear compound, and phenanthrene, the angular compound (p. 129). The linear compounds become increasingly reactive as more benzene rings are fused together and even anthracene behaves in many ways more like a diene than a benzenoid aromatic compound. We have included one example of a compound containing five condensed benzene rings, 3,4-benzopyrene. This is an extremely carcinogenic compound. If painted on the skin it produces a skin cancer, and if injected it gives rise to sarcomas (tumours of connective tissue). Benzopyrene is particularly dangerous as it has been shown to be formed in the combustion processes of many organic materials and there is little doubt that it is one of the agents responsible for lung cancer.

In the next chapter we will consider the chemical properties of benzene in greater detail. The chemistry of the polycyclic aromatic compounds will not be discussed further in this book. Note, however, that although we shall discuss in detail only the chemistry of benzene, there is a large number of polycyclic aromatic compounds which have somewhat similar chemical properties.

Finally, we turn back to the question we considered at the beginning of our discussion of cyclohexatriene. Can we expect other cyclic compounds to have the great stability characteristic of the benzene molecule?

We have already considered cyclobutadiene. The next possible cyclopolyene is cyclooctatetraene. To retain the 120° bond angle of ethylene the molecule is puckered. Two possible arrangements of the atoms are shown below:

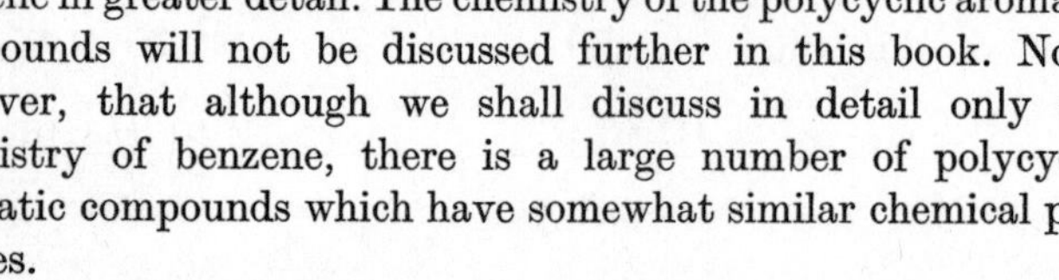

Possible conformations of cyclooctatetraene

It is impossible to draw two equivalent structures of cycloocta-tetraene retaining the 120° bond angle without moving the carbon atoms. Two equivalent structures can be drawn if we distort the molecule in such a way that all the carbon atoms lie in a plane (it is in fact a requirement of resonance theory that all the atoms participating in different canonical forms lie in the same plane); however, the energy required to distort cycloocta-tetraene into planar form is greater than the energy that would be gained by resonance, so that cyclooctatetraene is a puckered molecule and in consequence undergoes the normal reactions of a polyene.

At first sight, cyclodecapentaene could retain the 120° angle between the carbon atoms and still be planar; however, there must then be hydrogen atoms inside the ring and these are so close together that they 'overlap'; because of this, the molecule is not, in fact, perfectly planar. The smallest compound which will retain the 120° angle and remain planar is that compound containing 18 carbon atoms. Even here the hydrogen atoms inside the ring are so close that they probably cause slight non-planarity of the molecule.

Cyclodecapentaene   Cyclooctadecanonaene

Cyclooctadecanonaene has been synthesized recently and it proves to be a reasonably stable compound; it shows certain spectroscopic properties (especially nuclear magnetic resonance spectra) and to a lesser extent chemical properties characteristic of benzene.

In suggesting that the unique stability of benzene can be attributed to the planar nature of the molecule and the fact that the 120° angle of the ethylenic double bond is not distorted, we

10

are oversimplifying the problem. Nonetheless, these steric properties are key factors in determining the special properties of benzene.

Problems

1. What reaction would you predict between 2,3-dimethylbuta-1,3-diene and (*a*) 1 molar equivalent of bromine, (*b*) maleic anhydride, and (*c*) ozone followed by treatment with zinc and acetic acid.

2. How many compounds with the molecular formula $C_{18}H_{12}$ (from benzene rings fused together) can you draw?

CHAPTER 14

Reactions of the Aromatic Nucleus

In the last chapter we described how benzene, which does not react with bromine in the cold by itself, will react in the presence of a catalyst. The function of the catalyst is to produce an incipient bromine cation; suitable catalysts are metal halides capable of accepting an electron pair; ferric bromide is very commonly used. In the last chapter we depicted the reaction as follows:

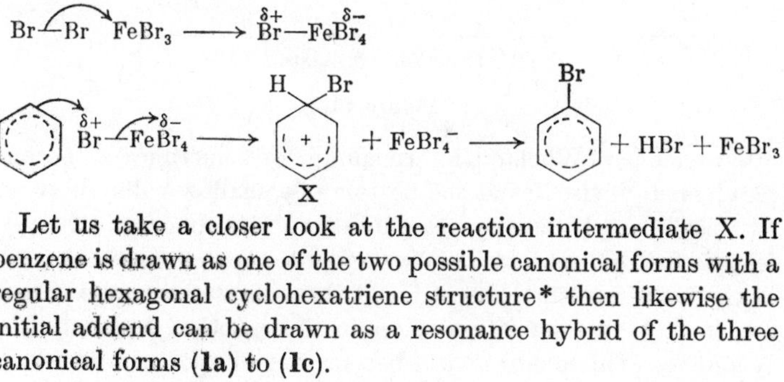

Let us take a closer look at the reaction intermediate X. If benzene is drawn as one of the two possible canonical forms with a regular hexagonal cyclohexatriene structure* then likewise the initial addend can be drawn as a resonance hybrid of the three canonical forms (1a) to (1c).

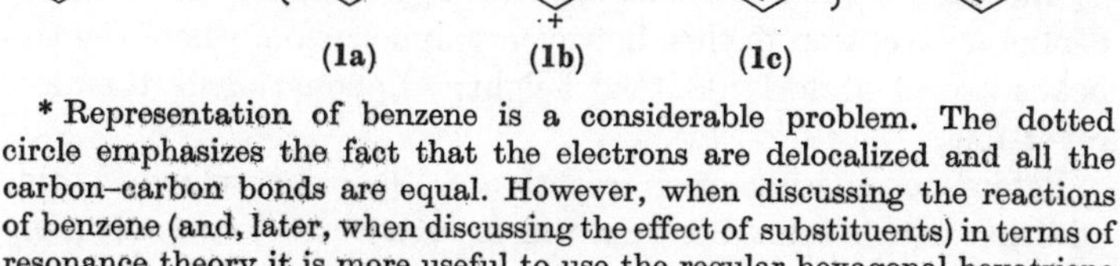

(1a) (1b) (1c)

* Representation of benzene is a considerable problem. The dotted circle emphasizes the fact that the electrons are delocalized and all the carbon–carbon bonds are equal. However, when discussing the reactions of benzene (and, later, when discussing the effect of substituents) in terms of resonance theory it is more useful to use the regular hexagonal hexatriene structure, usually called a 'Kekulé structure'.

133

According to resonance theory if a molecule can be represented by
more than one canonical form the complete resonance hybrid will
be more stable than any one of the single forms. This suggests
that the initial addend of an electrophilic addition to an aromatic
compound is more stable than an isolated carbonium ion. We can
represent this by a diagram of the kind we used in Chapter 2 when
discussing the chlorination of alkanes (Figure 14.1). The addend,

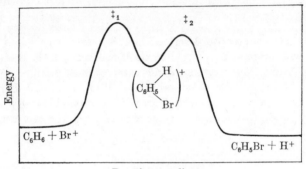

Figure 14.1

often called a 'Wheland intermediate' or sometimes a 'σ complex', energy-wise lies at the bottom of a shallow valley between
two peaks on the energy–reaction coordinate diagram. The first
feature to notice is that the Wheland intermediate does not occur
at the transition state, i.e. it is not the activated complex. There
are, in fact, two transition states in this reaction designated by
$\ddagger_1$ and $\ddagger_2$. (This diagram will become very important at a later
stage when considering the factors which control the rate and
orientation of these reactions.) In bromination, and in the majority
of other reactions that we shall discuss, $\ddagger_1$ is of higher energy than
$\ddagger_2$ and the reactions are thus not readily reversible. There is one
common exception to this, however: sulphonation, where the two
peaks are of almost identical height; sulphonation is therefore
reversible.

Before considering other reactions of benzene, which involve
addition-with-elimination resulting in substitution, we shall briefly
repeat our previous discussion. The first stage of these reactions

proceeds in an analogous manner to the additions which occur to olefinic double bonds. The difference between olefins on the one hand and benzene on the other is that the initial addend, which must always be a carbonium ion and therefore never a very stable species, stabilizes itself in the case of an olefin by adding an anion, but with benzene, because of the great stability of the aromatic nucleus, it ejects a proton. The most common electrophile is the proton itself. Such a reaction would therefore merely involve the interchange of two hydrogen atoms and we can only detect such a reaction by using a deuteron acid instead of a proton acid.

$$DF + BF_3 \longrightarrow D^+ - BF_4^-$$

If we do this the expected replacement of a hydrogen atom by a deuterium atom takes place.

The best known of these addition-with-elimination reactions of the aromatic nucleus is nitration, but before we can discuss nitration we must have a brief look at the chemistry of nitric acid. In water nitric acid is a strong acid, i.e. it is completely dissociated, and in this sense its strength is indistinguishable from that of sulphuric acid which is also completely dissociated. However, if we take a less basic solvent such as acetic acid, nitric acid is then only partially dissociated, i.e. it is behaving as a weak acid whereas sulphuric acid is still completely dissociated.

$$HNO_3 + H_2O \longrightarrow H_3O^+ + NO_2^-$$

$$H_2SO_4 + H_2O \longrightarrow H_3O^+ + HSO_4^-$$

Both acids completely dissociated in water.
(We are not concerned with the second dissociation of sulphuric acid.)

$$HNO_3 + CH_3CO_2H \xrightarrow{\longrightarrow} CH_3CO_2H_2^+ + NO_3^-$$

$$H_2SO_4 + CH_3CO_2H \longrightarrow CH_3CO_2H_2^+ + HSO_4^-$$

In acetic acid nitric acid is only slightly dissociated whereas sulphuric acid is still completely dissociated.

Notice that acetic acid, which behaves as a weak acid in water, becomes a base in nitric acid or in sulphuric acid. Nitric acid, which is a strong acid in water, becomes a weak acid in acetic acid. It is reasonable, therefore, to ask if nitric acid will become a base in sulphuric acid. The answer is 'yes', but the reaction is complicated by the fact that the conjugate acid is unstable and decomposes into a water molecule and a nitronium ion (NO_2^+). The water molecule produced in this reaction is immediately protonated by more sulphuric acid.

$$H_2SO_4 + HNO_3 \; \underset{\longleftarrow}{\overset{\longrightarrow}{}} \; H_2NO_3^+ + HSO_4^-$$
$$\text{Nitric acidium ion}$$

$$H_2NO_3^+ \; \underset{\longleftarrow}{\overset{\longrightarrow}{}} \; H_2O + NO_2^+$$
$$\text{Nitronium ion}$$

$$H_2SO_4 + H_2O \; \underset{\longrightarrow}{\overset{\longleftarrow}{}} \; H_3O^+ + HSO_4^-$$

$$\overline{2\,H_2SO_4 + HNO_3 \; \underset{\longrightarrow}{\overset{\longleftarrow}{}} \; NO_2^+ + H_3O^+ + 2\,HSO_4^-}$$

In a sulphuric acid solution nitric acid is converted largely into the nitronium ion. Notice that the nitronium ion can only exist in a medium in which there is no free water. The nitronium ion would react instantly with water to regenerate nitric acid. Further discussion of the properties of nitric acid are clearly not our concern at present. The important point is that in a solution of nitric acid in sulphuric acid we have a high concentration of this very reactive nitronium ion. This ion is an extremely powerful electrophile and we would therefore expect it to add electrophilically to the benzene nucleus. The ultimate product of this reaction is called nitrobenzene:

$$HNO_3 + 2\,H_2SO_4 \; \rightleftharpoons \; NO_2^+ + H_3O^+ + 2\,HSO_4^-$$

Nitrobenzene

The nitronium ion will add to olefinic double bonds but in the presence of such strong electrophiles most olefins tend to undergo complex polymerization (cf. Chapter 6). In sulphuric acid the main electrophile is, of course, a proton and we have already discussed the addition of a proton to benzene. In oleum, that is sulphuric acid containing sulphur trioxide, sulphur trioxide can behave as a very powerful electrophile:

Benzenesulphonic acid

This reaction, as we have already mentioned, is reversible, unlike most of the other reactions.

Alkyl halides react with aluminium chloride to form an ionic complex in which the carbon atom originally attached to the halogen carries a positive charge. This then is capable of acting as an electrophile to attack the benzene nucleus:

$$C_2H_5Cl + AlCl_3 \rightleftharpoons C_2H_5 \overset{\delta+}{-} \overset{\delta-}{AlCl_4}$$

Ethylbenzene

This reaction is called the *Friedel–Crafts reaction* and is of considerable practical importance. Notice that the aluminium chloride is regenerated at the end of the sequence and is therefore only required in catalytic amounts. If this reaction occurs with an alkyl halide, it is reasonable to ask whether it will occur with an acid chloride? The answer to this question is 'yes'. In this reaction the ketone produced forms a complex with the aluminium chloride and for this reason molecular quantities of aluminium chloride are required. Contrary to the suggestion in very many textbooks, the free acylium ion (CH_3CO^+) will not react with

$$CH_3COCl + AlCl_3 \rightleftharpoons CH_3\overset{\delta+}{CO}\!-\!\overset{\delta-}{AlCl_4}$$

$$+ 4\,HCl + Al(OH)_3$$

Acetophenone
(Methyl phenyl ketone)

benzene. It is only the complex with aluminium chloride or some similar metal halide which reacts. We can see that in the acylium ion the positive charge is not sited solely on the carbon atom:

$$CH_3\overset{+}{C}\!=\!O \longleftrightarrow CH_3C\!\equiv\!O^+$$

This makes the acylium ion more stable (less reactive) than a carbonium ion and this *acylation*, as it is called, proceeds less rapidly than the alkylation described above.

These so-called 'substitution reactions' we have been discussing are of great synthetic importance. Their basic feature is that the benzene nucleus undergoes electrophilic addition in the same way as a hydrocarbon olefin, but because of the great stability of the benzene ring the initial addend ejects a proton instead of adding an anion. This great stability of the benzene nucleus is manifest in many other reactions. Hydrocarbon olefins react rapidly with potassium permanganate solution in the cold (see Chapter 6); pure benzene undergoes no reaction with cold aqueous permanganate. Some idea of the stability of the benzene ring can be deduced from the experimental observation that methylbenzene (toluene) can be heated with a boiling solution of aqueous potassium permanganate to yield benzoic acid:

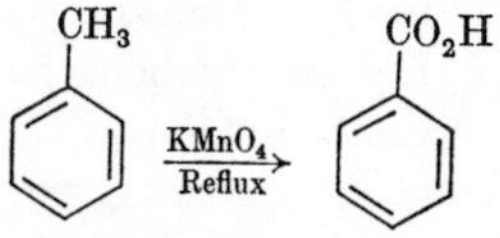

Toluene   Benzoic acid

Under forcing conditions benzene can be oxidized, and with ozone it yields a triozonide but the important point is that none of these reactions occur with the same facility that they do with hydrocarbon olefins. The same is true for hydrogenation. It is possible to hydrogenate benzene to cyclohexane, catalytically, but this reaction does not proceed anywhere near as readily as the hydrogenations of olefins described in Chapter 6. The resistance of benzene to hydrogen is important in many reactions, e.g. nitrobenzene can be reduced chemically or catalytically to aminobenzene (aniline):

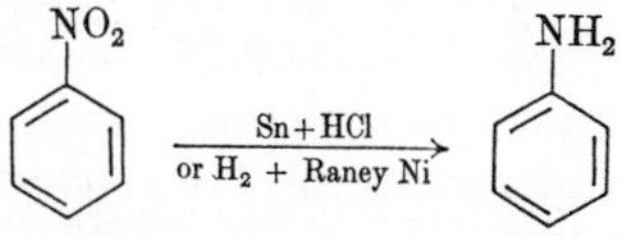

Nitrobenzene   Aniline

The difference in reactivity of the benzene nucleus and the olefinic double bond is best illustrated by the reactions of phenylethylene (styrene):

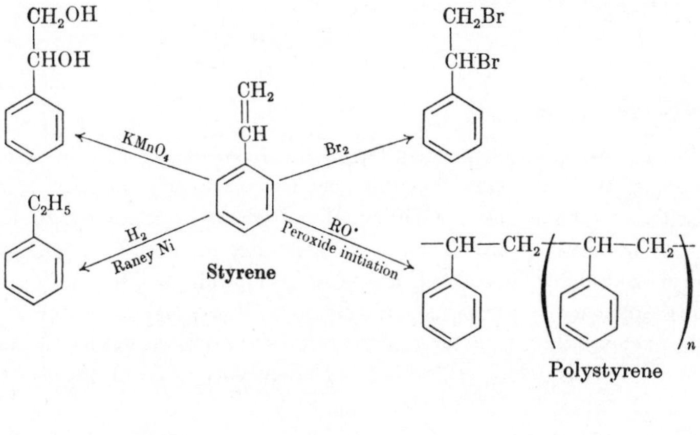

Polystyrene

Notice that styrene undergoes reactions of a hydrocarbon olefin described in Chapter 6, leaving the benzene nucleus unaffected.

The reaction of the benzene nucleus with free radicals and halogen atoms is slow; thus if toluene is treated with chlorine or bromine in the presence of ultraviolet light, reaction occurs only in the side-chain. This is identical with the chain-chlorination process we described in Chapter 2. In the absence of a side-chain,

or when the side-chain has been completely chlorinated, halogen atoms will attack the ring, and benzene with an excess of chlorine in the presence of ultraviolet (sun) light yields 1,2,3,4,5,6-hexa-chlorocyclohexane. This compound is sometimes most misleadingly called 'benzene hexachloride'. It will be apparent that there are a number of stereoisomers of this compound. One of them is a very powerful insecticide.

Derivatives of Benzene

So far we have been considering the reactions of the benzene nucleus. We must now consider the way in which the aromatic nucleus modifies the reactivity of substituents attached to it. Bromobenzene is called an aryl bromide as distinct from an alkyl bromide discussed in Chapter 3. Aryl halides will not undergo the displacement reactions of alkyl halides described in Chapter 3. If a nucleophile is to attack benzene we should expect it to add to the aromatic nucleus. However, we already know from Chapter 6 that hydroxyl anions do not add to hydrocarbon olefins and still less will they add to the stable aromatic nucleus. Thus, for laboratory purposes, a halogen atom attached to an aromatic hydrocarbon nucleus cannot be displaced by a nucleophile. In an industrial plant, where much higher temperatures and pressures are possible, this generalization is no longer true and chlorobenzene is converted into hydroxybenzene (phenol) as an industrial process.

Chlorobenzene   Phenol

Although the halogens cannot be replaced by ordinary nucleophiles under ordinary laboratory conditions, they can be replaced by metals; bromobenzene reacts with magnesium to form phenylmagnesium bromide, i.e. the corresponding Grignard reagent, although the reaction occurs less readily than it does with an alkyl bromide. Phenylmagnesium bromide will take part in all the reactions described in Chapter 11.

Bromobenzene   Phenylmagnesium bromide

A hydroxy group attached to an aromatic nucleus is greatly modified in its reactions. We argued in Chapter 8 that acetic acid was more acidic than ethanol because the acetate anion could be stabilized through resonance. It is possible to write four canonical forms for the phenoxide anion (**2a** to **2d**). Three of these structures have a negative charge on a carbon atom and will thus be of much higher energy than the first structure in which the negative charge is on the oxygen atom. Unlike the two canonical forms in the acetate ion, which are both equally stable, the structures

2b, **2c**, and **2d**, being appreciably less stable than **2a**, will only make a very small contribution to the overall resonance hybrid of the phenate anion. Nonetheless this is sufficient to make phenol

| Phenol | (2a) | (2b) | (2c) | (2d) |

very much more acidic than ethanol. Phenol behaves as a very weak acid in water (Table 14.1).

Table 14.1. Values of K_a at 25°c in water

Compound	K_a
Ethanol, C_2H_5OH	$\sim 10^{-18}$
Phenol, C_6H_5OH	$1 \cdot 3 \times 10^{-10}$
Acetic acid, CH_3CO_2H	$1 \cdot 8 \times 10^{-5}$

Note that if we add a proton to the nitrogen of aniline (amino-benzene) the positive charge cannot be distributed about the ring in the same way as the negative charge can be in phenol, and aniline is in fact a weaker (not a stronger) base than ethyl-amine:

Aniline

However, there is a derivative of aniline in which the stabilizing effect of the benzene ring is extremely important. In Chapter 10 we discussed the reaction of aliphatic primary amines with nitrous acid and we saw that the initial product of the reaction was a diazonium salt which decomposed spontaneously to yield a carbonium ion and nitrogen. With aniline, the diazonium salt is stabilized to some extent and aromatic diazonium salts can be prepared in cold aqueous solution. Crystalline diazonium salts can be isolated but they are usually very unstable. A proper discussion of the chemistry of aromatic diazonium salts is outside the scope of this introductory book. We have already inferred that

nitrogen is very readily lost from these compounds and the formulae below indicate how the elimination of nitrogen can be turned into a useful preparative reaction.

Heating an aqueous solution of benzenediazonium chloride yields a complex tarry mixture, of which phenol is the principal component. On treatment with cuprous salts, benzenediazonium salts lose nitrogen and give good yields of chlorobenzene (using cuprous chloride) or benzonitrile (using cuprous cyanide).

Apart from the ease with which a diazonium salt will lose nitrogen, the diazonium cation is clearly an electrophile and as such it will add to olefinic double bonds although this is a messy reaction; and although it will not undergo an addition-with-elimination reaction with benzene it will do so with the nucleophilic phenoxide anion:

Benzenediazonium   Phenoxide
       cation   anion

p-Hydroxyazobenzene

This coupling reaction, as it is called, is of immense importance. The product, *p*-hydroxyazobenzene, is a bright orange substance and is the simplest of the *azo dyes*. Dyes made by coupling diazonium salts with phenols, called azo dyes, are the largest single class of synthetic coloured materials used in the dyestuff industry.

Although the presence of the adjacent aromatic nucleus modifies the reactions of phenol by making it more acidic and modifies the reactions of aniline by stabilizing the diazonium salt, the main reactions of these two compounds are the same as those of their aliphatic analogues. Thus, treated with acetic anhydride or acetyl chloride, phenol will yield phenyl acetate, and aniline will yield acetanilide:

$$C_6H_5OH + CH_3COCl \longrightarrow CH_3C \overset{OC_6H_5}{\underset{O}{\big<}} + HCl$$

     Phenol   Acetyl chloride   Phenyl acetate

$$C_6H_5NH_2 + (CH_3CO)_2O \longrightarrow CH_3C \overset{NHC_6H_5}{\underset{O}{\big<}} + CH_3CO_2H$$

  Aniline   Acetic anhydride   Acetanilide

Similarly, benzoic acid, benzaldehyde, benzonitrile, and phenyl-acetylene all undergo the reactions described in Chapters 7, 8, and 10. Some books attempt to stress differences in the reactions of these compounds and their aliphatic analogues, but the important point is their similarity.

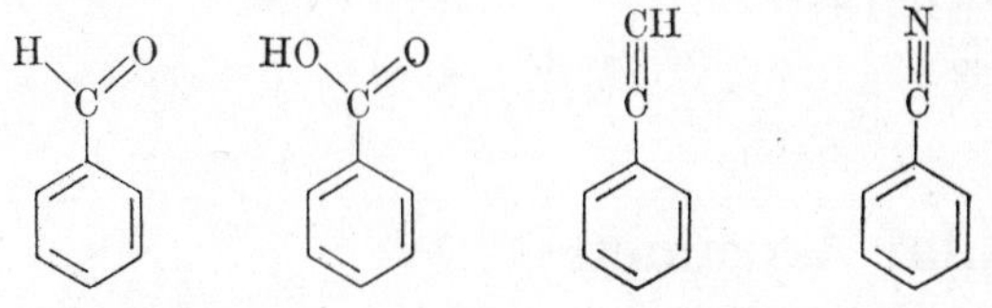

Benzaldehyde   Benzoic acid   Phenylacetylene   Benzonitrile

Problems

1. Predict the outcome of the following reactions:

(a) $C_6H_5CH=CHCH=CHC_6H_5 + Br_2 \longrightarrow$???

(b)

$+ KMnO_4 \xrightarrow{\text{Reflux}}$? ? ?

(c) $C_6H_5CH=CH-CH=CH_2 +$

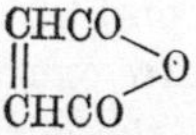

$\longrightarrow$? ? ?

2. Suggest steps for carrying out the following transformations:

(a) $C_6H_5Br \longrightarrow C_6H_5CO_2H$

(b) $C_6H_6 \longrightarrow C_6H_5NH_2$

(c) $C_6H_5COCH_3 \longrightarrow$

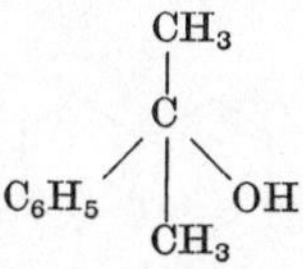

(d) $C_6H_5NH_2 \longrightarrow C_6H_5CH_2NH_2$

CHAPTER 15

Molecular Asymmetry and Optical Activity

In the first chapter, during a discussion on the tetrahedral arrangement of bonds around a tetravalent carbon atom, we drew attention to the fact that there are two forms of lactic acid (**1a** and **1b**).

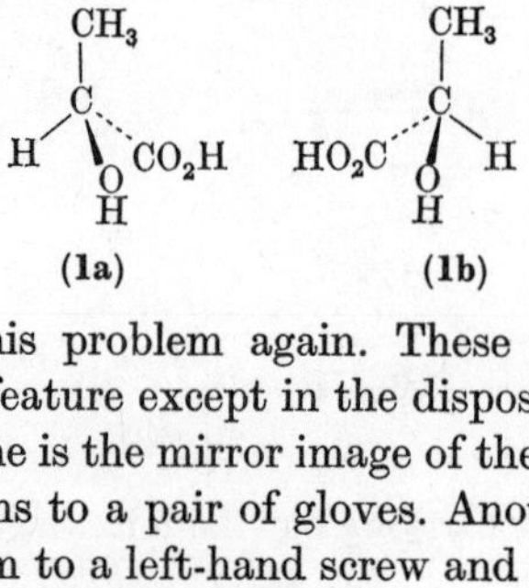

(1a)　　　　　(1b)

Let us look at this problem again. These two molecules are
identical in every feature except in the disposition of the various
groups in space. One is the mirror image of the other and we com-
pared the two forms to a pair of gloves. Another analogy would
be to compare them to a left-hand screw and a right-hand screw.
In fact a molecule with a helical shape is known and both the
left-hand helix and the right-hand helix have been separately
obtained.

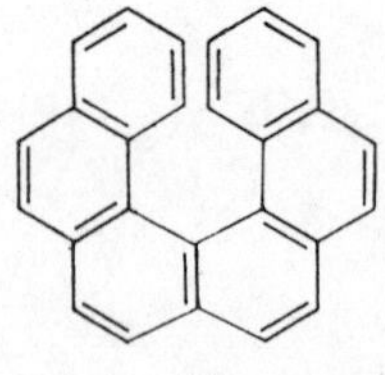

(2)

Compound **2**, correctly a phenanthrophenanthrene, was suitably
named 'hexahelicene'. In the formula shown above, the hydrogen

146

atoms attached to the benzene rings have been omitted and the two terminal benzene rings have deliberately been pulled apart in the diagram. In **3a** and **3b** we attempt to represent the two forms of the molecule in three dimensions. Benzene rings, of course, have no real thickness and they have only been drawn as plates to make it easier to visualize the helical nature of the molecule.

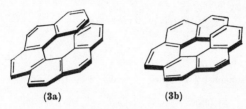

(3a)   **(3b)**

Other examples of molecules which exist in non-superimposable mirror images are 2,2′-dinitro-6,6′-diphenic acid and cyclopropane-1,2-dicarboxylic acid. In the former example (**4**) the bulky carboxyl and nitro groups prevent rotation about the bond joining the two benzene rings and thus it is possible to have two

No rotation about the bonds joining the benzene rings which are *not* in one plane

O_2N CO_2H
O_2N X CO_2H

CO_2H NO_2 NO_2 HO_2C

NO_2 HO_2C CO_2H O_2N

(4)

mirror images which are not superimposable. *trans*-Cyclopropane-1,2-dicarboxylic acid can exist in two non-superimposable mirror images (**5a**). The *cis* acid, on the other hand, only has one form; its mirror image is superimposable on itself (**5b**).

Molecules such as lactic acid, hexahelicene, 2,2′-dinitro-6,6′-
11

diphenic acid and *trans*-cyclopropane-1,2-dicarboxylic acid which can exist as two non-identical mirror images are called *asymmetric molecules* and the two forms are known as *enantiomorphs*. Asymmetric molecules do not necessarily contain carbon, but asymmetry is particularly common in carbon chemistry because a

trans-Cyclopropane-1,2-dicarboxylic acid   *cis*-Cyclopropane-1,2-dicarboxylic acid

(5a)   (5b)

tetrahedron which has four different groups attached to each corner of it is asymmetric and exists in non-superimposable mirror images (**6**).

It is obvious that a pair of molecules such as the two forms of lactic acid must have identical chemical properties. Likewise, their boiling point, melting point, solubility, and similar physical properties are identical. How then do we know that there are two

(6)

forms and how can we distinguish them? Before we can discuss this we must briefly remind ourselves of the nature of light and in particular of polarized light.

Polarized Light

There is ample physical evidence to make us associate light with wave motion. Wave motion may be caused by longitudinal vibrations or transverse vibrations. In a longitudinal vibration the vibrations are parallel to the direction of propagation. A familiar example of longitudinal vibrations are sound waves. In trans-

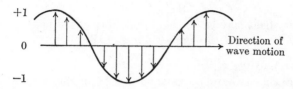

Figure 15.1. Transverse vibration

verse vibration the vibrations are perpendicular to the direction of propagation, such as ripples on the surface of water. In Figure 15.1 each vertical arrow represents a vector which maintains a fixed position and direction but varies continuously in magnitude from $+1$ through zero to -1 and back again during the passage of the wave. In an ordinary wave of light these transverse vectors are completely symmetrical to the direction of propagation (see Figure 15.2). Any single vector may be regarded

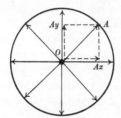

Figure 15.2

as the resultant of two components vibrating at right angles to each other, for example, vector $\overrightarrow{OA}$ may be regarded as the resultant of two vectors $\overrightarrow{OAy}$ and $\overrightarrow{OAx}$. Thus an ordinary ray of light may be divided into two separate rays in which the transverse vibrations are all in one direction, those of one ray being perpendicular to those of the other. The light wave in which all the transverse vibrations are in one direction is said to be *plane polarized*. There are many ways in which ordinary light may be decomposed into two plane polarized rays, the most common occurring when light passes from one medium into another. A parallel beam of ordinary light striking the surface of some transparent material at the critical angle is divided into two components, a reflected ray and a transmitted ray. These rays are both plane polarized at right angles to each other. Another way in which a beam of ordinary light may be divided into two beams of plane polarized light is by passage through certain crystals.

Optical Activity

If we shine a beam of plane polarized light through a solution of lactic acid containing only one form (i.e. one enantiomorph, say **1a**), we find the plane of polarization of the emergent light has been rotated to the right. If a beam of plane polarized light passes through a solution of the other enantiomer, i.e. **1b**, then the plane of polarization of the emergent light has been rotated to the left. This property of rotating the plane of polarized light is called *optical activity* and substances possessing this ability are said to be optically active. The number of degrees through which the plane of polarized light is rotated is called the *optical rotation* of the optically active substance and is given the symbol α. The direction of rotation of the plane of polarization is designated by a '$+$' sign for rotation to the right, and by a '$-$' sign for rotation to the left. So **1a** is ($+$)-lactic acid and **1b** is ($-$)-lactic acid. The words *dextro* and *laevo* are sometimes used as prefixes to the names of compounds to denote the sign of rotation, i.e. ($+$)-lactic acid is a shorter way of writing *dextro*-lactic acid. A single enantiomorph will rotate a plane of polarized light whether as a pure liquid in solution or as a vapour.

The extent of rotation of the plane of polarized light depends on the number of optically active molecules through which the light passes. Hence, the observed rotation is directly proportional to the length of the light path through the optically active material, and also to the concentration in weight per unit volume of the optically active substance in solution.

$$[\alpha] = \frac{\theta \times 100}{l \times c}$$

$[\alpha]$ = specific rotation of the substance

θ = the observed rotation

l = length of the light path through the solution in decimetres

c = concentration of the optically active substance in grams per c.c. of solution.

The specific rotation of a substance depends on the wavelength of the light, the nature of the solvent, the concentration, and the temperature. It is expressed in degrees. Sodium light is usually employed and thus a specific rotation at 25° is normally reported as $[\alpha]_D^{25}$.

Optical Isomerism

The two enantiomorphs of lactic acid are suitably called *optical isomers*. If we prepared lactic acid from the cyanohydrin, formed when hydrogen cyanide adds to acetaldehyde, we obtain a substance which shows no optical activity.

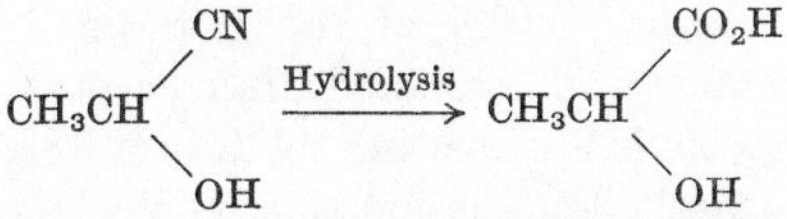

$$\underset{\text{OH}}{\overset{\text{CN}}{\text{CH}_3\text{CH}}} \quad \xrightarrow{\text{Hydrolysis}} \quad \underset{\text{OH}}{\overset{\text{CO}_2\text{H}}{\text{CH}_3\text{CH}}}$$

Lactic acid

This is hardly surprising for if we look at the reaction in which the asymmetric molecule was formed, i.e. the addition of hydrogen cyanide to acetaldehyde, we can clearly see that the cyanide ion may add to either side of the carbonyl group:

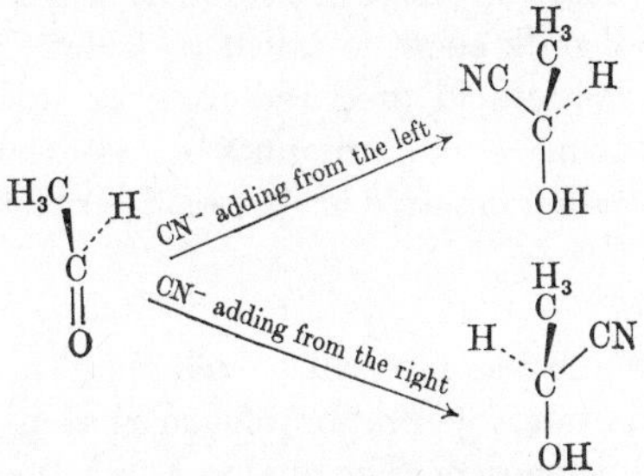

In the equation we have attempted to represent acetaldehyde with the methyl group projecting out of the plane of the paper and the hydrogen atom behind it. It is then possible for the cyanide anion to add either from the left or from the right to yield the two possible enantiomorphs of the cyanohydrin. Clearly addition at both sides of the acetaldehyde molecule is equally probable and therefore we obtain exactly equal amounts of the two enantiomorphs of the cyanohydrin. The subsequent hydrolysis of the cyanohydrin to yield lactic acid does not affect the asymmetric carbon atom. This is a completely general observation and any ordinary synthetic reaction in a laboratory will always produce exactly equal amounts of two enantiomorphs. Where then do we obtain samples containing only one enantiomorph and showing optical activity? The answer is from living organisms.

Lactic acid can be extracted from muscle tissue with water. On purification it yields hygroscopic crystals, melting at 26° and showing optical activity $[\alpha]_D^{25} + 4°$. Lactic acid can also be obtained from the action of certain microorganisms on milk sugar (lactose). This, on purification, is likewise a highly hygroscopic crystalline solid melting at 26°. It is also optically active ($[\alpha]_D^{25} - 4°$). Lactic acid prepared from acetaldehyde cyanohydrin is a hygroscopic low-melting solid, m.p. 18°. It is not optically active. If exactly equal proportions of the lactic acid derived from muscle and the lactic acid derived by fermentation of milk are mixed together the solution is optically inactive and the solid obtained from the solution melts at 18°. To distinguish between the two naturally occurring acids, that derived from muscle which rotates the plane of polarized light towards the right is called (+)-lactic acid (or *dextro*-lactic acid) while that obtained by fermentation of milk sugar is called (−)-lactic acid (or *laevo*-lactic acid). The lactic acid prepared from acetaldehyde cyanohydrin or by mixing equal amounts of (+)-lactic acid and (−)-lactic acid is called inactive or *racemic* (±) lactic acid.

Conclusions

A compound which has molecules such that the mirror image of one molecule is not superimposable on that molecule is said to exhibit optical isomerism. The analogy with the pair of gloves should always be remembered. Any ordinary chemical synthesis of an asymmetric compound will produce the two mirror images in equal amounts and the resulting compound will not exhibit optical activity. If, however, it is possible to obtain a sample of that compound containing only one form (e.g. left-hand gloves only) then solutions of this sample will exhibit optical activity, i.e. they will rotate the plane of plane polarized light. Molecular asymmetry is particularly common in the chemistry of carbon compounds because a carbon atom with four different groups attached to it is asymmetric. However, molecular asymmetry is, as we have clearly indicated, by no means necessarily associated with the tetrahedral carbon atom.

Methods for separating enantiomorphs and what happens when there is more than one asymmetric centre in a molecule must await a more detailed discussion of polarized light and the experimental techniques involved.

Problems

1. Assuming you could separate the enantiomorphs, which of the following compounds would show optical activity?

(*a*) $CHFClSO_3H$ (*b*) $CH_3CH_2CH(NH_2)CO_2H$

(*c*)

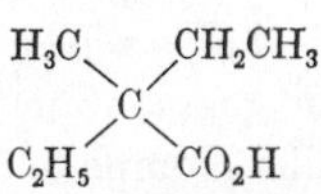

(*d*)

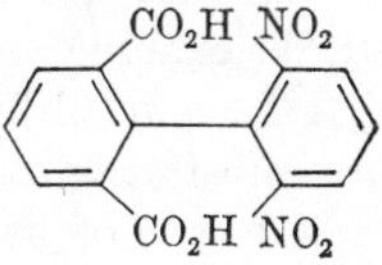

(*e*)

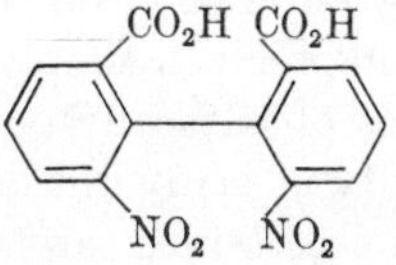

(*f*) $CH_2OHCHOHCHO$

2. Emil Fischer completed the following reaction sequence:

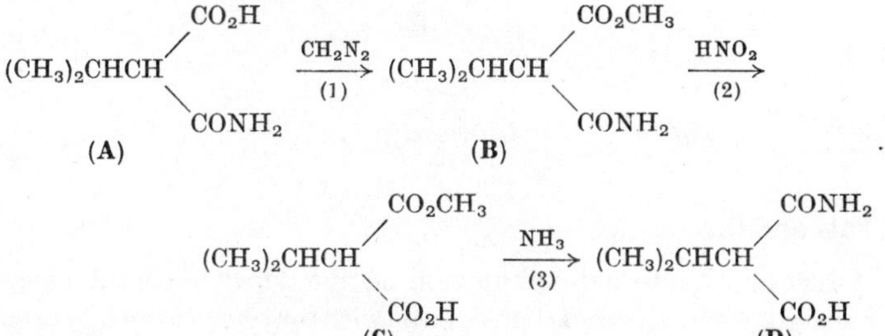

If compound **A** had a specific rotation of 49° 40′ what was the specific rotation of compound **D**? (Reactions (1) and (2) have not been discussed in this book; reaction (3) is the normal aminolysis of an ester discussed in Chapter 8.)

CHAPTER 16

Naturally Occurring Organic Compounds

At the beginning of Chapter 1, we said that life is a complex series of chemical processes and these invariably involve the compounds of carbon. Many simple carbon compounds are involved in living processes, carbon dioxide occupying a key position in the carbon cycle. On the other hand, many extremely complex molecules are also involved; for example, vitamin B_{12} has a molecular formula $C_{63}H_{90}O_{14}N_{14}PCo$, and all living organisms contain highly complex polymeric substances called proteins. Complete discussion of even the simplest type of naturally occurring compound is outside the scope of this book. This chapter will simply attempt to outline a few of the simpler classes of naturally occurring substances, for in spite of the complexity of many of them, they can often be regarded as belonging to a class which can be defined by some chemical feature. For example, the first class we consider are fats which are all esters of glycerol (propane-1,2,3-triol):

$$
\begin{array}{c}
OH \\
| \\
CH \\
\diagup \quad \diagdown \\
HOCH_2 \quad\quad CH_2OH
\end{array}
$$

Fats and Oils

Just as an internal combustion engine depends on the energy released when hydrocarbons react with oxygen to yield carbon dioxide and water, so an animal obtains energy by the oxidation of its food. Although a great deal of food may be degraded directly, some is converted into compounds which can be stored in the body as a kind of reserve. One of the body's energy reserves is fat. Fat is a mixture of glycerol esters, the formulae of which can be written in the following way:

$$
\begin{array}{c}
O \\
\parallel \\
C \\
\diagup \diagdown \\
O \quad R'' \\
\mid \\
CH \\
\diagup \quad \diagdown \\
CH_2 \quad\quad CH_2 \\
\diagdown \quad\quad \diagdown \\
R' \quad O \quad\quad O \quad R''' \\
\diagdown \diagup \quad\quad \diagdown \diagup \\
C \quad\quad C \\
\parallel \quad\quad \parallel \\
O \quad\quad O
\end{array}
$$

where R′, R″, and R‴ represent long straight hydrocarbon chains. These esters, occurring in animal and plant fats and oils, can be

$$
\begin{array}{c}
O \\
\parallel \\
C \\
\diagup \diagdown \\
O \quad R'' \\
\mid \\
CH \\
\diagup \quad \diagdown \\
CH_2 \quad\quad CH_2 \\
\diagdown \quad\quad \diagdown \\
R' \quad O \quad\quad O \quad R''' \\
\diagdown \diagup \quad\quad \diagdown \diagup \\
C \quad\quad C \\
\parallel \quad\quad \parallel \\
O \quad\quad O
\end{array}
\quad + \; 3\,\overset{+}{Na}OH^- \longrightarrow
$$

$$
\begin{array}{c}
OH \\
\mid \\
CH \\
\diagup \quad \diagdown \\
CH_2 \quad\quad CH_2 \\
\mid \quad\quad \mid \\
OH \quad\quad OH
\end{array}
\quad + \quad
\begin{array}{c}
O \\
\parallel \\
R'C \; - \; Na^+ \\
\diagdown \\
O \\[4pt]
O \\
\parallel \\
R''C \; - \; Na^+ \\
\diagdown \\
O \\[4pt]
O \\
\parallel \\
R'''C \; - \; Na^+ \\
\diagdown \\
O
\end{array}
$$

Glycerol   **Soap**

hydrolysed with hot aqueous sodium hydroxide to glycerol and the sodium salts of the long-chain acids. This process is used commercially to produce soap and is known as *saponification*.

Among the acids commonly obtained by the hydrolysis of fats are:

$$\text{Saturated} \begin{cases} CH_3(CH_2)_{10}COOH & \text{Lauric acid} \\ CH_3(CH_2)_{12}COOH & \text{Myristic acid} \end{cases} \Big\} \text{from butter}$$
$$\begin{cases} CH_3(CH_2)_{14}COOH & \text{Palmitic acid} \\ CH_3(CH_2)_{16}COOH & \text{Stearic acid} \end{cases} \Big\} \text{from beef dripping}$$

$$\text{Unsaturated} \begin{cases} CH_3(CH_2)_7CH{=}CH(CH_2)_7COOH \quad \text{Oleic acid} \qquad \text{from olive oil} \\ CH_3(CH_2)_4CH{=}CHCH_2\,CH{=}CH(CH_2)_7COOH \\ \qquad \text{Linoleic acid} \\ CH_3\,CH_2CH{=}CHCH_2CH{=}CHCH_2CH{=}CH(CH_2)_7COOH \\ \qquad \text{Linolenic acid} \end{cases} \Big\} \begin{matrix}\text{from}\\ \text{linseed}\\ \text{oil}\end{matrix}$$

In general, plants and fish produce oils in which the glycerol esters contain unsaturated straight chains, while animal fat contains mainly saturated esters. The more unsaturated a glycerol ester is, the lower is its melting point, and in countries where vegetable oils are not widely used for cooking, these oils are hardened on a commercial scale by partial hydrogenation using hydrogen and a finely divided nickel catalyst (cf. Chapter 6). The hardened oil is used for making margarine and synthetic cooking fat.

$$\overset{\displaystyle H}{\underset{\displaystyle H}{\diagdown}}C{=}C\overset{\displaystyle}{\underset{\displaystyle}{\diagup}} \quad \xrightarrow[\text{Ni}]{H_2} \quad -CH_2-CH_2-$$

Soap is made both from animal fat and from hardened vegetable oil. The soap is separated from the aqueous glycerol solution by salting out with sodium chloride, and filtering the precipitated sodium salts; these are pressed into cakes of soap.

The cleaning action of soap is a complex one involving surface forces. In simple terms it can be ascribed to the fact that the fatty acid anion has a long hydrocarbon tail attached to an ionic group. Dirt adheres to the skin and other surfaces mainly by films of oil. The hydrocarbon chains are adsorbed by such oil films leaving the ionic carboxylate groups in the aqueous phase.

The presence of the carboxylate ion at the head of this tail renders the oil film partly soluble in water, enabling the oil and the dirt sticking to it to be dispersed to give a colloidal suspension, which may be rinsed away.

The waterproof nature of plant leaves is due to a surface layer of wax. This wax contains long-chain hydrocarbons (about C_{30}) as well as esters of long-chain monohydric alcohols (ROH) with long-chain acids ($R'CO_2H$).

Carbohydrates

A quite different class of organic molecules is used by plants and also by animals as energy reserves and by plants as their main structural building material. These compounds, many of which have the empirical formula $(CH_2O)_n$, are called *carbohydrates*. For example, plant seeds and roots contain reserves of energy in the form of starch which is a polymer having a complex structure, roughly represented in the following way:

where n is about 300.

Sucrose (cane sugar), another energy reserve of plants, can be extracted from sugar cane and from sugar beet. It is a *disaccharide*, having two multihydroxy C_6 units joined together. Starch is called a *polysaccharide*, having many of the six-carbon units linked in a chain.

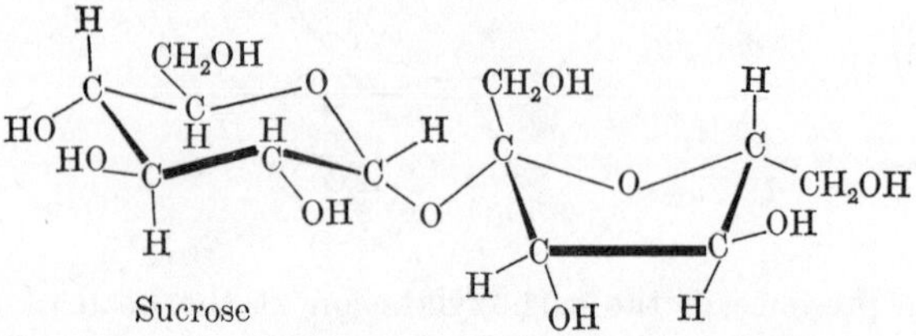

Sucrose

Cellulose is a polysaccharide formed by plants as a structural building material and is similar to starch in chemical make-up, differing principally in the stereochemistry of the link between the C_6 units and in the length of the chain. Both starch and cellulose can be hydrolysed and broken down into identical C_6 units, called *glucose*, a monosaccharide which also forms one half of the sucrose molecule and which occurs free in many living cells.

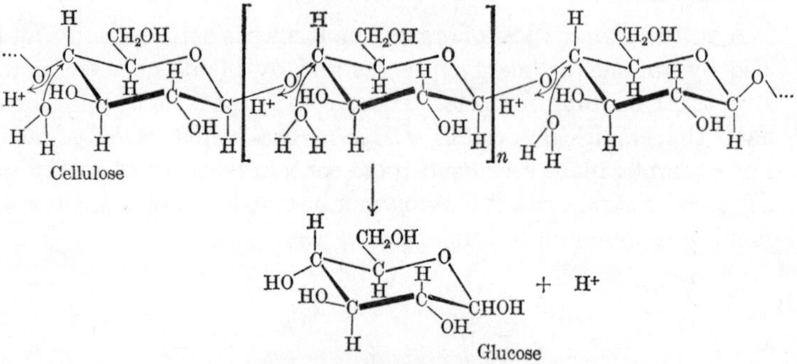

Hydrolysis of cellulose

This hydrolysis can be achieved with dilute mineral acids such as sulphuric acid. (This is why laboratory coats—made of cellulose fibres—are so easily rotted by acid splashes.) Hydrolysis can also be achieved by enzymes. The enzymic hydrolysis of polysaccharides to monosaccharides such as glucose, followed by enzymic breakdown of glucose to ethanol and carbon dioxide (fermentation):

$$C_6H_{12}O_6 \text{ (aq)} \longrightarrow 2\,C_2H_5OH \text{ (aq)} + CO_2 + \text{heat}$$

is of widespread importance for the production of beer and other dilute solutions of ethanol which are used as beverages. It is also employed for the preparation of pure ethanol for the chemical industry.

To prepare industrial ethanol, starch, and sometimes cellulose, are hydrolysed by acids rather than enzymes. The formation of ethanol from glucose by fermentation is brought about by an enzyme in yeast. This step cannot be achieved by synthetic chemical reagents. The resulting dilute (10%) solution of ethanol is concentrated by fractional distillation to give 'rectified spirit' which is an azeotrope of water and ethanol (95·6% ethanol by weight). The remaining water is usually removed by addition of benzene and refractionating the mixture. The ternary mixture containing 18·5% ethanol, 74·1% benzene, and 7·4% water by weight distils at 65° and permits complete dehydration if just sufficient benzene is added.

A dilute solution of ethanol, if exposed to the air, is bacterially oxidized to a dilute acetic acid solution. This is the reason why wine and beer go sour if left uncorked, and it is the basis for the production of vinegar, the chief component of which is acetic acid.

If we look carefully at the structure of a typical monosaccharide such as glucose, we see it is a hemi-acetal and it is thus sensitive

to either acids or bases, and even in aqueous solution of pH 7 the following equilibrium is quickly established:

We would thus expect glucose to exhibit the properties of an aldehyde as well as those of a polyhydroxy compound, which it does. Most carbohydrates are asymmetric molecules and usually only one enantiomorph is found in nature.

Proteins

Unlike plants, the structural material of animal tissues is proteins which are polyamides of high molecular weight. These polyamides can be hydrolysed by acids, alkalis, and enzymes to give α-amino acids. Proteins have many functions besides their structural use and are important constituents of all living cells.

$$\cdots NH-CH(R)-C(=O)-NH-CH(R')-C(=O)-NH-CH(R'')\cdots \xrightarrow{H_2O}$$

$$\cdots NH_2 + HO-C(=O)-CH(R) \quad + \quad HO-CH(R')-C(=O)-NH_2 \quad + \quad HO-C(=O)-CH(R'')\cdots$$

Simple proteins such as egg albumin and keratin from hair yield just α-amino acids, $RCHNH_2CO_2H$, when hydrolysed. About 20 such amino acids form the structural units of all the animal proteins that have been investigated. The molecular weight of proteins varies from $1 \cdot 2 \times 10^4$ for insulin to 3×10^8 for influenza virus. Notice that the α-amino acids contain an asymmetric carbon atom and that only one enantiomorph of any one amino acid occurs in a protein, and in general all naturally occurring amino acids have the same relative distribution in space of the four groups R, NH_2, H, and CO_2H.

Silk is a fibrous protein produced by the silk worm. After several years of research in the 1930's, Carrothers of du Pont matched the skill of the silk worm and made a polyamide in the laboratory which had the properties of silk, called nylon.

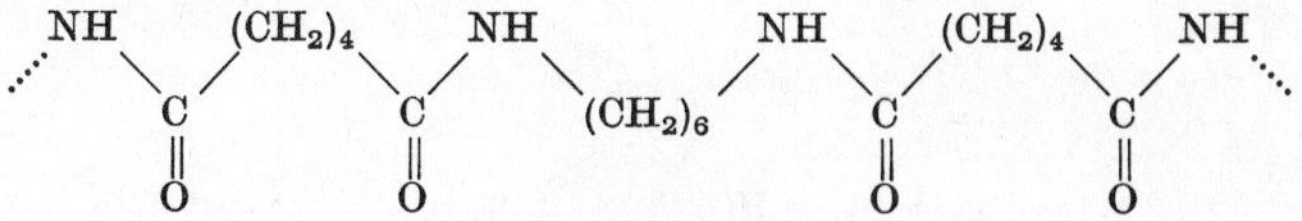

Nylon 66

Nylon 66 is prepared by the reaction of adipic acid, $HO_2C(CH_2)_4CO_2H$, with hexamethylenediamine, $H_2N(CH_2)_6NH_2$.

Terpenes

Many plants and trees, particularly conifers, produce a class of organic compounds called terpenes. These compounds, often fragrant oils, are contained in the essential oils obtained by solvent extraction of plant blooms or steam distillation of leaves or resinified sap.

Rose oil contains citronellol, lemon oil contains limonene, and

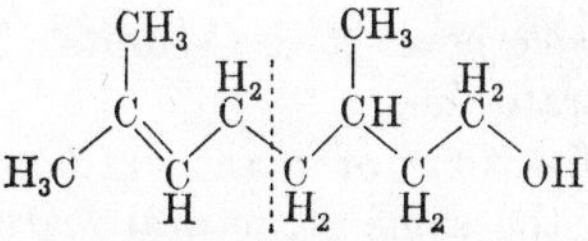

Citronellol

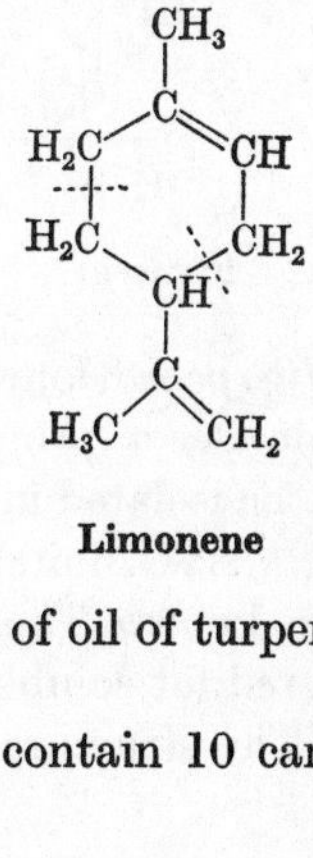

Limonene

the principal component of oil of turpentine, the paint thinner, is α-pinene.

All these compounds contain 10 carbon atoms and exhibit a

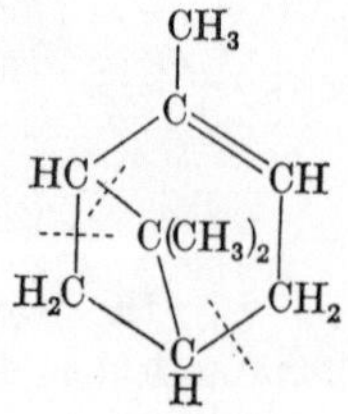

α-Pinene

typical structure pattern which is based on two 5 carbon isopentane skeletons joined together

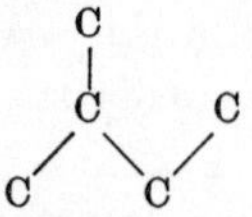

Isopentane skeleton
(2-Methylbutane)

and are called *monoterpenes* (two C_5 units). The dashed lines on the formulae illustrate this.

Higher-boiling fractions of plant extracts contain C_{15} compounds exhibiting the same structural feature of the monoterpenes and are called *sesquiterpenes* (three C_5 units). Farnesol is present in many perfume oils including rose oil.

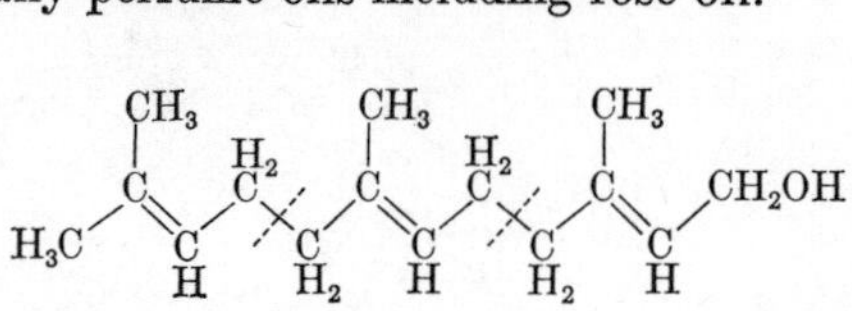

Farnesol

C_{20} compounds, called *diterpenes* (four C_5 units), also exhibit this structure pattern; vitamin A, a primary alcohol essential to the process of vision, may be isolated in high yield from fish oils.

C_{30} compounds, *triterpenes* (six C_5 units) and C_{40} compounds, *tetraterpenes* (eight C_5 units), are known. The latter, called *carotenoids*, constitute the yellow and red fat-soluble pigments of plants such as carrots and tomatoes. The structure of these compounds can

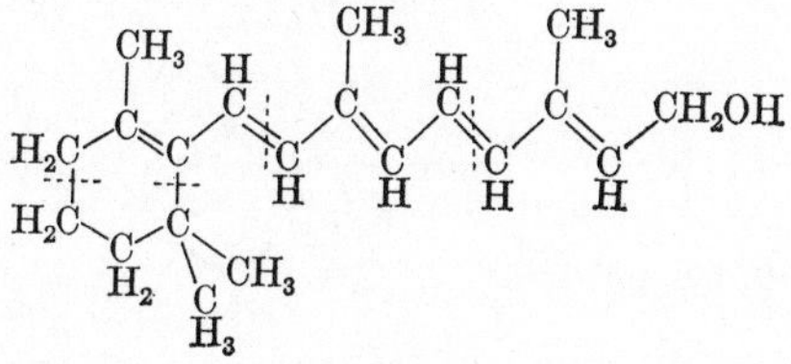

Vitamin A

be represented as dimers of vitamin A, and the body can convert some carotenoids into vitamin A; hence the belief that a diet of carrots improves vision.

Natural rubber is a *polyterpene* (about 10^4 C_5 units):

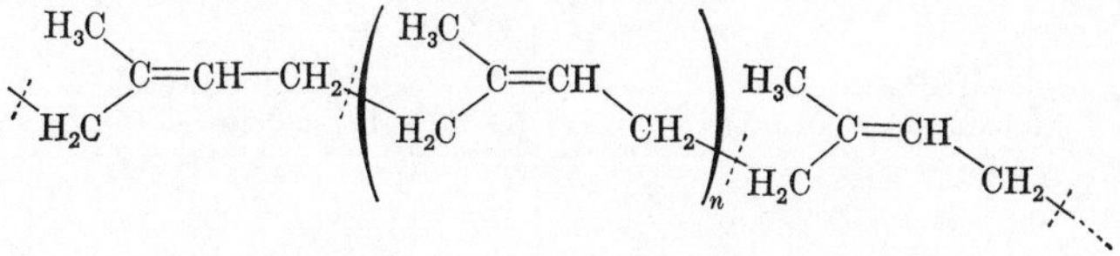

Natural rubber

This polymeric molecule shares with many terpenes the property of giving isoprene when destructively distilled.

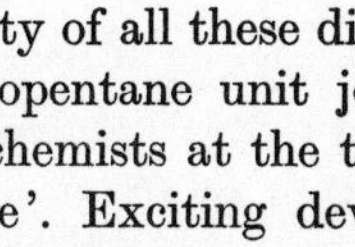

Isoprene (2-Methylbuta-1,3-diene)

The structural similarity of all these different compounds containing the repeating isopentane unit joined head to tail was appreciated by organic chemists at the turn of the century and called the 'isoprene rule'. Exciting developments in the last decade have shown how the living organisms build these compounds from acetate units. This discovery has shown that the terpenes are biosynthetically related to the steroids, a class of compounds of great physiological significance which include sex hormones, adrenal hormones, and heart poisons.

12

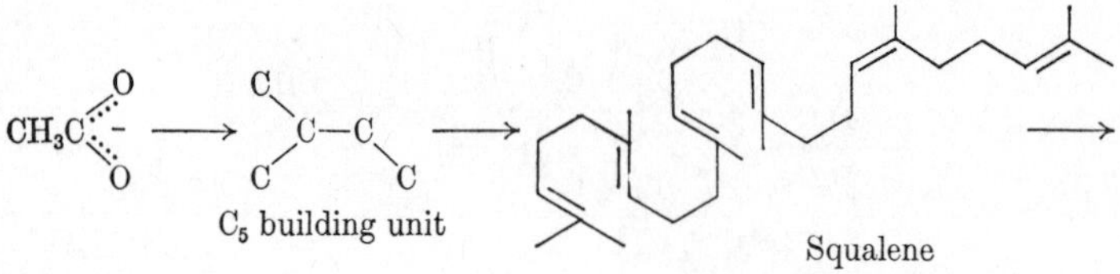

C₅ building unit

Squalene

(a triterpene; carbon atoms omitted—
skeleton only shown)

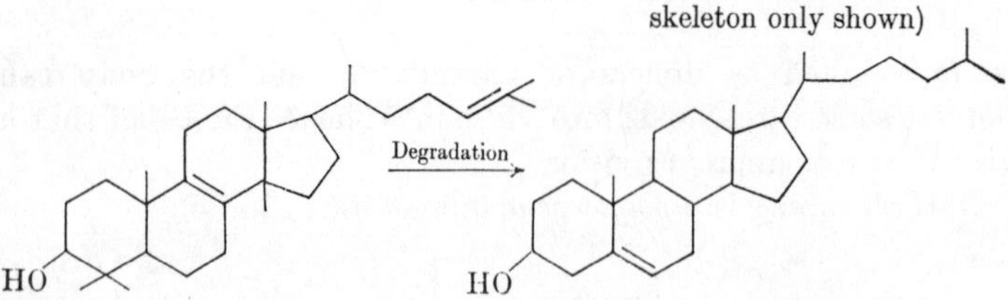

Lanosterol
(occurs in wool fat)

Cholesterol
(typical steroid found in
gall stones)

Alkaloids

A wide variety of basic substances containing nitrogen occur in plants. These compounds are loosely grouped together under the heading *alkaloids*. For example, opium (obtained from poppies) contains over 24 alkaloids, one of the most important medicinally being morphine.

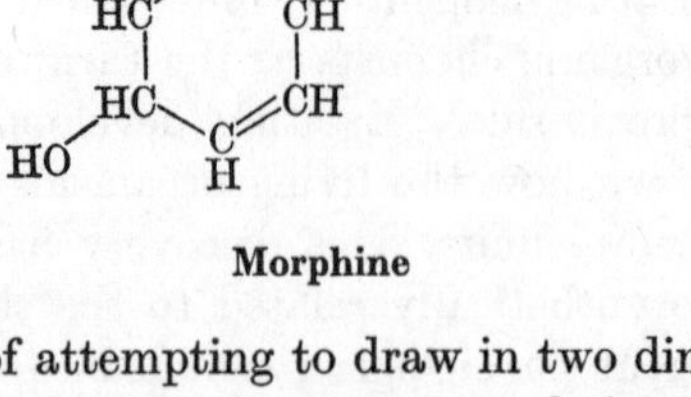

Morphine

The difficulty of attempting to draw in two dimensions such a three dimensional structure is even more obvious here than with the carbohydrates. Organic chemistry has been very much concerned with the determination of the structure and subsequent synthesis of natural products, a very few of which have been mentioned in this section. Of recent years attention has been focused on how the plant or animal makes these complicated compounds.

Organic compounds produced today by living organisms are usually too complex to serve as raw material for the production of simple organic compounds to form the basis of organic chemical synthesis. The one notable exception is the formation of ethanol from such carbohydrates as cellulose or starch.

For the production of organic compounds on a scale vast enough to satisfy the requirements of industry, we must turn to substances which were produced by living organisms many millions of years ago, and which, during the course of time, have been modified by heat and pressure. In the next chapter we will deal with the compounds obtained from petroleum and coal, both of which are believed to be the remains of prehistoric plants and animals.

Note

The structures given in this chapter are not meant to be committed to memory, but are given to illustrate structural types and chemical reactivity of the groups of natural products.

Problems

1. Show, by means of equations, the chemistry of the following processes:

    (a) The production of soap and glycerol from a liquid vegetable oil.

    (b) The production of ethanol from starch.

2. Ozonization of natural rubber and hydrolysis of the ozonide leads to the formation of laevulinic aldehyde (pentan-4-onal, $CH_3CCH_2CH_2CH{=}O$) in about 95 per cent yield. Natural rubber
$$\overset{\|}{O}$$
adds 1 molecule H_2 for each 5 carbon atoms of the molecule, and yields isoprene when destructively distilled. Show how these facts can be used to derive a structure for natural rubber.

3. Show how the following compounds may be classified by dividing into isopentane units:

(a)

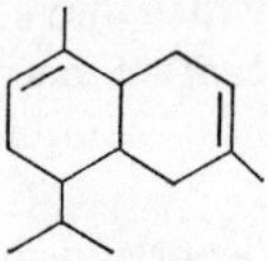

Cadinene
(from cade oil)

(b)

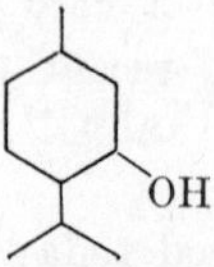

OH

Menthol
(from mint oil)

(c)

OH

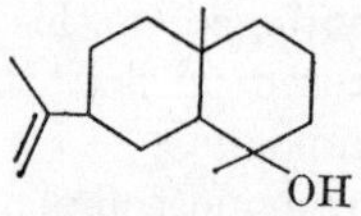

Eudesmol
(from eucalyptus
oil)

CHAPTER 17

Coal and Petroleum as Sources of
Organic Compounds

In the first 13 chapters we discussed the reactions of various types
of organic molecule without considering from where such compounds might be derived. In the last chapter we considered a few
examples of the vast range of organic compounds present in
living organisms. However, it was indicated that industry does
not obtain the many simple organic compounds needed for
synthetic purposes from complicated natural products. The two
main sources, coal and petroleum, are believed to be the remains
of prehistoric living material.

Coal

Coal is the product of the gradual anaerobic decomposition of
vegetable material which has been subjected to high pressure and
temperature during geological changes in the surface of the earth.
Coal is formed in the following stages: peat, lignite or brown coal,
bituminous or soft coal (formerly used in open grates for inefficient
domestic heating), and anthracite or hard coal. The age of the
deposit increases from peat to anthracite, as does the carbon
content. Apart from carbon there are small percentages of other
elements present (e.g. H, 5%; N, 2%; S, 2%; O, 5%).

The products formed by the destructive distillation of coal vary
according to the temperature, but the following diagrammatic
generalization gives an idea of the chemical nature of the various
fractions obtained. There are three groups of substances present
in each of the condensible fractions: (1) neutral compounds,
chiefly aromatic hydrocarbons; (2) tar acids, weakly acidic

Table 17.1. Fractions obtained by the distillation of coal tar

Fraction	B.p.	Main components		
		Neutral	Acidic	Basic
Light oil	up to 200°	benzene 	phenol 	pyridine
		toluene 	cresols 	methylpyri- dines
		xylenes 		
		a little cyclo- hexane and ole- fins		
		thiophene 		
		pyrrole 		
Middle oil	200–250	naphthalene 	phenol and cresols	pyridine and methylpyri- dines
Heavy oil	250–300	naphthalene	cresols and xylenols 	quinoline

Table 17.1 (*contd.*)

Fraction	B.p.	Main components		
		Neutral	Acidic	Basic
Anthracene oil	300–350	phenanthrene anthracene and carbazole		weakly basic and extracted by solvents
Residual pitch	—			

phenols; and (3) tar bases, weakly basic heterocyclic aromatic compounds.

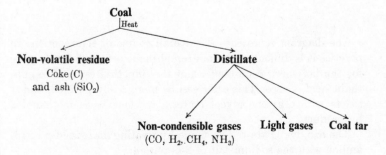

The coal tar is then distilled into 4 or 5 fractions (Table 17.1). In order to isolate the many organic compounds present, the fractions are further separated into their main components by a combination of physical and chemical means; the fractions may be redistilled. Phenols can be extracted by washing with alkali; extraction with acid will separate organic bases.

The organic chemical industry, founded in the last half of the nineteenth century, was originally concerned mainly with chemicals derived from coal. Today, so many useful materials are made from aromatic compounds that coal does not satisfy the needs of industry, and petroleum also serves as a supplementary source of aromatic starting materials.

We will briefly consider some simple commercial products derived from aromatic compounds. The artificial polyester fibre 'Terylene' is made from *p*-xylene (1,4-dimethylbenzene) and ethylene glycol:

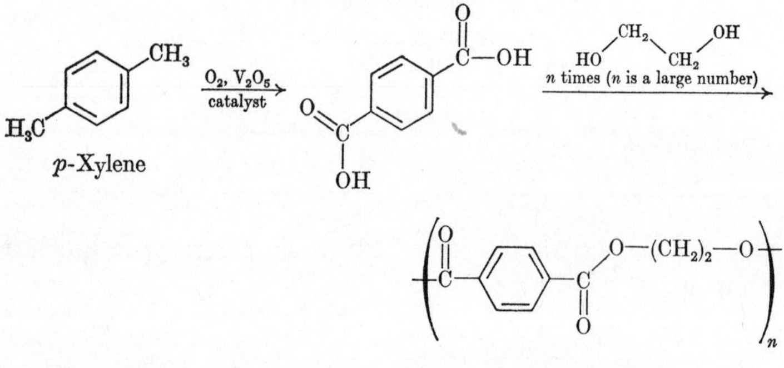

The diagram represents the overall course of the reaction. In practice it is difficult to obtain terephthalic acid sufficiently pure for the polymerization stage, and the dimethyl ester of terephthalic acid is used. This ester can be more easily purified, and it reacts with ethylene glycol to form terylene, with methanol a by-product.

The azo dye 'Para-red' is made by treating diazotized *p*-nitro-aniline with the sodium salt of 2-naphthol:

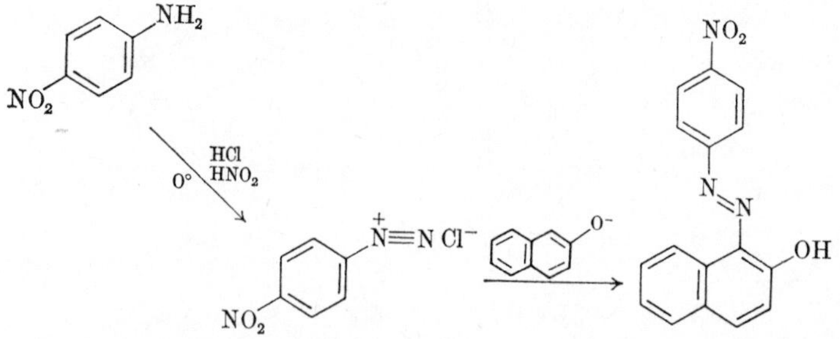

The cross-linked polymer 'Bakelite', much used in the electrical industry and for laminating wood, is made from phenol and formaldehyde:

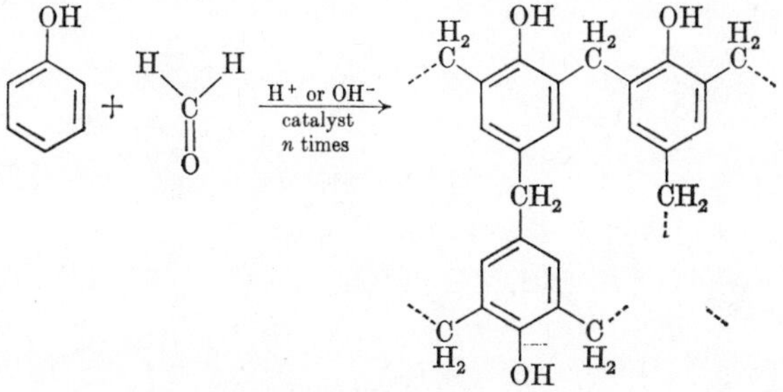

Phenol, obtained from coal (see p. 168), may be used as a raw material for the polyamide fibre 'Nylon 66' (see top of next page). The '66' indicates that there are 6 carbon atoms in both the acid and amine component. Other useful nylons are manufactured which contain a different number of carbon atoms in both fragments.

Petroleum

In this century the emphasis has shifted from the use of coal as a source of energy for industry to the other major fossil fuel, petroleum, which is more easily handled. Petroleum is believed to be formed by the decomposition of organic material, possibly marine in origin, and the products of this decomposition have accumulated in porous strata subsequently capped by impervious

Phenol $\xrightarrow{Ni/H_2}$ Cyclohexanol $\xrightarrow{Oxidation}$ Adipic acid

Cyclohexanol   Adipic acid

$$\begin{matrix} COOH \\ | \\ (CH_2)_4 \\ | \\ COOH \end{matrix} \xrightarrow{NH_3} \begin{matrix} CONH_2 \\ | \\ (CH_2)_4 \\ | \\ CONH_2 \end{matrix} \xrightarrow{Dehydration} \begin{matrix} N \\ \| \\ C \\ | \\ (CH_2)_4 \\ | \\ C \\ \| \\ N \end{matrix} \xrightarrow{H_2/catalyst} \begin{matrix} NH_2 \\ | \\ (CH_2)_6 \\ | \\ NH_2 \end{matrix}$$

Adipic acid   Adipamide   Adiponitrile   Hexamethylene-diamine

$$HO_2C-(CH_2)_4-CO_2H + H_2N-(CH_2)_6-NH_2$$

$\downarrow$ Heat

$$\left[OC-(CH_2)_4-CO-NH-(CH_2)_6-NH \right]_n$$

Nylon 66

layers of rock. High pressures and temperatures have probably not been a part of the process forming petroleum, as is the case in coal formation.

The formation of petroleum is probably analogous to the process which can be observed in any stagnant pond where rotting vegetation gives off methane, CH_4 (marsh gas). In fact the treatment of sewage results in the formation of sufficient methane to provide power to fire the boilers of the sewage disposal works.

Refineries are familiar parts of the present day industrial landscape. What does petroleum consist of and what are the chemical reactions that go on in these refineries?

Petroleum contains a mixture of hydrocarbons, mainly alkanes, ranging from CH_4 (the major constituent of natural gas) to compounds containing over 100 carbon atoms. Some petroleums contain a small proportion of cycloalkanes; others, found in central Europe, contain some 5% or so of aromatic hydrocarbons. The first operation that petroleum is subjected to is that of fractional distillation. In the fractionating column the petroleum is separated roughly according to molecular weight into fractions of increasing boiling point (Table 17.2).

Table 17.2. Fractions obtained from the distillation of petroleum

Fraction	B.p. (°c)	Range of number of carbon atoms in the constituent hydrocarbons
Gas	up to 40°	1– 4
Petrol (Gasoline)	40–180°	5–10
Paraffin (Kerosine)	180–230°	10–13
Fuel oil	230–300°	13–17
Gas oil	300–400°	18–25[a]
Lubricating oil	400–500°	20–30[a]
Residue	non-volatile	> 30

[a] These fractions are often further refined by distillation under vacuum at a lower temperature.

Let us now look at some of the reactions and the utility of these fractions.

Natural gas

Consists of mainly CH_4 and C_2H_6 with traces of C_3H_8 and C_4H_{10}. It is burnt as a fuel, and used for the enrichment of town gas obtained from the destructive distillation of coal.

$$CH_4(g) + 2\,O_2\,(g) \longrightarrow$$
$$CO_2(g) + 2\,H_2O\,(l) \quad \varDelta H = -212{\cdot}8 \text{ kcal mole}^{-1}$$

The combustion can be controlled to produce:

(*a*) methanol

$$CH_4 + \tfrac{1}{2}\,O_2 \longrightarrow CH_3OH$$

which is also produced by synthesis:

$$CO + 2\,H_2 \xrightarrow[\text{high pressure}]{\text{Oxide catalyst}} CH_3OH$$

(b) formaldehyde

$$CH_4 + O_2 \longrightarrow \begin{matrix} H \\ \diagdown \\ C=O \\ \diagup \\ H \end{matrix} + H_2O$$

(c) carbon black, finely divided carbon particles used in tyres to improve the mechanical properties of the rubber

$$CH_4 + O_2 \longrightarrow C + 2\,H_2O$$

or (d) 'cracked' to serve as a source of hydrogen

$$CH_4 \xrightarrow[\substack{\text{decomposition} \\ 1200°}]{\text{Thermal}} C + 2\,H_2$$

These are all very complex reactions and the equations only summarize the overall process. It is thought that the reactions are free radical in nature.

Petrol

The main use for petrol is in spark-ignition engines. It is found that straight-chain hydrocarbons such as heptane $CH_3(CH_2)_5CH_3$ ('octane value' = 0) give rough running with 'pinking' or 'knocking' under load in a spark-ignition engine. This characteristic pinking can be ascribed to the explosive detonation, rather than the smooth combustion, of the fuel–air mixture. Branched-chain hydrocarbons such as the so-called 'isooctane'

Isooctane (2,2,4-Trimethylpentane)

(octane rating = 100) give very smooth running even in engines with a high compression ratio. The octane number or rating of a petrol is defined as the proportion of isooctane which has to be added to heptane to match the running characteristics of the petrol under test.

Unlike spark-ignition engines, the reverse is true for diesel (compression-ignition) engines. Here, straight-chain hydrocarbons give smoother running than branched-chain hydrocarbons and different standard fuels are used to rate diesel fuels. With the spread of motoring, not enough branched-chain hydrocarbons were available to make high-octane petrol, and refineries now operate several reactions to turn unwanted straight-chain hydro-carbons into branched-chain hydrocarbons, and also to convert surplus high-boiling fractions (fuel oils) into more volatile hydro-carbons.

a. Isomerization. At room temperature, branched-chain hydro-carbons are thermodynamically more stable than straight chain. $AlCl_3$ is used to catalyse this isomerization which takes place by way of a hydride shift, and involves a carbonium ion intermediate and the migration of a methyl group with an electron pair:

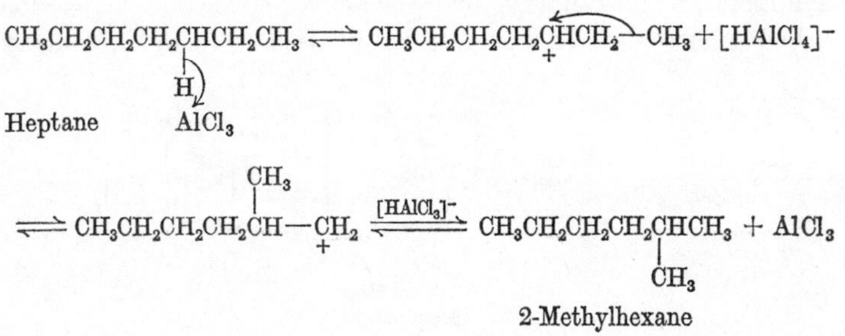

$$CH_3CH_2CH_2CH_2CHCH_2CH_3 \rightleftharpoons CH_3CH_2CH_2CH_2\overset{+}{C}HCH_2\frown CH_3 + [HAlCl_4]^-$$

Heptane $AlCl_3$

$$\rightleftharpoons CH_3CH_2CH_2CH_2\overset{CH_3}{\overset{|}{CH}} - \overset{+}{CH_2} \xrightleftharpoons{[HAlCl_3]^-} CH_3CH_2CH_2CH_2\overset{|}{\underset{CH_3}{CH}}CH_3 + AlCl_3$$

2-Methylhexane

The reaction is more complex than has been indicated, as traces of HCl and alkenes are essential for the reaction to start.

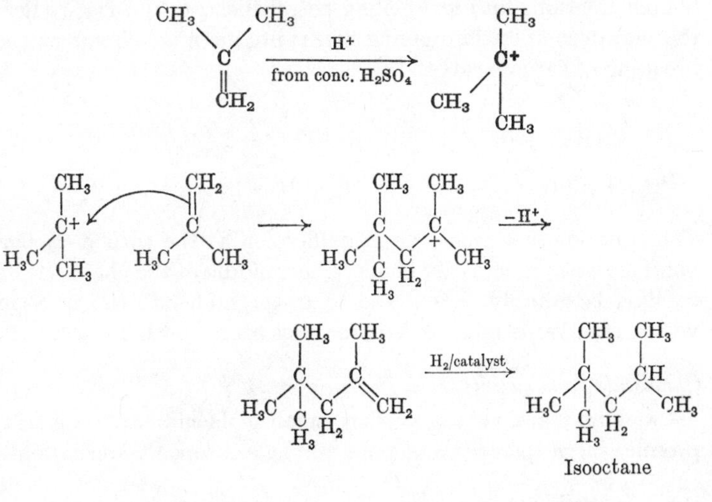

Isooctane

b. Alkylation. Branched-chain hydrocarbons are prepared from alkenes, e.g. isooctane from 2-methylpropene (isobutene). The reaction (see above) involves the addition of one C_4 unit to another, catalysed by a strong acid (see Chapter 6, p. 65). The resulting branched-chain alkene is hydrogenated. Alkenes have high octane ratings, but are too reactive, and may polymerize, so clogging pipes and carburettors.

c. Reforming. Aromatic hydrocarbons have high octane values and can be used in petrols. They may be obtained either from coal distillation, or from alkanes containing from 6 to 7 carbon atoms available in the refinery, by cyclodehydrogenation, a reaction called 'reforming'. This process can be used to render a country

$$CH_3(CH_2)_5CH_3 \xrightleftharpoons[500°]{\text{Mo and Al oxides}} \left[\begin{array}{c} CH_3 \\ \bigcirc \end{array} \right] \rightleftharpoons \begin{array}{c} CH_3 \\ \bigcirc \end{array} + H_2$$

Methyl-
cyclohexane
intermediate   Toluene

less dependent on coal as a source of aromatic hydrocarbons.

d. Thermal cracking. This process is used to turn surplus high-boiling fractions into low-boiling petrol fuels. It is a free-radical thermal decomposition, giving many products and involves the breaking of carbon–carbon bonds.

$$CH_3(CH_2)_3\overset{.}{C}H_2 \overgroup{\quad} CH_2(CH_2)_3CH_3 \xrightarrow[450-500°]{\text{Al, Si oxides}} 2\ CH_3(CH_2)_3\overset{.}{C}H_2$$

$$2\ CH_3(CH_2)_2CH_2\overset{.}{C}H_2 \longrightarrow CH_3(CH_2)_2CH{=}CH_2 + CH_3(CH_2)_2CH_2CH_3$$

The equation is a gross oversimplification as the carbon–carbon bond does not necessarily break in the middle of the chain. If the catalyst is suitably chosen and hydrogen added to the reaction vessel, the alkene mixture is reduced as soon as it is formed.

Chemicals from petroleum

Cracking reactions can produce small molecules, and refineries produce large quantities of pure ethylene, propene, and butenes which are used not as fuels but as the starting points of chemical syntheses.

Ethylene can be converted into ethyl chloride, which when reacted with a lead/sodium alloy forms tetraethyllead which is used as an anti-knock additive to petrol when branched-chain hydrocarbons are in short supply or too expensive.

$$CH_2{=}CH_2 \xrightarrow{\text{HCl}} CH_3CH_2Cl \xrightarrow{\text{Pb/Na}} Pb(C_2H_5)_4$$

The tetraethyllead suppresses knocking by forming a fog of PbO in the combustion chamber. This fog must not be allowed to collect on the valves and cylinder head, so ethyl bromide is also added to the petrol, to form volatile $PbBr_2$ after the combustion is complete, which passes out into the atmosphere.

Ethylene is converted by H_2SO_4 followed by hydrolysis into ethanol (Chapter 6, p. 56), used by industry as a solvent and as a starting material for other solvents such as esters.

$$CH_2{=}CH_2 \xrightarrow{\text{H}_2\text{SO}_4} CH_3CH_2OSO_2OH \xrightarrow{\text{H}_2\text{O}} CH_3CH_2OH$$

Ethylene itself is the monomer of polyethylene

$$n\,CH_2{=}CH_2 \xrightarrow[\text{RX}]{\text{Initiator}} R{-}(CH_2CH_2)_n{-}X$$

a plastic used on a vast scale for domestic articles such as washing-up basins and squeezable bottles (Chapter 6, p. 66). Polypropylene, made by polymerization of propene, has better mechanical strength and a higher melting point than polyethylene.

Several other organic molecules of everyday importance, such as ethylene glycol (ethane-1,2-diol), are made from ethylene by simple reactions (Chapter 6, p. 61).

Acetylene, an important starting material for the syntheses of acetic acid, vinyl chloride, and acrylonitrile, is obtained on a large scale by the thermal decomposition of ethane. At high temperature the following equilibrium is established:

$$CH_3{-}CH_3 \xrightleftharpoons[1500°]{1000-} CH{\equiv}CH + 2\,H_2$$

The ethane can be converted either by partial combustion in a restricted supply of air or by passing the alkane through an electric arc. The conversion only occurs to the extent of 5% but the acetylene can be removed from the issuing gases and unchanged ethane recycled. This process is competitive with the calcium carbide method for producing acetylene,

$$\text{Coke} + \text{CaO} \xrightarrow[\text{furnace}]{\text{Electric}} \underset{\substack{\text{Calcium} \\ \text{carbide}}}{\text{CaC}_2} \xrightarrow{2\ \text{H}_2\text{O}} \text{CH}\equiv\text{CH}\uparrow + \text{Ca(OH)}_2$$

especially in countries with a plentiful supply of natural gas.

Both vinyl chloride and acrylonitrile are monomers for plastics. Polyvinyl chloride is used as a substitute for leather, in long-playing records, and for plastic baby pants. Polyacrylonitrile is used in the production of artificial fibres such as 'Acrilan'.

Phenol from petroleum

An example of how petroleum can supplement or even replace coal as a source of aromatic compounds is the preparation of

Cumene   Cumene hydroperoxide

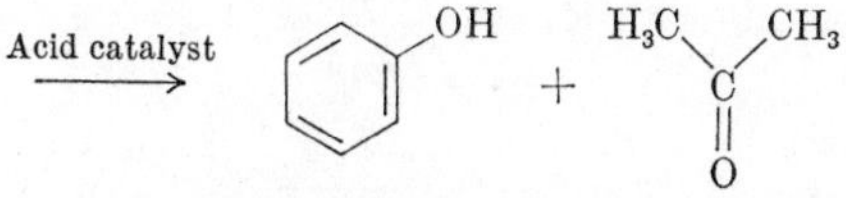

Acid catalyst $\longrightarrow$ Phenol + Acetone

phenol on an industrial scale from benzene and propene. The reactions involve alkylation, followed by oxidation. Acetone, an important solvent, is a useful by-product of this reaction.

Detergents from petroleum

Synthetic detergents are usually the sodium salts of long-chain sulphonic acids. These detergents are often more successful cleansing agents in hard-water areas than soap, as their Ca^{2+} and Mg^{2+} salts are soluble in water in contrast to the Ca^{2+} and Mg^{2+} salts of the fatty acids in soap, the latter being insoluble in water.

Long-chain aliphatic hydrocarbons can be treated in the gas phase at high temperatures with a mixture of SO_2 and Cl_2, to give the following sequence of free-radical reactions:

$$Cl_2 \longrightarrow 2\ Cl\cdot$$

$$CH_3(CH_2)_{12}CH_3 + Cl\cdot \longrightarrow CH_3(CH_2)_{12}\overset{.}{C}H_2 + HCl$$

$$CH_3(CH_2)_{12}\overset{.}{C}H_2 + SO_2 \longrightarrow CH_3(CH_2)_{12}CH_2\overset{\overset{O}{\|}}{\underset{\underset{O}{\|}}{S}}\cdot$$

$$CH_3(CH_2)_{12}CH_2\overset{\overset{O}{\|}}{\underset{\underset{O}{\|}}{S}}\cdot + Cl_2 \longrightarrow CH_3(CH_2)_{12}CH_2\overset{\overset{O}{\|}}{\underset{\underset{O}{\|}}{S}}-Cl + Cl\cdot$$

Alkanesulphonyl chloride

The resulting alkanesulphonyl chloride can be hydrolysed to

13

the detergent, an aqueous solution of sodium alkanesulphonate by sodium hydroxide solution:

$$CH_3(CH_2)_{12}CH_2-\overset{\overset{O}{\|}}{\underset{\underset{O}{\|}}{S}}-Cl + H-OH \longrightarrow$$

$$CH_3(CH_2)_{12}CH_2-\overset{\overset{O}{\|}}{\underset{\underset{O}{\|}}{S}}-O-H$$

$$+ H^+ + Cl^-$$

$$CH_3(CH_2)_{12}CH_2\overset{\overset{O}{\|}}{\underset{\underset{O}{\|}}{S}}-O-H + Na^+OH^- \longrightarrow$$

$$CH_3(CH_2)_{12}CH_2\overset{\overset{O}{\|}}{\underset{\underset{O}{\|}}{S}}-O^- Na^+$$

A more common type of detergent, used in household washing powders and liquids, is prepared by alkylating benzene with an alkyl halide (about C_{12}), sulphonating the product, and treating this with sodium carbonate.

$$C_6H_6 + RX \xrightarrow{AlCl_3} RC_6H_5 + HX$$

$$RC_6H_5 \xrightarrow[\text{or } SO_3]{H_2SO_4} RC_6H_4-\overset{\overset{O}{\|}}{\underset{\underset{O}{\|}}{S}}-OH$$

$$RC_6H_4-\overset{\overset{O}{\|}}{\underset{\underset{O}{\|}}{S}}-OH \xrightarrow{Na_2CO_3} RC_6H_4-\overset{\overset{O}{\|}}{\underset{\underset{O}{\|}}{S}}-O^-Na^+ + CO_2$$

Detergent (an alkyl aryl sulphonate)

This is a very incomplete survey intended to give some idea of how coal and petroleum are used as sources of small, reactive molecules which are in time used for starting materials for industrial syntheses. Some of the reactions described here appear different from those discussed in previous lectures. This is because in industrial plant very high temperatures and pressures can be used and reactions improbable in the ordinary laboratory can become feasible. However, all these reactions do in fact involve the principles we have discussed earlier, and many of the reactions are exactly the same as can be performed in the laboratory, but are merely scaled up to produce tons of product instead of grams.

Problems

   1. Indicating where possible the type of reaction involved, show the steps involved in forming the following from petroleum:

     (*a*) tetraethyllead   (*d*) toluene
     (*b*) polyethylene   (*e*) polyvinyl chloride
     (*c*) ethyl alcohol   (*f*) acetic acid

   2. Show how coal tar serves as a source of starting compounds for the production of:

     (*a*) Nylon 66   (*c*) Bakelite
     (*b*) Terylene   (*d*) an azo dye

CHAPTER 18

Synthesis

The first 14 chapters have been concerned with the chemical
reactions of different types of bonds and groupings attached to a
carbon chain. Chapters 16 and 17 gave an account of the natural
sources from which carbon compounds are obtained. It is the
purpose of this chapter to draw together all the reactions we considered earlier in order to see how we can convert one carbon compound into another, bearing in mind always the kind of compounds we have to start with from natural sources. Conventional
textbooks have lists of methods of preparation for each class of
organic compound. It should already be clear, however, that with
the possible exceptions of methanol and acetylene, we would
never, in a strict sense, prepare any carbon compound. If we
want a molecule which is not readily available from some natural
source such as petroleum, we take a petroleum product as closely
related as possible and convert it by a series of chemical reactions
into the compound we desire. Thus, this chapter is really not
concerned with the preparation but with the interconversion of
different types of groupings. Very few new reactions will be introduced and those which are will not involve any new principles.
We will work through the different types of bonds and groupings
in the same order as they have been discussed, considering in each
case how a particular grouping can be introduced into an organic
molecule. When a reaction has been described in a previous chapter a reference will be given to the appropriate chapter and page
and, in such cases, the electron transfers will not be detailed, since
these can be found by looking up the reference.

The Carbon–Hydrogen Bond

It should be clear from Chapter 16 that, in general, there is no need to attempt to synthesize hydrocarbons. These are readily available from petroleum, although to obtain one particular hydrocarbon free from any of the others may be a difficult business. There may be occasions when we wish to remove a particular grouping from a molecule and replace it by a hydrogen atom and we shall briefly consider ways in which this can be done.

(1) A carbon–halogen bond can be replaced by a carbon–hydrogen bond via the Grignard reaction (see Chapter 12, p. 116):

$$RCH_2Br \xrightarrow[(C_2H_5)_2O]{Mg} \underset{\substack{\text{Grignard} \\ \text{reagent}}}{RCH_2MgBr} \xrightarrow{H_2O} RCH_3$$

(2) There are three reactions by which we can convert a carbonyl group into a methylene group. The first of these, described in Chapter 7, p. 80, is the Wolff–Kishner reaction:

$$\underset{R'}{\overset{R}{\diagdown}}C{=}O + NH_2NH_2 \longrightarrow \underset{\underset{\text{Hydrazone}}{R'}}{\overset{R}{\diagdown}}C{=}NNH_2 \xrightarrow[\text{Glycol}]{NaOH} \underset{R'}{\overset{R}{\diagdown}}CH_2 + N_2 \uparrow$$

$$\text{Hydrazine} \qquad \text{Hydrazone}$$

A closely related reaction described in Chapter 7 involves the reaction of the carbonyl compound with a thiol, followed by treatment of the thioacetal with hydrogen and nickel:

$$\underset{R'}{\overset{R}{\diagdown}}C{=}O + 2\,C_2H_5SH \longrightarrow \underset{\underset{\text{Thioacetal}}{R'}}{\overset{R}{\diagdown}}\underset{SC_2H_5}{\overset{SC_2H_5}{C}} \xrightarrow[Ni]{H_2}$$

$$\text{Ethyl mercaptan} \qquad \text{Thioacetal}$$

$$\underset{R'}{\overset{R}{\diagdown}}CH_2 + 2\,NiS + 2\,C_2H_6$$

A third method of carrying out this transformation via the Clemmensen reaction is described in Chapter 7, p. 81, and involves the reaction of the carbonyl compound with hydrochloric acid and amalgamated zinc:

$$\underset{R'}{\overset{R}{\diagdown}}C{=}O + HCl + Zn(Hg) \longrightarrow \underset{R'}{\overset{R}{\diagdown}}CH_2$$

Zinc amalgam

(3) Olefins and acetylenes can of course be converted into saturated hydrocarbons by hydrogenation and this is described in Chapter 6, p. 63, for olefins and Chapter 11, p. 109, for acetylenes.

The Carbon–Halogen Bond

Alkyl halides are reagents of great value in synthesis and therefore methods of obtaining them from other compounds are very important.

(1) The replacement of an alcoholic hydroxyl group by a halogen can be carried out in a number of ways. These are discussed in Chapter 4, pp. 36 and 37.

$$RCH_2OH + HBr \longrightarrow RCH_2Br + H_2O$$

It is important to remember that the reaction between an alcohol and hydrogen chloride or hydrogen bromide requires the anyhdrous hydrogen halide and not its aqueous solution. It is also important to remember that a halide anion will not replace a hydroxyl group from an alcohol but that the reaction involves the halide anion replacing the water molecule in a protonated alcohol or oxonium ion. This is discussed in Chapter 4, p. 37. In place of the free acid we can use inorganic acid halides such as phosphorus halides or thionyl chloride:

$$3\ ROH + PBr_3 \longrightarrow 3\ RBr + H_3PO_3$$
$$ROH + SOCl_2 \xrightarrow{\text{Pyridine}} RCl + HCl + SO_2$$

Thionyl
chloride

(2) The carbon–halogen bond is readily formed by the addition of a hydrogen halide to an olefin (see Chapter 6, p. 54):

$$RCH{=}CHR + HF \longrightarrow RCH_2CHFR$$

(3) Carbon–halogen bonds are formed in a reaction, not previously discussed, in which the silver salt of a carboxylic acid and a halogen (especially Br_2 or I_2) are heated together in boiling carbon tetrachloride. This reaction probably involves free radicals.

$$RCO_2Ag + Br_2 \xrightarrow{CCl_4} RC \overset{OBr}{\underset{O}{\diagup\diagdown}} + AgBr \longrightarrow$$

$$RBr + CO_2 + AgBr$$

Notice that in this reaction we have lost one carbon atom, breaking a carbon–carbon bond, so that we can consider this reaction as a method of degrading the carbon chain.

(4) The direct reaction of molecular halogen with a hydrocarbon is not an important method for making a carbon–halogen bond in the laboratory because such a reaction normally results in the formation of a number of isomers. If, for example, we cause propane to react with chlorine, initiating the reaction by light or by heat, we obtain a mixture of 1- and 2-chloropropane (see Chapter 2, p. 17).

$$CH_3CH_2CH_3 \xrightarrow[\text{light}]{Cl_2} CH_3CHClCH_3 \quad \text{and} \quad CH_3CH_2CH_2Cl$$

(5) In many cases it is possible to change one carbon–halogen bond by another and this is described in Chapter 3, pp. 22 and 23.

$$RCl + KF \xrightarrow[\text{glycol}]{\text{Dry}} RF + KCl$$

$$RCl + NaI \xrightarrow{\text{Acetone}} RI + NaCl$$

With the exception of reaction (3), i.e. the reaction of the silver salt of a carboxylic acid with molecular halogen in carbon tetrachloride, none of the other reactions described above can be used for making an aromatic carbon–halogen bond. We have described two reactions by which this can be done (Chapter 14, pp. 134 and 143), namely:

(6) Chloro- and bromobenzene can be prepared by the direct

reaction of benzene with the halogen and a suitable metal halide catalyst (Chapter 14, p. 133).

$$C_6H_6 + Br_2 \xrightarrow{\text{FeBr}_3} C_6H_5Br + HBr$$

(7) The amino group in aniline can be replaced by a halogen via the diazonium salt as described in Chapter 14, p. 143.

$$C_6H_5NH_2 \xrightarrow[\text{HCl}]{\text{HNO}_2} C_6H_5\overset{+}{N}\equiv N\ Cl^- \xrightarrow{\text{CuCl}} C_6H_5Cl + N_2$$

The Hydroxyl Group

We have seen in Chapters 16 and 17 that methanol, ethanol, and propan-2-ol are produced industrially on a large scale and so we must think of these compounds as starting points from which we can attempt to synthesize other molecules and not as compounds that we should ever want to prepare. The introduction of OH groups is, however, often of great importance in more complex molecules.

(1) The replacement of a halogen by a hydroxyl group is described in Chapter 3, p. 21. This is the classic example of a displacement reaction. For preparative purposes this reaction works best with primary alcohols where the danger of an accompanying elimination reaction (see Chapter 5, p. 44) is less likely.

$$RBr + OH^- \longrightarrow ROH + Br^-$$

(2) Ethanol is prepared industrially by the hydration of ethylene (see Chapter 6, p. 56) and this hydration is a reaction which can be of general synthetic importance.

$$RCH{=}CHR + H_2SO_4 \longrightarrow \underset{OSO_3H}{RCH_2CHR} \xrightarrow{H_2O} \underset{OH}{RCH_2CHR}$$

Closely related to this reaction is the reaction of olefins with aqueous potassium permanganate or with osmium tetroxide to produce vicinal dihydroxy compounds, i.e. glycols.

$$RCH{=}CHR \xrightarrow[H_2O]{\text{KMnO}_4} \underset{OH\quad OH}{RCH{-}CHR}$$

(3) Alcohols can be prepared by the reduction of carbonyl compounds, aldehydes yielding primary alcohols, ketones yielding secondary alcohols (see Chapter 7, p. 77)

$$
\left.\begin{array}{c} RCHO \\[4pt] \overset{R}{\underset{R}{\diagdown}}C{=}O \end{array}\right\} \quad \xrightarrow[\text{or chemical reduction}]{\text{Cat. hydrogenation}} \quad \left\{\begin{array}{c} RCH_2OH \\[4pt] \overset{R}{\underset{R}{\diagdown}}CHOH \end{array}\right.
$$

(4) Esters can also be reduced to primary alcohols although, as discussed in Chapter 9, p. 97, reduction of carboxylic acid derivatives is not normally a satisfactory reaction (see Chapter 9, p. 98).

$$
RCO_2C_2H_5 \xrightarrow[\text{or Na} + C_2H_5OH]{LiAlH_4} RCH_2OH
$$

(5) Two methods for the industrial preparation of phenol have been described (see Chapter 14, p. 141, and Chapter 17, p. 178). Neither of these processes is practical in the laboratory but aniline can be converted into phenol via the diazonium salt (see Chapter 14, p. 143).

$$
C_6H_5NH_2 \xrightarrow[\text{HCl}]{HNO_2} C_6H_5\overset{+}{N}{\equiv}N\ Cl^- \xrightarrow[\text{Heat}]{H_2O} C_6H_5OH
$$

The Amino Group

It is not possible to prepare a primary amine by the reaction of ammonia and an alkyl halide because, as described in Chapter 3, pp. 26 and 27, the reaction goes further and the products of such a reaction are a mixture of primary, secondary, and tertiary amines together with some of the quaternary salt. Similarly, it is not possible to prepare a primary aliphatic amine by the reaction of an alkyl halide with sodamide because the amide anion, NH_2^-, is a very powerful base and the result of such a reaction will be elimination rather than displacement (see Chapter 5, p. 46).

(1) In Chapter 8, p. 91, we described how amides were amphoteric substances and how, acting as weak acids, they would form salts with the alkali metals. Benzene-1,2-dicarboxylic acid is called *phthalic acid* and although this compound will form a

normal diamide called *phthalamide*, it more readily forms an imide in which the nitrogen atom is attached to two carbonyl groups.

Phthalic acid   Phthalic anhydride   Phthalimide

Phthalimide is very much more acidic than acetamide and readily forms a potassium salt with potassium hydroxide or even potassium carbonate. The phthalimide anion is a suitable nucleophile with which to react an alkyl halide. The product of this reaction, an *N*-alkylphthalimide, can then be hydrolysed to yield a primary amine and phthalic acid.

This reaction is known as the *Gabriel phthalimide synthesis* of amines.

(2) Primary amines can also be prepared by the reduction of nitriles (see Chapter 11, p. 111), but the reaction may be accompanied by undesirable side-reactions giving secondary and even tertiary amines in addition to the desired primary amine. It is used industrially in the preparation of 1,6-diaminohexane (see Chapter 17, page 172).

$$RCN \xrightarrow[\text{or LiAlH}_4]{\text{Cat. H}_2} RCH_2NH_2$$

Likewise, amides can be hydrogenated and this enables us to prepare secondary or tertiary amines from secondary or tertiary amides.

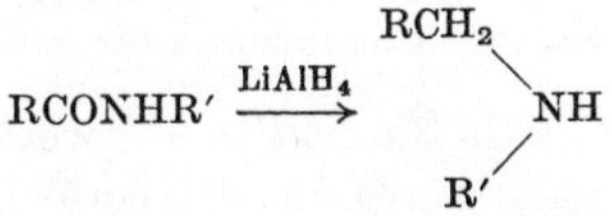

$$RCONHR' \xrightarrow{\text{LiAlH}_4} \begin{array}{c} RCH_2 \\ \diagdown \\ \diagup \\ R' \end{array} NH$$

(3) Amines can also be prepared by the hydrogenation of oximes or hydrazones formed by the reaction of aldehydes and ketones with hydroxylamine or hydrazine derivatives.

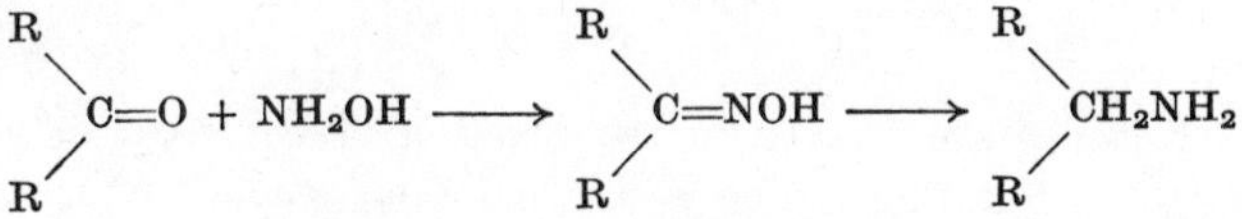

$$\begin{array}{c} R \\ \diagdown \\ \diagup \\ R \end{array} C{=}O + NH_2OH \longrightarrow \begin{array}{c} R \\ \diagdown \\ \diagup \\ R \end{array} C{=}NOH \longrightarrow \begin{array}{c} R \\ \diagdown \\ \diagup \\ R \end{array} CH_2NH_2$$

Oxime

(4) Aniline cannot be prepared by any of the above reactions, but is readily formed by the hydrogenation of nitrobenzene (see Chapter 14, p. 139).

$$C_6H_6 \xrightarrow[\text{H}_2\text{SO}_4]{\text{HNO}_3} C_6H_5NO_2 \xrightarrow[\text{or chemical reduction}]{\text{Cat. reduction}} C_6H_5NH_2$$

The Carbonyl Group

(1) The main method for introducing the carbonyl group is by the oxidation of an alcohol. Primary alcohols yield aldehydes and secondary alcohols yield ketones whereas tertiary alcohols are not readily oxidized (see Chapter 10, p. 101).

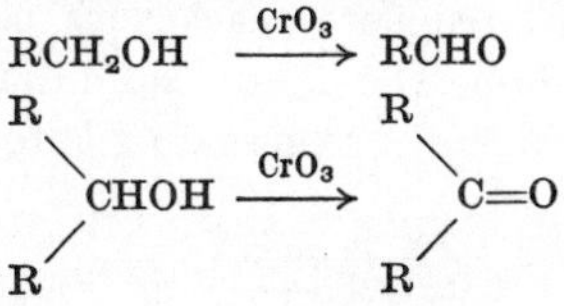

$$RCH_2OH \xrightarrow{\text{CrO}_3} RCHO$$

$$\begin{array}{c} R \\ \diagdown \\ \diagup \\ R \end{array} CHOH \xrightarrow{\text{CrO}_3} \begin{array}{c} R \\ \diagdown \\ \diagup \\ R \end{array} C{=}O$$

(2) An acetylenic group can be converted into a methylene group and an adjacent carbonyl group and this is the way in which acetaldehyde can be manufactured from acetylene (see Chapter 11, p. 108).

$$RC{\equiv}CR \xrightarrow[\text{H}_2\text{SO}_4]{\text{Hg}^{2+}} RCH_2COR$$

These two reactions are the only simple conversion reactions which result in the formation of the carbonyl group. However, carbonyl groups are formed in a wide variety of other reactions which involve either the breaking or forming of carbon–carbon bonds.

(3) An example of the formation of a carbonyl group as the result of a degradation or breaking of a carbon chain, we have the ozonolysis of an olefinic bond described in Chapter 6, p. 62.

$$
\begin{array}{c}
R \\ \diagdown \\ \diagup \\ R
\end{array}
C = C
\begin{array}{c}
R' \\ \diagup \\ \diagdown \\ R'
\end{array}
\xrightarrow[H_2O]{O_3}
\begin{array}{c}
R \\ \diagdown \\ \diagup \\ R
\end{array}
C = O \; + \; O = C
\begin{array}{c}
R' \\ \diagup \\ \diagdown \\ R'
\end{array}
$$

(4) Ketones are formed in the reaction of Grignard reagents with esters, but the ketone so formed then reacts further with more Grignard reagent to yield the tertiary alcohol. The reaction of Grignard reagents with nitriles, however, can be used to prepare ketones (see Chapter 12, p. 119).

$$
RCN + C_2H_5MgBr \longrightarrow
\begin{array}{c}
R \quad C_2H_5 \\ \diagdown \; \diagup \\ C \\ \parallel \\ N \\ \diagdown \\ MgBr
\end{array}
\xrightarrow{H_2O}
\begin{array}{c}
R \quad C_2H_5 \\ \diagdown \; \diagup \\ C \\ \parallel \\ O
\end{array}
$$

Grignard reagents react with acid chlorides to yield ketones but, as in the case of esters, the resulting ketone then reacts further with more Grignard reagent to yield the tertiary alcohol. A method of avoiding this difficulty is to use a less reactive organometallic derivative. Grignard reagents react with cadmium chloride to yield a dialkylcadmium. The dialkylcadmium then reacts with an acid chloride to yield the corresponding ketone.

$$
2\,C_2H_5MgBr + CdCl_2 \longrightarrow (C_2H_5)_2Cd + MgBrCl
$$
$$
(C_2H_5)_2Cd + 2\,RCOCl \longrightarrow 2\,RCOC_2H_5 + CdCl_2
$$

(5) Phenyl ketones can be prepared by the reaction of an acid chloride and aluminium chloride in the Friedel–Crafts acylation reaction (see Chapter 14, p. 137).

$$
C_6H_6 + CH_3COCl + AlCl_3 \longrightarrow C_6H_5COCH_3
$$
$$
\text{Acetophenone}
$$

The Carboxyl Group

Acetic acid is a commercial product produced in large quantities from the oxidation of acetaldehyde derived from acetylene, or by the oxidation of ethanol from ethylene, or by the direct oxidation of short-chain hydrocarbons from the petroleum refinery. Long-chain carboxylic acids are obtained by the hydrolysis of fats, as described in Chapter 16, and by the oxidation of long-chain hydrocarbons.

(1) The main method of introducing a carboxyl group into a straight carbon chain is by oxidation of the appropriate primary alcohol to the aldehyde which is then oxidized to the carboxylic acid (see Chapter 7, p. 81).

$$RCH_2OH \longrightarrow RCHO \longrightarrow RCO_2H$$

(2) Another very important way of preparing carboxylic acids is the hydrolysis of a cyanide by either acid or base (see Chapter 11, p. 110).

$$RCN \xrightarrow[\text{Acid or base}]{H_2O} RCO_2H$$

(3) Of equal importance is the conversion of an alkyl halide into a carboxylic acid containing one more carbon atom via the Grignard reagent (see Chapter 12, p. 118).

$$RBr \xrightarrow[(C_2H_5)_2O]{Mg} RMgBr \xrightarrow{CO_2} RCO_2H$$

It is a good opportunity, while we are discussing the carboxyl group, to consider how we can make esters and amides. The direct interaction of a carboxylic acid and an alcohol is discussed in Chapter 8, pp. 86–7, and this section should be carefully re-read. It will be clear from this discussion that the direct preparation of an ester from an alcohol and a carboxylic acid is a somewhat limited reaction. The alternative is to make the acid halide or the acid anhydride (see Chapter 9, p. 95). This is the only way in which tertiary alcohols can be esterified and also the only way in which phenol can be esterified. The method of preparing esters of very limited application was described in Chapter 3, p. 25, and involves the reaction of the sodium salt of the carboxylic acid with an alkyl halide. Primary amides can be prepared from esters and ammonia as described in Chapter 8, p. 89. The 'acylation' of primary and secondary amines to secondary and tertiary amides requires the use of either an acid chloride or an acid anhydride.

The Nitrile Group

(1) The most important route to an alkyl cyanide is to use an alkyl halide and treat this with potassium cyanide (Chapter 3, p. 24).

$$RBr + KCN \xrightarrow{C_2H_5OH} RCN + KBr$$

α-Hydroxy cyanides are prepared by the reaction of an aldehyde or ketone with aqueous hydrogen cyanide (Chapter 7, p. 71).

$$RCHO + HCN \longrightarrow RCHOHCN$$

(2) Nitriles can also be prepared by the dehydration of amides in a reaction that we have not described previously. This simply involves treating the amide with a very powerful dehydrating agent such as phosphorus pentoxide.

$$RCONH_2 \xrightarrow[P_2O_5]{-H_2O} RCN$$

The Olefinic Double Bond

Elimination reactions and the formation of the olefinic bond form the subject of Chapter 5; a brief discussion of when displacement and when elimination are likely to occur is given on p. 46 of that chapter. An important point is that the stronger the base, the more likely reaction with an alkyl halide is to result in elimination. Thus the reaction between an alkyl halide and a sodamide results in elimination whereas the reaction between sodium acetate and an alkyl halide almost invariably results in displacement. The structure of the alkyl halide is also extremely important and the more branched the alkyl halide, the more likely is elimination. From a practical point of view, the most convenient way of making olefins is from alcohols, either by direct dehydration as described on p. 49, or (better) by way of the ester, particularly the xanthate esters as described on the same page.

$$RCH_2CH_2OH + CS_2 \xrightarrow{NaOH} RCH_2CH_2OCS_2^- + Na^+$$

Sodium xanthate ester

$$RCH_2CH_2OCS_2^- \ Na^+ \ \overset{\curvearrowright}{CH_3}\overset{\curvearrowleft}{-I} \longrightarrow RCH_2CH_2OCS_2CH_3 + Na^+I^-$$

Methyl xanthate ester

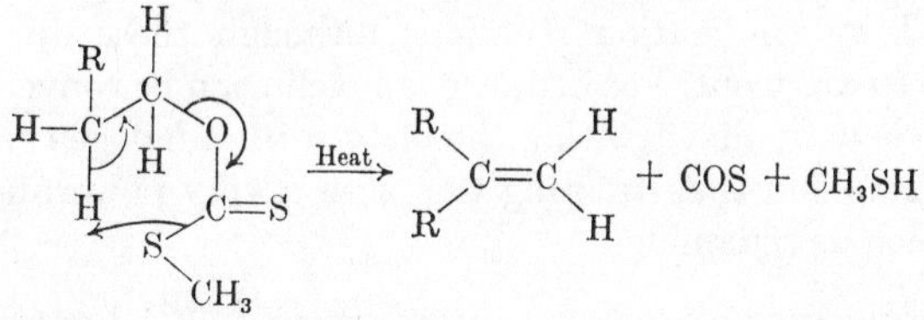

The Hofmann elimination described in Chapter 5, p. 48, is also of considerable practical importance.

$$RCH_2CH_2NH_2 \xrightarrow{\text{Excess } CH_3I} RCH_2CH_2\overset{+}{N}(CH_3)_3 \ I^- \xrightarrow{Ag_2O}$$

$$RCH_2CH_2\overset{+}{N}(CH_3)_3 \ OH^- \xrightarrow{Heat} RCH=CH_2 + (CH_3)_3N + H_2O$$

The hydrogenation of acetylenes described in Chapter 11, p. 109, is very important because it is possible in this way to prepare an olefin in a stereospecific fashion.

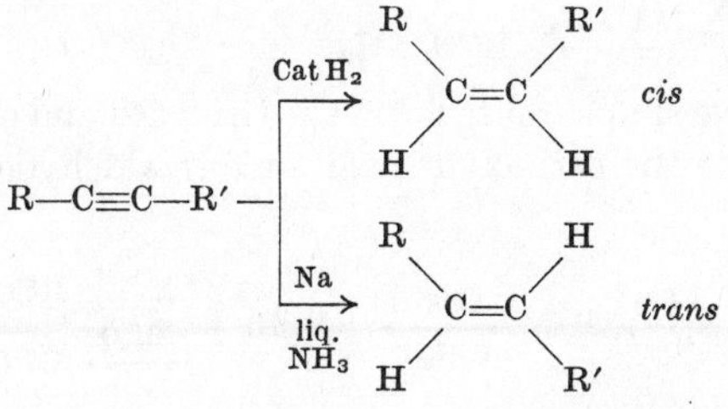

The Acetylenic Bond

Acetylenes are normally prepared by the reaction of sodium acetylide with an alkyl halide in liquid ammonia, as described in

Chapter 11, p. 111. The extension of this reaction to give a disubstituted acetylide is also described there:

$$RBr + Na^+ \ \bar{C}{\equiv}CH \xrightarrow{\text{Liq. NH}_3} RC{\equiv}CH + Na^+Br^- \xrightarrow[\text{liq. NH}_3]{\text{NaNH}_2}$$

$$RC{\equiv}\bar{C} \ Na^+ \xrightarrow{R'Br} RC{\equiv}CR'$$

as is the formation of acetylenic alcohols by the nucleophilic addition of an acetylide anion to a ketone. Acetylenes can also be prepared by elimination reactions although these are usually difficult to carry out. For instance, an olefin can be converted into an acetylene by first treating the olefin with a halogen to form a 1,2-dihalide and then treating this with a very powerful nucleophile, such as sodamide.

$$RCH{=}CHR + Cl_2 \longrightarrow RCHClCHClR \xrightarrow{\text{NaNH}_2} RC{\equiv}CR$$

This reaction may give indifferent yields.

Chain-lengthening Sequences

We now finally wish to consider how we can take a sequence of reactions to build up or degrade a carbon chain. The simplest method of increasing the length of a carbon chain by one carbon atom at a time involves the use of cyanide.

$$ROH \xrightarrow{\text{PBr}_3} RBr \xrightarrow[\text{C}_2\text{H}_5\text{OH}]{\text{KCN}}$$

$$RCN \xrightarrow[\text{LiAlH}_4]{\overset{\text{HOH}}{}} \begin{array}{l} RCO_2H \longrightarrow RCO_2C_2H_5 \longrightarrow RCH_2OH \\ RCH_2NH_2 \end{array}$$

The alternative simple route is via the Grignard and either carbon dioxide to give the carboxylic acid, or formaldehyde to give the alcohol.

$$ROH \xrightarrow{\text{PBr}_3} RBr \xrightarrow[\text{(C}_2\text{H}_5\text{)O}]{\text{Mg}} RMgBr \overset{\text{CO}_2}{\underset{\text{CH}_2\text{O}}{\Big|}} \begin{array}{l} RCO_2H \\ RCH_2OH \end{array}$$

Lengthening of the carbon chain by two or more carbon atoms can be achieved by using sodium acetylide.

$$ROH \xrightarrow{\text{PBr}_3} RBr \xrightarrow{\text{NaC}{\equiv}\text{CH}} RC{\equiv}CH \overset{}{\underset{\text{H}_2\text{SO}_4}{\overset{}{\Big|}_{\text{Hg}^{2+}}}} \begin{array}{l} RC{\equiv}CNa \longrightarrow RC{\equiv}CR' \\ RCOCH_3 \end{array}$$

An alkyl chain can be attached to an aromatic nucleus by means of the Friedel–Crafts reaction.

With the exception of the last reaction, all the reactions we have discussed lead to straight chains. Branched chains can be obtained by the reaction of ketones with hydrogen cyanide:

or by the reactions of carbonyl compounds with Grignard reagents.

$$R_2C{=}O + R'MgBr \longrightarrow R'{-}\underset{R}{\overset{R}{C}}{-}OH \qquad \text{Tertiary alcohol}$$

$$RCHO + R'MgBr \longrightarrow \underset{R'}{\overset{R}{C}}HOH \qquad \text{Secondary alcohol}$$

$$RCO_2C_2H_5 + 2\,R'MgBr \longrightarrow R{-}\underset{R'}{\overset{R'}{C}}OH \qquad \text{Tertiary alcohol}$$

Shortening of the Carbon Chain

One of the best methods for degrading the carbon chain one carbon atom at a time is the so-called Barbier–Wieland degradation

14

which simply consists of treating the ester of a carboxylic acid with a Grignard reagent, preferably phenylmagnesium bromide.

$$RCH_2CO_2C_2H_5 + 2\ C_6H_5MgBr \longrightarrow RCH_2-\overset{\overset{\displaystyle C_6H_5}{|}}{\underset{\underset{\displaystyle C_6H_5}{|}}{C}}-OH \xrightarrow{-H_2O}$$

$$RCH{=}C\overset{\displaystyle C_6H_5}{\underset{\displaystyle C_6H_5}{\big\backslash}} \xrightarrow[CrO_3]{O_3} RCO_2H + (C_6H_5)_2CO$$
Benzophenone

The acid produced in this reaction can be separated from the neutral benzophenone by dissolving it in sodium bicarbonate solution from which the free acid can be recovered. It can then be reesterified and the same reaction repeated. Stepwise degradation of carbon chains by this reaction has been extremely important in the past in studying the structures of natural products. If the chain terminates in an amino group then it is convenient to begin the series of degradations with a Hofmann elimination.

$$RCH_2CH_2NH_2 \xrightarrow[CH_3I]{Excess} RCH_2CH_2\overset{+}{N}(CH_3)_3I^- \longrightarrow$$
$$RCH_2CH_2\overset{+}{N}(CH_3)_3OH^- \xrightarrow{Heat} RCH{=}CH_2 \xrightarrow{O_3} RCHO \longrightarrow$$
$$RCO_2H$$

Many textbooks describe the decarboxylation of a carboxylic acid both as a method of preparing alkanes and as a method of degrading the carbon chain. Decarboxylation proceeds satisfactorily with acetic acid; sodium acetate treated with soda lime and heated does yield methane, and benzoic acid will decarboxylate readily to yield benzene. In general, however, this is not a satisfactory reaction and usually all sorts of other products are formed as well.

Note to the Student

We have endeavoured throughout the previous chapters to describe the reactions of different types of groups attached to a carbon chain and consider how they react and what makes them react in the way they do. In this last chapter we have listed nearly fifty sets of equations, but heaven forbid that any student should sit down and try and memorize these by rote! Of the fifty equations, only three are reactions which have not been described before. Our purpose in writing out again these reactions described in the previous chapters is simply to give you an opportunity of thinking about these reactions in a different light. Previously we were concerned with how and why the reactions occurred. Now we have looked at the reactions again with a view to seeing what practical application we could put them to. Many of the reactions described in this chapter you will have felt you were already familiar with but many more you have probably forgotten. At the end of most chapters we suggested problems which usually involved thinking of reactions in this utilitarian or synthetic light. It is only by doing problems of this kind that a student can hope to become familiar with the vast number of reactions which organic compounds undergo. It is our hope, however, that having worked through the book thus far, you will feel you understand what is happening and why it is happening and are not just memorizing a lot of dull dry facts. By becoming familiar with how and why the reactions occur you should find it possible to devise sensible synthetic sequences without having to memorize endless lists of reactions. On page 199 are two charts in which some of the principal reactions are represented diagrammatically, illustrating how different compounds can be interconverted. First attempt some of the problems with this chart in front of you and then when you become more familiar with the reactions cover up the chart and do the problems without any help.

The study of the chemistry of the compounds of carbon involving as it does, on the one hand, the most rapidly developing sector of industry and, on the other hand, the study of life itself, is one of the most thrilling branches of science today. In this book we have been able to do little more than introduce you to the ABC of organic chemistry. Learning the alphabet is a dull business at the best of times. It is only when we realize that the sequences of letters joined together spell out words that it becomes interesting. We have endeavoured in these lectures to make the alphabet of organic chemistry as interesting as possible. It is up to you to now go on to learn to spell out the words, and finally make the words into sentences.

Problems

1. Starting from ethanol (C_2H_5OH) how would you prepare the following:

      (a) Ethyl bromide (C_2H_5Br) (c) Diethyl ether $((C_2H_5)_2O)$
      (b) Ethylamine $(C_2H_5NH_2)$ (d) Propyl alcohol (C_3H_7OH)
               (e) Ethyl propionate $(C_2H_5CO_2C_2H_5)$

2. Starting from benzene (C_6H_6) how would you prepare the following:

      (a) Bromobenzene (C_6H_5Br) (c) Aniline $(C_6H_5NH_2)$
      (b) Nitrobenzene $(C_6H_5NO_2)$ (d) Benzonitrile [phenyl cyanide] (C_6H_5CN)

3. A liquid X $(C_6H_{13}N)$ was treated with excess methyl iodide followed by moist silver oxide to yield an ionic substance Y $(C_9H_{21}NO)$ On heating, Y yielded trimethylamine, $(CH_3)_3N$, water, and Z (C_6H_{10}). Z reacted rapidly with bromine (to yield a compound $C_6H_{10}Br_2$), with osmium tetroxide (to yield on hydrolysis $C_6H_{12}O_2$), and with ozone to yield on hydrolysis of the ozonide a dialdehyde which could be further oxidized to yield adipic acid, $HO_2C(CH_2)_4CO_2H$. Deduce the structures of X, Y, and Z and elucidate the various reactions.

4. Starting from butan-1-ol $(CH_3CH_2CH_2CH_2OH)$ how would you prepare the following compounds:

      (a) $CH_3(CH_2)_4NH_2$ (c) $CH_3CH_2CHOHCH_2OH$
      (b) $CH_3(CH_2)_2CH(CH_3)OH$ (d) $CH_3CH_2CO_2H$
          (e) $CH_3(CH_2)_3C{\equiv}C(CH_2)_3CH_3$

5. How do nucleophiles react with a carbonyl bond? Starting from acetone how could the following be prepared:

(a)
$$\begin{array}{c} CH_3 \\ | \\ C \\ \diagup \; | \; \diagdown \\ CH_3 \quad \; \; OH \\ COOH \end{array}$$

(c)
$$\begin{array}{c} CH_3 \\ | \\ C \\ \diagup \; | \; \diagdown \\ C_2H_5 \quad \; \; OH \\ CH_3 \end{array}$$

(b)
$$\begin{array}{c} CH_3 \\ \diagdown \\ CHNH_2 \\ \diagup \\ CH_3 \end{array}$$

(d)
$$\begin{array}{c} CH_3 \\ \diagdown \\ CHBr \\ \diagup \\ CH_3 \end{array}$$

The Main Synthetic Sequences of Organic Compounds

Aliphatic Compounds

$$RCH_2OCOCH_3 \xleftarrow{CH_3COCl} RCH_2OH \xrightarrow{CrO_3} RCHO \xrightarrow[KMnO_4]{CrO_3} RCO_2H$$

$$RCH_2OH \underset{OH^-}{\overset{PBr_3}{\rightleftarrows}} RCH_2Br$$

$$RCH_2F \xleftarrow[Glycol]{K^+F^-} \mathbf{RCH_2Br} \xrightarrow{K^+CN^-} RCH_2CN \xrightarrow{[H]} RCH_2CH_2NH_2$$

$$RCH_2CN \xrightarrow[\substack{Acid \\ or \\ base}]{H_2O} RCH_2CO_2H$$

From $\mathbf{RCH_2Br}$:

- $\xrightarrow{Na^+I^- \text{ in } (CH_3)_2CO}$ RCH_2I
- $\xrightarrow[C_2H_5OH]{Na^+O^-C_2H_5}$ $RCH_2OC_2H_5$
- $\xrightarrow[\substack{2.\ Hydrolysis}]{1.\ \text{(phthalimide) } N^-K^+}$ RCH_2NH_2

$$RCH_2Br \xrightarrow[(C_2H_5)_2O]{Mg} RCH_2MgBr \xrightarrow{CO_2} RCH_2CO_2H$$

From RCH_2MgBr:

- $\xrightarrow{(CH_3)_2CO}$ $RCH_2\underset{\underset{CH_3}{|}}{\overset{\overset{CH_3}{|}}{C}}-OH$
- $\xrightarrow{HCHO}$ RCH_2CH_2OH
- $\xrightarrow{CH_3CHO}$ $\underset{\underset{CH_3}{|}}{\overset{RCH_2}{|}}CHOH$

Aromatic Compounds

199

Answers to Problems

Chapter 1

1. Isomers of C_7H_{16}:

$$CH_3CH_2CH_2CH_2CH_2CH_2CH_3 \quad \text{n-Heptane}$$

$$CH_3CH_2CH_2CH_2\underset{\underset{CH_3}{|}}{C}HCH_3 \quad \text{2-Methylhexane}$$

$$CH_3CH_2CH_2\underset{\underset{CH_3}{|}}{C}HCH_2CH_3 \quad \text{3-Methylhexane}$$

$$CH_3CH_2\underset{\underset{CH_2CH_3}{|}}{C}HCH_2CH_2 \quad \text{3-Ethylpentane}$$

$$CH_3CH_2CH_2\overset{\overset{CH_3}{|}}{\underset{\underset{CH_3}{|}}{C}}CH_3 \quad \text{2,2-Dimethylpentane}$$

$$CH_3CH_2\underset{\underset{CH_3}{|}}{C}H-\underset{\underset{CH_3}{|}}{C}HCH_3 \quad \text{2,3-Dimethylpentane}$$

$$CH_3\underset{\underset{CH_3}{|}}{C}HCH_2\underset{\underset{CH_3}{|}}{C}HCH_3 \quad \text{2,4-Dimethylpentane}$$

$$CH_3CH_2\overset{\overset{CH_3}{|}}{\underset{\underset{CH_3}{|}}{C}}CH_2CH_3 \quad \text{3,3-Dimethylpentane}$$

$$CH_3\underset{\underset{CH_3}{|}}{C}H-\overset{\overset{CH_3}{|}}{\underset{\underset{CH_3}{|}}{C}}-CH_3 \quad \text{2,2,3-Trimethylbutane}$$

2. Possible conformations of methyl cyclohexane:

(a)

(b)

(c)

(d)

These four structures represent conformations of methylcyclohexane in which the tetrahedral arrangement of the carbon atoms is
maintained. These are not *isomers*, but different arrangements which
this molecule can assume. At normal temperatures the molecule is
changing very rapidly from one form to the other. At any one moment
the most probable conformation is **b** followed by **a**; **d** and **c** are much
less probable, and represent the extreme conformations of a 'twist'
form.

Chapter 2

1. If iodination of methane were to take place it would involve the
same steps as chlorination:

$$I_2 + h\nu \xrightarrow{\ 1\ } 2\,I\cdot \qquad \text{Initiation}$$

$$\left.\begin{array}{l} CH_4 + I\cdot \xrightarrow{\ 2\ } CH_3^{\bullet} + HI \\[4pt] CH_3^{\bullet} + I_2 \xrightarrow{\ 3\ } CH_3I + I\cdot \end{array}\right\} \text{Propagation}$$

$$\left.\begin{array}{l} I\cdot + I\cdot + M \xrightarrow{\ 4\ } I_2 + M \\[4pt] CH_3^{\bullet} + I\cdot \xrightarrow{\ 5\ } CH_3I \\[4pt] CH_3^{\bullet} + CH_3^{\bullet} \xrightarrow{\ 6\ } C_2H_6 \end{array}\right\} \text{Termination}$$

Taking the values of the bond-dissociation energies given in the
question and the value $D(CH_3-H) = 103$ kcal mole^{-1} we have:

$$\Delta H_2 = +103 - 71 = +32 \text{ kcal mole}^{-1}$$
$$\Delta H_3 = \ \ +36 - 50 = -14 \text{ kcal mole}^{-1}$$

Reaction 2 is endothermic to the extent of 32 kcal mole^{-1}. It is therefore a most unfavourable reaction and iodination of methane is not practicable.

2. We have seen that the bromination (at 150°) at the secondary position in propane occurs 90 times faster than attack at the primary position. There are 4 hydrogen atoms attached to secondary carbon atoms and 6 attached to primary carbon atoms in n-butane. Therefore if we brominate n-butane at 150° we would expect to obtain 2-bromobutane and 1-bromobutane in the proportions 60:1. Hydrogen atoms attached to a tertiary carbon atom are the least strongly bound. We therefore expect bromination at a tertiary site to occur considerably faster than a secondary site. In isobutane (2-methyl-propane) there is one tertiary site, the remainder being unreactive primary sites. Thus there is one site very much more reactive than all the others and we would expect bromination of isobutane to yield *t*-butyl bromide (2-bromo-2-methylpropane) almost exclusively, which it does.

Fluorination of n-propane at room temperature favours attack at the secondary position by a factor of 1·5:1. Fluorination of n-butane under the same conditions yields equal amounts of 1-fluoro- and 2-fluorobutane. Fluorination is so much less selective that, in spite of the fact that a hydrogen atom bonded to a tertiary carbon atom is appreciably less tightly bound than a hydrogen atom bonded to a primary carbon, fluorination of isobutane yields more 1-fluoro-2-methylpropane (isobutyl fluoride) than 2-fluoro-2-methylpropane (*t*-butyl fluoride).

Chapter 3

1. In ethyl bromide the bromine atom is more electronegative than carbon, and the C—Br bond is polarized:

$$\overset{\delta+\ \ \delta-}{C—Br}$$

It will react with *nucleophiles*, i.e. electron-donating species, e.g. anions (a), (d), (h):

Ethanol

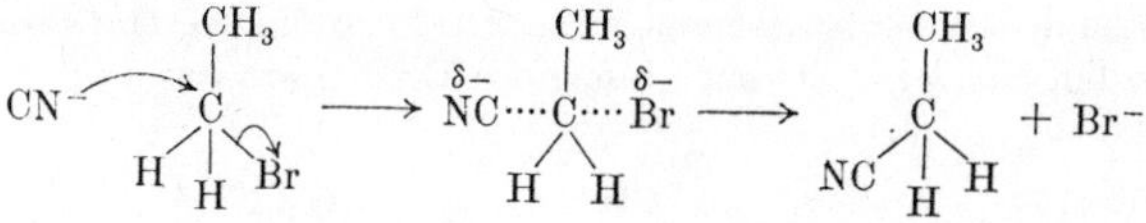

Ethyl cyanide

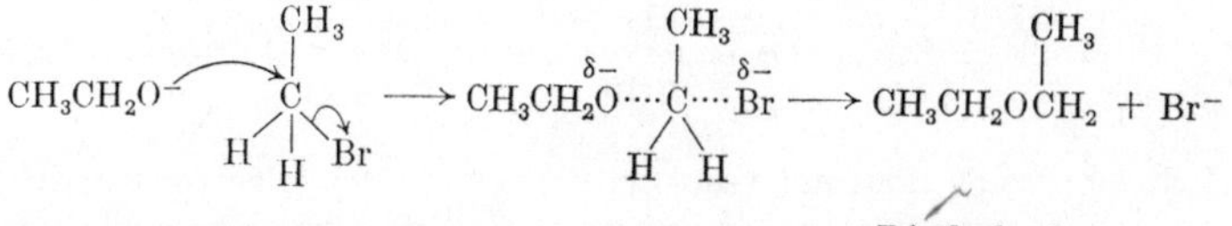

Diethyl ether

With the halogen anions (g) and (i) the reaction is similar but reversible:

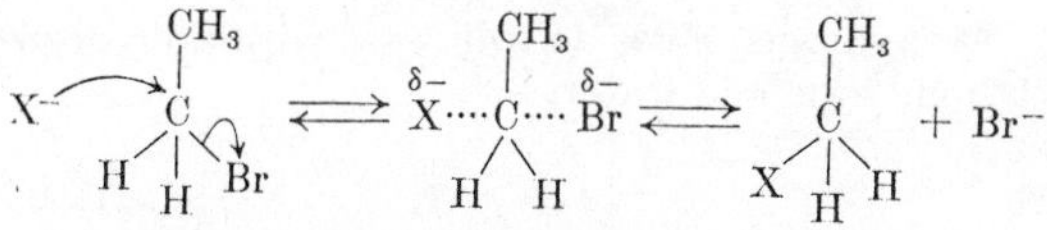

$$K_c = \frac{[RX][Br^-]}{[RBr][X^-]} \qquad (R = C_2H_5)$$

For fluoride K_c is large, and provided the reaction is carried out in a solvent in which F^- is only weakly solvated (e.g. glycol) the reaction goes almost to completion. For iodide $K_c < 1$, but NaI is soluble in acetone and NaBr is not, so that by carrying out the reaction in acetone it may be forced to completion.

Ammonia (e) carries no negative charge, but it does possess a pair of el. ctrons which are readily donated:

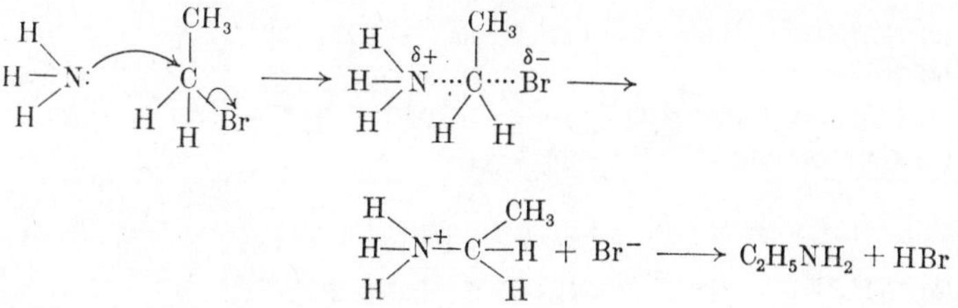

Ethylamine

Ethylamine will then react with further ethyl bromide to yield diethylamine, and this in turn will give triethylamine and ultimately tetraethylammonium bromide.

A chlorine atom (c) will react with ethyl bromide in the same way as it will react with ethane, but note that there are two possible products:

$$
\begin{array}{c}
CH_3 \\
\mid \\
CH_2Br
\end{array}
+ Cl\cdot -
\left\langle
\begin{array}{l}
\xrightarrow{-HCl}
\begin{array}{c}
CH_2\cdot \\
\mid \\
CH_2Br
\end{array}
\xrightarrow{Cl_2}
\begin{array}{c}
CH_2Cl \\
\mid \\
CH_2Br
\end{array}
+ Cl\cdot
\\[2em]
\xrightarrow{-HCl}
\begin{array}{c}
CH_3 \\
\mid \\
CHBr\cdot
\end{array}
\xrightarrow{Cl_2}
\begin{array}{c}
CH_3 \\
\mid \\
CHBrCl
\end{array}
+ Cl\cdot
\end{array}
\right.
$$

Ethyl bromide does not react with electrophiles (electron-seeking species, i.e. cations (b) or nitric acid (f) which ionizes as $H_3O^+ + NO_3^-$ in aqueous solution).

Chapter 4

1. 1 (*a*) Dry hydrogen chloride will react with anhydrous alcohol to yield ethyl chloride and water:

$$
\begin{array}{c}
CH_3 \\
\mid \\
C \\
H\ \big/\ \big\backslash\ O \\
H
\end{array}
H + HCl \longrightarrow
Cl^-
\begin{array}{c}
CH_3 \\
\mid \\
C \\
H\ \big|\ H \\
\overset{+}{O} \\
\mid \\
H
\end{array}
H \longrightarrow
\begin{array}{c}
CH_3 \\
\mid \\
C \\
Cl\ \big|\ H \\
H
\end{array}
+ H_2O
$$

Note that ethanol will not react with hydrochloric acid (aqueous solutions of hydrogen chloride) nor will a solution of sodium chloride react with ethanol; i.e.

$$Cl^- + C_2H_5{-}OH \longrightarrow C_2H_5Cl + OH^-$$

does not occur (see second paragraph of Chapter 4).

(*b*) $C_2H_5OH + Na \longrightarrow C_2H_5O^-Na^+ + \frac{1}{2}H_2$

(*c*) No reaction.

(*d*) $C_2H_5OH + Na^+NH_2^- \longrightarrow C_2H_5O^- + Na^+ + NH_3$

(*e*) No reaction.

2 (*a*) $C_2H_5NH_2 + HCl \longrightarrow C_2H_5\overset{+}{N}H_3Cl^-$

(*b*) $C_2H_5NH_2 + Na \xrightarrow{\text{Slow}} C_2H_5NH^-Na^+ + \frac{1}{2}H_2$

(*c*) $C_2H_5NH_2 + H_2O \rightleftharpoons C_2H_5NH_3^+ + OH^- \qquad K_b = 4 \times 10^{-4}$

(*d*) No reaction. (Ethylamine is a stronger base than ammonia.)

(Carrying out these reactions would be complicated by the fact that ethylamine is a gas at room temperature.)

(e)

$$C_2H_5\overset{\cdot\cdot}{N}H_2 \quad \overset{CH_3}{\underset{H\ H}{\overset{|}{C}}} \, Br \longrightarrow C_2H_5\overset{+}{N}H_2C_2H_5 + Br^- \xrightarrow[\text{}]{C_2H_5NH_2}$$

$$(C_2H_5)_2NH + C_2H_5\overset{+}{N}H_3Br^-$$

$$(C_2H_5)_2\overset{\cdot\cdot}{N}H \quad C_2H_5{-}Br \longrightarrow (C_2H_5)_2\overset{+}{N}HC_2H_5 + Br^- \xrightarrow[\text{}]{C_2H_5NH_2}$$

$$(C_2H_5)_3N + C_2H_5\overset{+}{N}H_3Br^-$$

$$(C_2H_5)_3\overset{\cdot\cdot}{N} \quad C_2H_5{-}Br \longrightarrow (C_2H_5)_4\overset{+}{N} + Br^-$$

2. *(a)*

$$\underset{C_2H_5}{\overset{C_2H_5}{>}}O + HBr \longrightarrow \underset{C_2H_5}{\overset{C_2H_5}{>}}\overset{+}{O}{-}H \ Br^-$$

Rewriting the diethylhydroxonium ion, we get:

$$Br^- \quad \underset{H\ H}{\overset{CH_3}{\overset{|}{C}}}\overset{+}{\underset{|}{O}}C_2H_5 \longrightarrow \underset{Br\ \ H}{\overset{CH_3}{\overset{|}{C}}} H + HOC_2H_5$$

Note that this cleavage of ethers by hydrogen halides will only occur when the anhydrous hydrogen halide is used. Dilute aqueous solutions of hydrogen bromide (i.e. hydrobromic acid) would not react.

(b) $Cl_2 + (C_2H_5)_2O \longrightarrow$ no reaction in the dark

$$Cl_2 + h\nu \longrightarrow 2\ Cl\cdot \qquad \text{Initiation}$$

$$Cl\cdot + CH_3CH_2OC_2H_5 \longrightarrow \dot{C}H_2CH_2OC_2H_5$$

$$Cl\cdot + CH_3CH_2OC_2H_5 \longrightarrow CH_3\dot{C}HOC_2H_5$$

$$CH_3\dot{C}HOC_2H_5 \text{ (or } \dot{C}H_2CH_2OC_2H_5) + Cl_2 \longrightarrow$$

$$CH_3CHClOC_2H_5 \text{ (or } CH_2ClCH_2OC_2H_5) + Cl\cdot$$

Chain propagation

There will be the usual termination steps, e.g.

$$Cl\cdot + Cl\cdot + M \longrightarrow Cl_2 + M$$
$$R\cdot + R\cdot \longrightarrow R_2$$
$$R\cdot + R'\cdot \longrightarrow R\text{---}R'$$
$$R'\cdot + R'\cdot \longrightarrow R'_2$$
$$(R'\cdot)\, R\cdot + Cl\cdot \longrightarrow RCl\ (R'Cl)$$

In practice the chlorination of ethers at low temperatures in the liquid phase yields predominantly the α-chloro ether (i.e. $CH_3CHClOC_2H_5$). In the gas phase the reaction is much more complicated and outside the scope of this book.

(c) No reaction.

Chapter 5

1. Alkenes with the molecular formula C_5H_{10}:

$CH_3CH_2CH_2CH{=}CH_2$ Pent-1-ene

$CH_3CH_2CH{=}CHCH_3$ Pent-2-ene

$\begin{array}{l} CH_3CH_2 \\ C{=}CH_2 \\ CH_3 \end{array}$ 2-Methylbut-1-ene

$CH_3CH{=}C\begin{array}{l} CH_3 \\ \\ CH_3 \end{array}$ 2-Methylbut-2-ene

$\begin{array}{l} CH_3 \\ CHCH{=}CH_2 \\ CH_3 \end{array}$ 3-Methylbut-1-ene

2. (*a*) To ensure elimination from ethyl bromide, a primary alkyl halide, it is necessary to use a very strong base; e.g.

$$Na^+NH_2^- \cdots H$$

$$\longrightarrow Na^+ + NH_3 + CH_2{=}CH_2 + Br^-$$

(*b*) 2-Bromopropane is a secondary alkyl halide and thus undergoes elimination fairly readily, so it is not necessary to use such a strong base:

$$\begin{array}{c} CH_3 \\ \diagdown \\ \qquad CHBr + Na^+ OC_2H_5{}^- \xrightarrow{C_2H_5OH} \\ \diagup \\ CH_3 \end{array}$$

$$CH_3CH{=}CH_2 + Na^+Br^- + C_2H_5OH$$

(*c*) Methyl 2-propyl ether (2-methoxypropane) cannot be prepared by the reaction of 2-bromopropane with sodium methoxide (we have just used sodium ethoxide to promote elimination). Very careful treatment with an aqueous alkaline solution will result in some elimination, but the predominant reaction will be substitution.

Treatment of the propan-2-ol as formed with sodium metal will yield the corresponding alkoxide which we may then react with methyl iodide.

$$CH_3CHOHCH_3 + Na \longrightarrow (CH_3)_2CHO^- + Na^+ + \tfrac{1}{2} H_2$$

$$\longrightarrow (CH_3)_2CHOCH_3 + I^-$$

Chapter 6

1. (*a*)

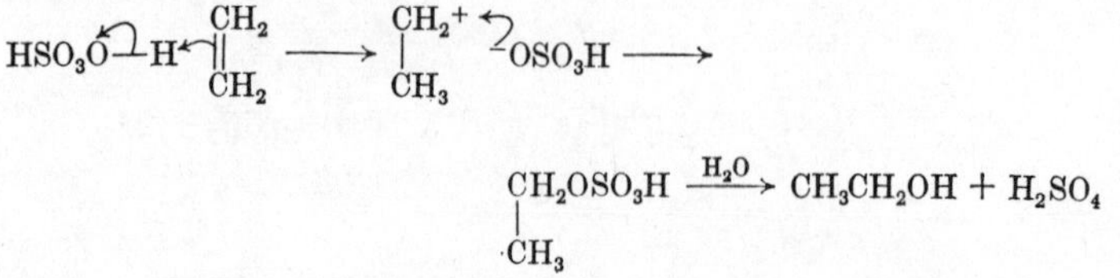

$$HSO_3O-H \quad \overset{CH_2}{\underset{CH_2}{\|}} \longrightarrow \overset{CH_2^+}{\underset{CH_3}{|}} \quad OSO_3H \longrightarrow$$

$$\overset{CH_2OSO_3H}{\underset{\cdot CH_3}{|}} \xrightarrow{\text{H}_2\text{O}} CH_3CH_2OH + H_2SO_4$$

(*b*)

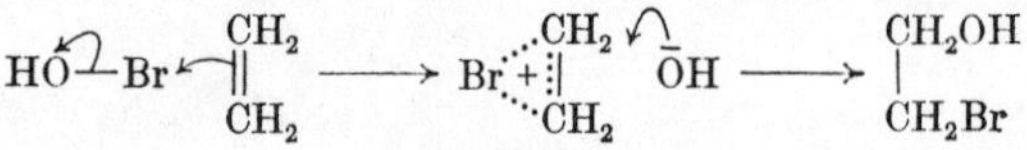

$$HO-Br \quad \overset{CH_2}{\underset{CH_2}{\|}} \longrightarrow \overset{\cdot\cdot CH_2}{Br^+ \underset{\cdot\cdot CH_2}{:\|}} \quad \bar{O}H \longrightarrow \overset{CH_2OH}{\underset{CH_2Br}{|}}$$

(*c*)

$$\overset{CH_2}{\underset{CH_2}{\|}} \quad \overset{O}{\underset{O}{\diagdown}} Mn^{VII} \overset{O}{\underset{O^-}{\diagup}} \longrightarrow \overset{CH_2-O}{\underset{CH_2-O}{|}} Mn^V \overset{O}{\underset{O^-}{\diagup}} \xrightarrow{2\ \text{H}_2\text{O}}$$

$$\overset{CH_2OH}{\underset{CH_2OH}{|}} + \overset{HO}{\underset{HO}{\diagdown}} Mn^V \overset{O}{\underset{O^-}{\diagup}}$$

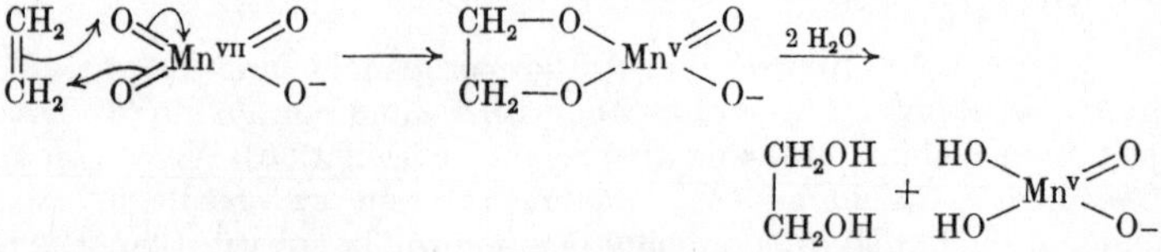

(*N.B.* This represents a possible mechanism; the reactions in alkaline permanganate are extremely complex.)

(*d*)

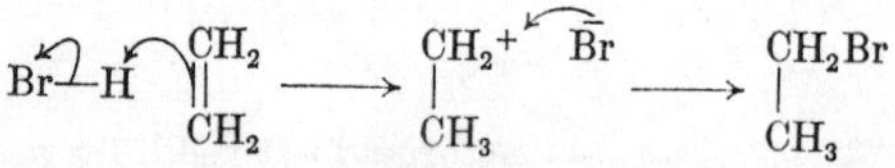

$$Br-H \quad \overset{CH_2}{\underset{CH_2}{\|}} \longrightarrow \overset{CH_2^+}{\underset{CH_3}{|}} \quad \bar{Br} \longrightarrow \overset{CH_2Br}{\underset{CH_3}{|}}$$

(*e*)

$$R\cdot \quad CH_2=CH_2 \longrightarrow R-CH_2-\dot{C}H_2 \xrightarrow{CH_2=CH_2}$$

$$R-(CH_2CH_2)\dot{}_2 \xrightarrow{CH_2=CH_2} \text{etc.}$$

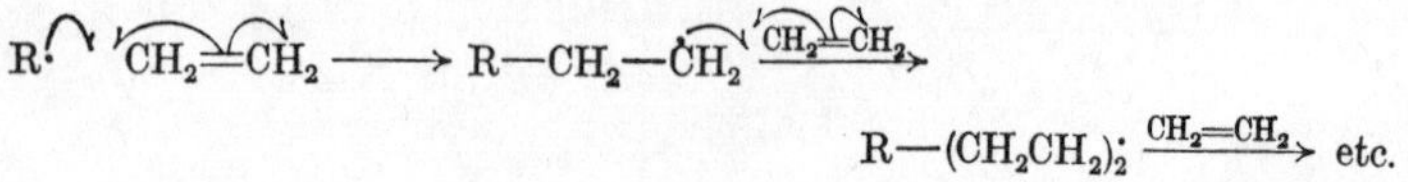

(R· = initiating radical)

2. Heterolytic addition (*a*) Electrophilic attack:

(*a'*) Electrophilic attack:

(*b*) Nucleophilic attack (uncommon in hydrocarbon olefins):

Homolytic attack:

Half-headed arrow represents the transfer of *one* electron

Heterolytic addition of bromine to but-2-ene (in solution in the dark):

Homolytic addition of bromine to but-2-ene (in the gas phase in the light):

$$Br_2 \xrightarrow{h\nu} 2\,Br\cdot$$

$$CH_3CH{=}CHCH_3 \quad Br\cdot \longrightarrow CH_3CHBr\dot{C}HCH_3$$

$$CH_3CHBr\dot{C}HCH_3 \quad Br{-}Br \longrightarrow CH_3CHBrCHBrCH_3 + Br\cdot \quad \text{Chain}$$
$$\text{reaction}$$

Under these conditions hydrogen abstraction is also possible:

$$Br\cdot \quad H{-}CH_2CH{=}CHCH_3 \longrightarrow BrH + \dot{C}H_2CH{=}CHCH_3$$

$$Br{-}Br \quad \dot{C}H_2CH{=}CHCH_3 \longrightarrow Br\cdot + BrCH_2CH{=}CHCH_3$$

The chain-terminating steps are discussed in Chapter 2.

From the heterolytic addition of bromine to but-2-ene, only 2,3-dibromobutane can be formed. In the homolytic reaction, in addition to 2,3-dibromobutane, 1-bromobut-2-ene and 1,2,3-tribromobutane may also be found (the latter as a result of addition of bromine to 1-bromobut-2-ene).

Chapter 7

1. This question is to illustrate the difference in reactivity of the carbon–carbon and carbon–oxygen double bonds. Three of the reagents are nucleophilic in character: (1) aqueous sodium cyanide, (4) aqueous hydroxylamine, and (5) aqueous ammonia. These reagents will not react with ethylene but will add to the carbonyl bond of formaldehyde attacking the carbon atom. Hydrogen chloride is an electrophilic reagent which will add to ethylene and to formaldehyde (attacking the oxygen atom). Aqueous sodium chloride will add neither to ethylene nor to formaldehyde.

(1) No reaction

(2) No reaction   No reaction

(3)

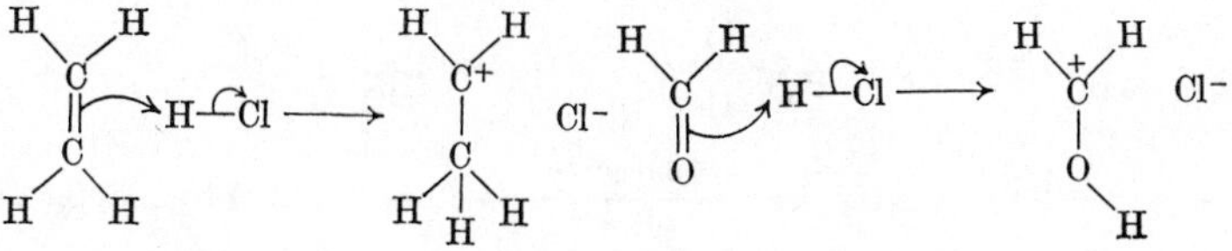

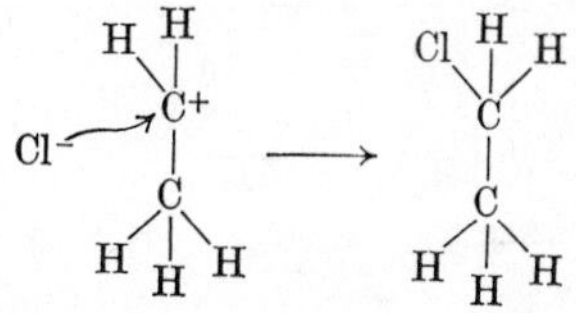

Formaldehyde undergoes further reaction in the presence of strong acids, but we will not be concerned with this at present.

(4) No reaction

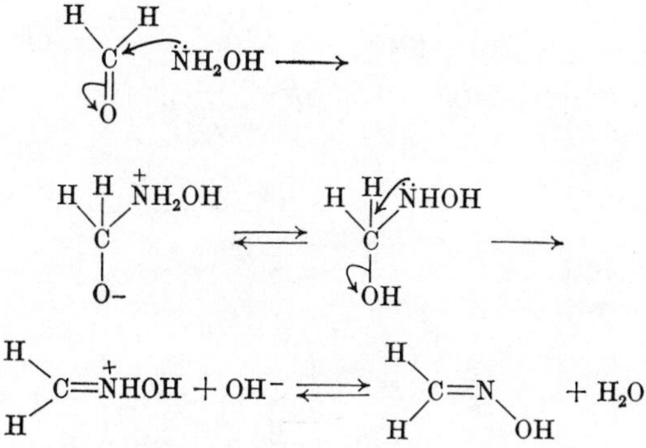

(5) No reaction

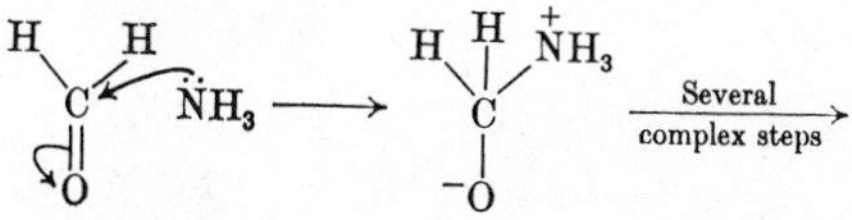

$$[(CH_2)_6(NH_2)_4]$$

Hexamethylene-
tetramine

2. This question illustrates the similarity of the nucleophilic reagents which react with alkyl halides by a substitution reaction with those which react with aldehydes and ketones by addition.

15

(1*a*)

$$H_3\ddot{N} + \underset{\underset{H}{\overset{CH_3}{|}}}{C}\!\!-\!Br \longrightarrow \overset{CH_3}{\underset{\underset{H}{\overset{|}{H}}}{\overset{+}{H_3N}\!-\!C}} \; Br^- \xrightarrow{NH_3} \overset{CH_3}{\underset{\underset{H}{\overset{|}{H}}}{H_2N\!-\!C}} +$$

$$NH_4{}^+Br^- \xrightarrow[\text{steps}]{\text{Subsequent}} (\text{see Problem 2(c) to Chapter 4})$$

(1*b*)

$$H_3\ddot{N} + \overset{H_3C\quad CH_3}{\underset{\underset{O}{\|}}{C}} \longrightarrow \overset{H_3}{\underset{\underset{O^-}{|}}{\overset{+}{H_3N}\!-\!C\!-\!CH_3}} \rightleftharpoons \overset{H_3}{\underset{\underset{OH}{|}}{H_2\dot{N}\!-\!C\!-\!CH_3}} \longrightarrow$$

$$\overset{CH_3}{\underset{CH_3}{H_2\overset{+}{N}\!=\!C}} + OH^- \rightleftharpoons \overset{CH_3}{\underset{CH_3}{HN\!=\!C}} + H_2O \longrightarrow$$

Polymer of $(CH_3)_2C\!=\!NH$

(2*a*)

$$Na^+NC^- + \underset{\underset{H}{\overset{CH_3}{|}}}{C}\!\!-\!Br \longrightarrow \overset{CH_3}{\underset{\underset{H}{\overset{|}{H}}}{NC\!-\!C}} + Br^-Na^+$$

(2*b*)

$$H^+NC^- + \overset{H_3C\quad CH_3}{\underset{\underset{O}{\|}}{C}} \longrightarrow \overset{H_3}{\underset{\underset{O^-}{|}}{NC\!-\!C\!-\!CH_3}} \xrightarrow{H^+} \overset{H_3}{\underset{\underset{OH}{|}}{NC\!-\!C\!-\!CH_3}}$$

(Although both (2*a*) and (2*b*) involve attack by CN⁻, (2*a*) goes to completion if ethyl bromide is treated with potassium cyanide in ethanol, whereas (2*b*) goes to completion in aqueous sodium or potassium cyanide solution to which 1 mole of acid has been added.)

(3a)

$$Na^+C_2H_5O^- \quad \underset{H}{\overset{CH_3}{\underset{|}{C}}} \!\! \overset{|}{\underset{Br}{H}} \longrightarrow \underset{C_2H_5O}{\overset{CH_3}{\underset{|}{C}}} \!\! \overset{|}{H} \ \ H + Na^+Br^-$$

Diethyl ether

(3b)

$$Na^+C_2H_5O^- \quad \underset{O}{\overset{H_3C \quad CH_3}{\underset{\parallel}{C}}} \longrightarrow \underset{O^-}{\overset{C_2H_5O \ \ \overset{H_3}{C} \ \ CH_3}{\underset{\mid}{C}}} \quad Na^+$$

The product of this reaction is on acidification a hemi-acetal which is unstable in water and hydrolyses to regenerate acetone and ethanol.

(4a) No reaction.

(4b) Electrophiles add to the carbonyl bond attacking the oxygen atom and leaving a carbonium ion:

$$\underset{O}{\overset{H_3C \quad CH_3}{\underset{\parallel}{C}}} \to H^+Cl^- \rightleftharpoons \underset{OH}{\overset{H_3C \quad CH_3}{\underset{\mid}{C^+}}} + Cl^-$$

The carbonium ion is much more susceptible to nucleophilic attack and weak nucleophiles such as methanol react readily.

$$\underset{H}{\overset{H_3C}{\underset{\mid}{O:}}} \ \underset{OH}{\overset{H_3C \quad CH_3}{\underset{\mid}{C^+}}} \ Cl^- \longrightarrow \underset{H}{\overset{H_3C \ \overset{+}{O} \ \overset{H_3}{C} \ CH_3}{\underset{OH}{\underset{\mid}{C}}}} \ Cl^- \rightleftharpoons$$

$$\underset{OH}{\overset{CH_3O \ \overset{H_3}{C} \ CH_3}{\underset{\mid}{C}}} + H^+Cl^-$$

Hemi-acetal

The difference between this reaction and the base-catalysed addition (3*b*) is that this reaction goes further:

$$CH_3O - \overset{\overset{\displaystyle CH_3}{|}}{\underset{\underset{\displaystyle H}{|}{O}}{C}} - CH_3 \longrightarrow H^+Cl^- \rightleftharpoons CH_3O - \overset{\overset{\displaystyle CH_3}{|}}{\underset{\underset{\displaystyle H \quad H}{|}{O^+}}{C}} - CH_3 \quad Cl^- \longrightarrow$$

$$CH_3O - \overset{\overset{\displaystyle CH_3}{|}}{\underset{\underset{\displaystyle +}{}}{C}} - CH_3 \quad + H_2O + Cl^-$$

$$Cl^- \quad CH_3O - \overset{\overset{\displaystyle CH_3}{|}}{\underset{\underset{\displaystyle +}{}}{C}} - CH_3 \xrightarrow{\quad \overset{\displaystyle H}{\underset{\displaystyle CH_3}{O}} \quad} Cl^- \quad CH_3O - \overset{\overset{\displaystyle CH_3}{|}}{\underset{\underset{\underset{\displaystyle H_3C \quad H}{}}{O^+}}{C}} - CH_3 \rightleftharpoons$$

$$CH_3O - \overset{\overset{\displaystyle CH_3}{|}}{\underset{\underset{\displaystyle OCH_3}{|}}{C}} - CH_3 \quad + H^+Cl^-$$
Acetal

All these steps are reversible although we have only put double arrows for reactions involving proton transfer, because these are extremely rapid. Although the acetal can be hydrolysed back to acetone and two moles of ethanol this reaction is very much slower than the hydrolysis of the hemi-acetal.

Chapter 9

1. (*a*) The reaction between ethanol and acetic acid is a reversible one, the equilibrium being established very slowly.

$$CH_3CO_2H + C_2H_5OH \rightleftharpoons CH_3CO_2C_2H_5 + H_2O$$

The reaction can be greatly accelerated by the addition of a strong mineral acid as catalyst:

If, instead of adding just a trace of mineral acid as a catalyst, we add an excess of sulphuric acid then all the water will be converted into hydroxonium sulphate ($H_3\overset{+}{O}$ HSO_4^-) and so the reaction will go to completion.

(*b*) Acetamide is most conveniently prepared by the direct reaction of ethyl acetate with ammonia

Alternatively, both ethyl acetate and acetamide may be prepared by the reaction of acetyl chloride (see below) with ethanol and ammonia respectively. Acetamide can also be prepared by heating ammonium acetate but this reaction is restricted to acetamide and is not general for other amides.

(*c*) Acetic anhydride can be prepared in the laboratory by treating acetyl chloride with sodium acetate, i.e.

$$CH_3CO_2H + SOCl_2 \longrightarrow CH_3COCl + HCl + SO_2 \text{ (cf. page 94)}$$

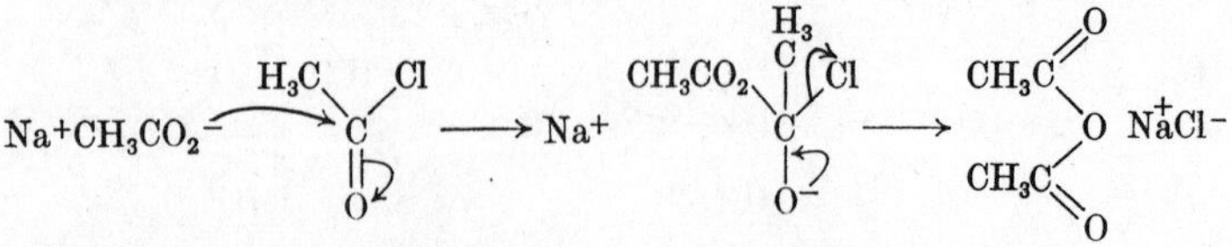

(d) *N,N*-Dimethylacetamide can be prepared by treating *N,N*-dimethylamine with either acetic anhydride or acetyl chloride:

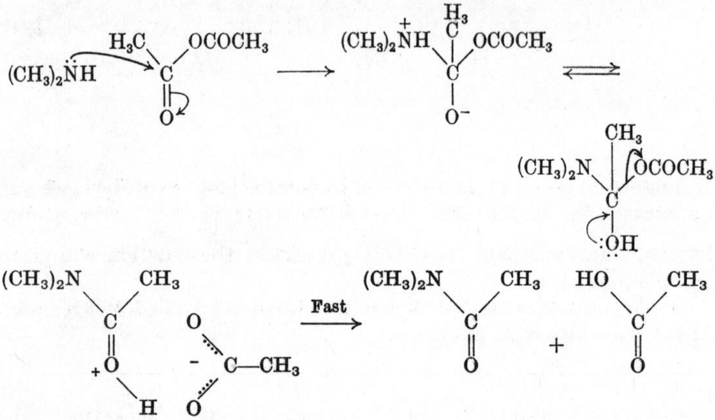

Chapter 10

1. The simplest laboratory test to distinguish between primary, secondary, and tertiary amines is to treat the unknown substance with dilute aqueous nitrous acid. If the unknown base is a primary aliphatic amine, nitrogen will be evolved.

$$RCH_2NH_2 + HONO \longrightarrow [RCH_2NHNO] \longrightarrow [RCH_2N_2OH] \longrightarrow$$
$$[RCH_2N_2{}^+ OH^-] \longrightarrow [RCH_2{}^+] + N_2 \uparrow \xrightarrow{H_2O}$$
$$RCH_2OH + \text{other products}$$

The compounds in square brackets are transient intermediates, none of them capable of isolation.

If the unknown base is a secondary amine, a nitrosamine will be formed. Nitrosamines are yellow oils, insoluble in dilute aqueous acid if there are more than five carbon atoms. (If the secondary amine is diethylamine, for example, no oil will be precipitated but the solution will turn deep yellow.)

If the unknown base is a tertiary aliphatic amine, no reaction will occur and the free base may be recovered from the aqueous nitrous acid solution by treatment with aqueous sodium hydroxide.

Chapter 11

1. (i) Ethyl bromide is treated with a solution of potassium cyanide in ethanol (cf. Chapter 3):

$$C_2H_5Br + KCN \xrightarrow{C_2H_5OH} C_2H_5CN + KBr$$

Hydrolysis of ethyl cyanide, preferably using an acid catalyst:

$$C_2H_5CN + H_2O \xrightarrow{H^+ A^-} C_2H_5CO_2H$$

(ii)

$$CH_3CH_2C\equiv CH + Na^+NH_2^- \xrightarrow[\text{ammonia}]{\text{Liquid}} CH_3CH_2C\equiv C^-Na^+ + NH_3$$
But-1-yne

This reaction may be carried out in two stages without separating the butyne. The first stage involves the preparation of sodamide in liquid ammonia. Acetylene gas is then passed through the liquid ammonia suspension of sodamide and sodium acetylide is formed. Alternatively, acetylene gas may be passed directly into a solution of sodium in liquid ammonia, but the reaction is rather vigorous and much ethylene is formed:

$$C_2H_2 + Na \longrightarrow C_2HNa + \tfrac{1}{2}H_2; \quad C_2H_2 \xrightarrow{H_2} C_2H_4$$

Ethyl bromide is added to the solution of sodium acetylide in liquid ammonia and but-1-yne is formed. A fresh suspension of sodamide in liquid ammonia is made in a separate reaction vessel and added to the butyne–ammonia mixture. The butyne reacts rapidly with the sodamide to form the sodium butylacetylide and the second portion of ethyl bromide is now added. The hex-3-yne is isolated by allowing most of the ammonia to evaporate and then adding water. The water dissolves the sodium bromide and leaves the hexyne floating on a dilute aqueous solution of ammonia.

(iii) Treatment of hex-3-yne with mercuric sulphate in aqueous sulphuric acid:

$$C_2H_5C{\equiv}CC_2H_5 \xrightarrow[H_2O+H_2SO_4]{Hg^{2+}} C_3H_7COC_2H_5$$

(iv) Hydrogenation of ethyl cyanide will yield n-propylamine:

$$C_2H_5C{\equiv}N \xrightarrow{H_2} C_3H_7NH_2$$

Chapter 12

1. All these reactions involve butylmagnesium bromide:

$$C_4H_9Br + Mg \xrightarrow[\text{solution}]{(C_2H_5)_2O} C_4H_9MgBr$$

(a) $C_4H_9MgBr + HCHO \longrightarrow C_5H_{11}OMgBr \xrightarrow{H_2O} C_5H_{11}OH$

(b) $C_4H_9MgBr + CO_2 \longrightarrow C_4H_9CO_2H$

(c) $C_4H_9MgBr + CH_3CHO \longrightarrow$

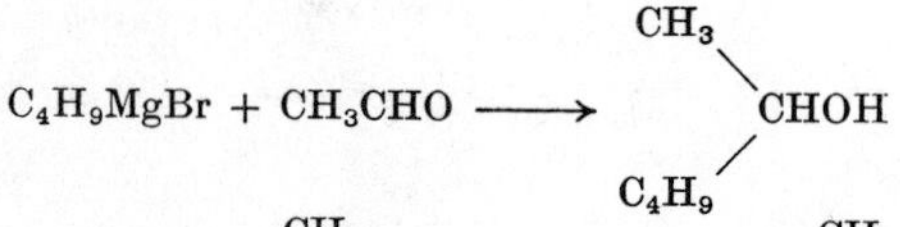

(d) $C_4H_9MgBr +$

(e) $C_4H_9MgBr + CH_3CO_2C_2H_5 \longrightarrow$

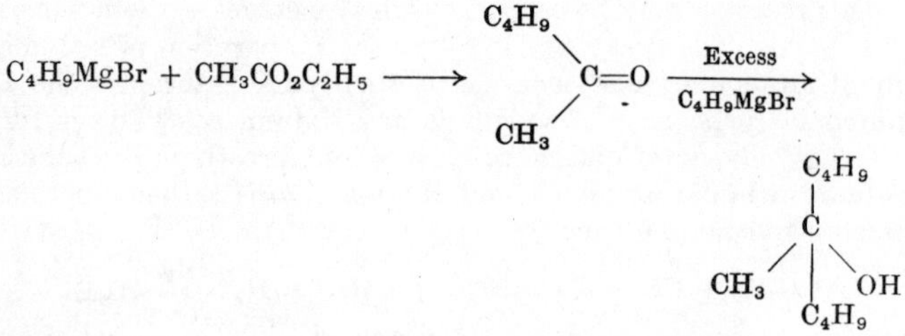

Chapter 13

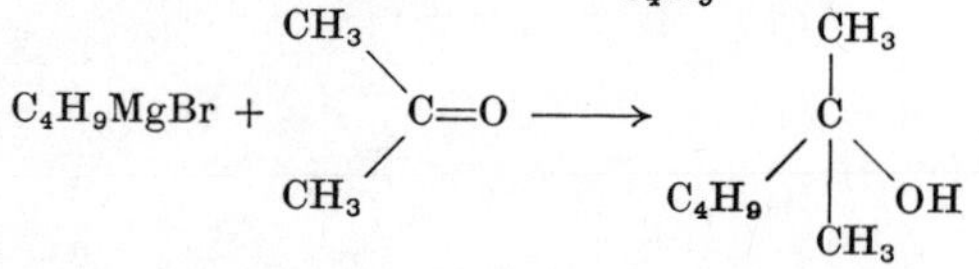

1. (a)
Mixture

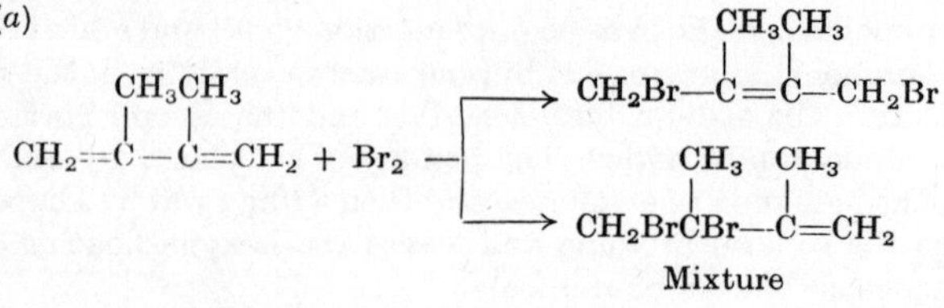

(b)

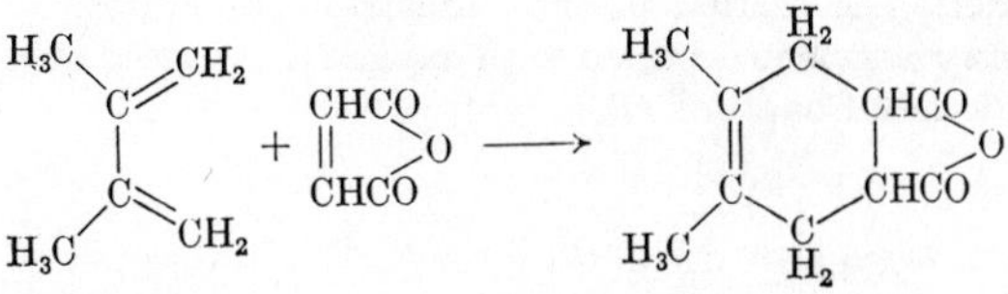

(c)

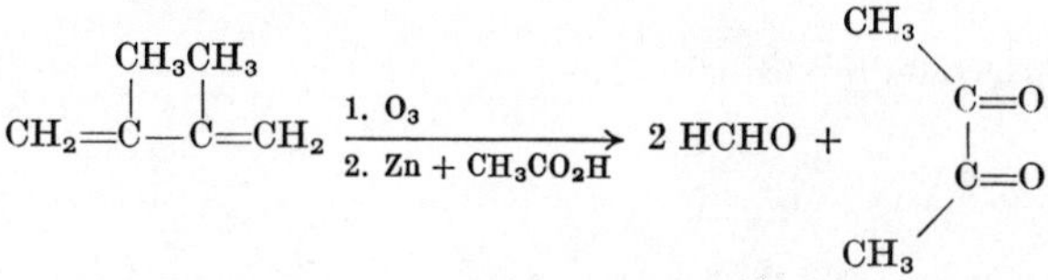

$$CH_2=C-C=CH_2 \xrightarrow[\text{2. Zn + CH}_3\text{CO}_2\text{H}]{\text{1. O}_3} 2\ HCHO +$$

2.

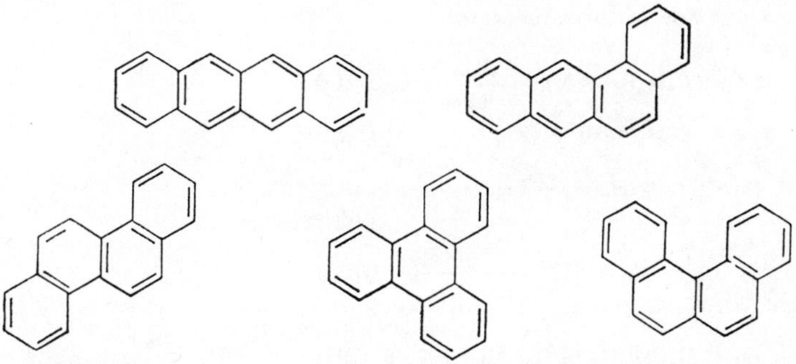

(Note that

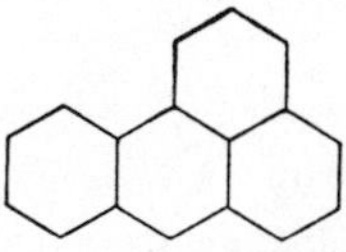

will not be a stable molecule. Try drawing Kekulé, i.e. cyclohexatriene, rings keeping each carbon atom surrounded by eight electrons in its outer shell.)

Chapter 14

1. (a) $C_6H_5CH=CH-CH=CHC_6H_5 + Br_2 \longrightarrow$
$C_6H_5CHBrCH=CHCHBrC_6H_5 + C_6H_5CHBrCHBrCH=CHC_6H_5$

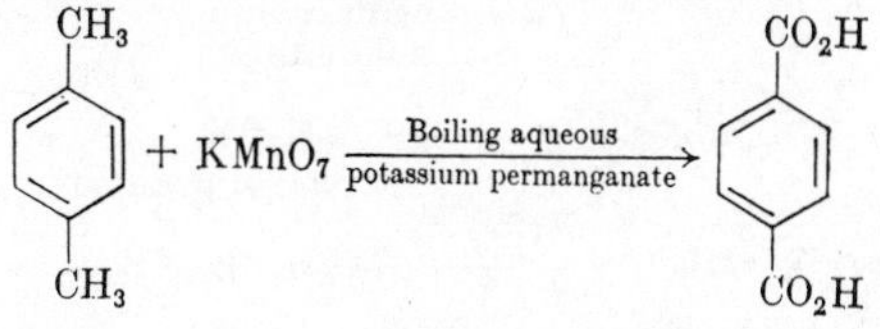

This reaction is carried in the industrial preparation of Terylene. In industry p-xylene is mixed with oxygen and passed over vanadium pentoxide (see Chapter 17).

(c)

$$C_6H_5CH{=}CH{-}CH{=}CH_2 + \begin{matrix}CHCO\\||\quad\ \ \rangle O\\CHCO\end{matrix} \longrightarrow$$

Notice that the 'double bonds' of the benzene nucleus do not take part in any of these reactions.

2. (a) $C_6H_5Br + Mg \xrightarrow[\text{solution}]{(C_2H_5)_2O} C_6H_5MgBr$

   $C_6H_5MgBr + CO_2 \longrightarrow C_6H_5CO_2H$

(b) $C_6H_6 + HNO_3 + H_2SO_4 \longrightarrow C_6H_5NO_2$
                                        Nitrobenzene

   $C_6H_5NO_2 + H_2 \xrightarrow[\text{or Sn + HCl}]{\text{Catalyst (Ni)}} C_6H_5NH_2$

(c) $C_6H_5COCH_3 + CH_3MgI \longrightarrow$

(d) $C_6H_5NH_2 + NaNO_2 + 2\,H_2SO_4 \xrightarrow[\substack{\text{aqueous}\\\text{solution}}]{\text{In dilute}}$

   $C_6H_5N_2{}^+ HSO_4{}^- + Na^+ HSO_4{}^- + 2\,H_2O$
   Benzenediazonium
   sulphate

   $C_6H_5N_2{}^+ HSO_4{}^- + CuCN \longrightarrow C_6H_5CN$
                                        Phenyl cyanide

   $C_6H_5CN + LiAlH_4 \longrightarrow C_6H_5CH_2NH_2$

Chapter 15

1. (*a*)

$$
\begin{array}{cc}
\text{H} & \text{H} \\
| & | \\
\text{F}-\text{C}-\text{SO}_3\text{H} \qquad & \text{HO}_3\text{S}-\text{C}-\text{F} \\
| & | \\
\text{Cl} & \text{Cl} \\
\text{(i)} & \text{(ii)}
\end{array}
$$

ii is the mirror image of **i** and is not superimposable upon **i**.

Similarly with (*b*) when the structure is written out more fully, **i** and **ii** are optically active.

$$
\begin{array}{cc}
\text{H} & \text{H} \\
| & | \\
\text{CH}_3\text{CH}_2-\text{C}-\text{COOH} \qquad & \text{HOOC}-\text{C}-\text{CH}_2\text{CH}_3 \\
| & | \\
\text{NH}_2 & \text{H}_2\text{N} \\
\text{(i)} & \text{(ii)}
\end{array}
$$

(*c*)

$$
\begin{array}{cc}
\text{CH}_3 & \text{CH}_3 \\
| & | \\
\text{CH}_3\text{CH}_2-\text{C}-\text{CH}_2\text{CH}_3 \qquad & \text{CH}_3\text{CH}_2-\text{C}-\text{CH}_2\text{CH}_3 \\
| & | \\
\text{CO}_2\text{H} & \text{HO}_2\text{C} \\
\text{(i)} & \text{(ii)}
\end{array}
$$

This compound has two ethyl groups attached to the central carbon atom and **ii** can be made to coincide with **i**. The molecule is not asymmetric and does not show optical activity.

(*d*)

$$
\begin{array}{cc}
\text{CO}_2\text{H} \quad \text{NO}_2 \qquad\qquad & \text{O}_2\text{N} \quad \text{HO}_2\text{C} \\
\\
\text{CO}_2\text{H} \quad \text{NO}_2 \qquad\qquad & \text{O}_2\text{N} \quad \text{HO}_2\text{C} \\
\text{(i)} & \text{(ii)}
\end{array}
$$

ii, the mirror image of **i**, is superimposable upon **i**. The molecule is not optically active, even though the bulky carboxyl and nitro groups do not allow the two benzene rings to lie in the same plane.

(e)

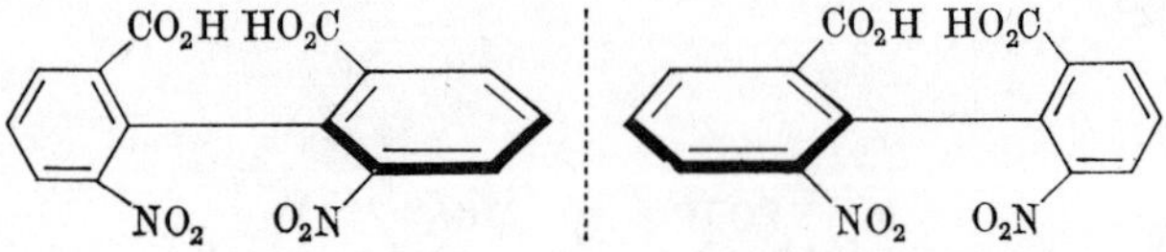

(i)   (ii)

The two mirror images are not superimposable in this case and the molecule is optically active.

(f)

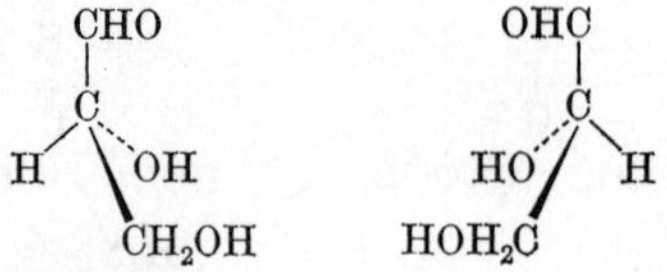

(i)   (ii)

The molecule has 4 different groups attached to the central carbon atom and as in (a) and (b) it is asymmetric.

2.

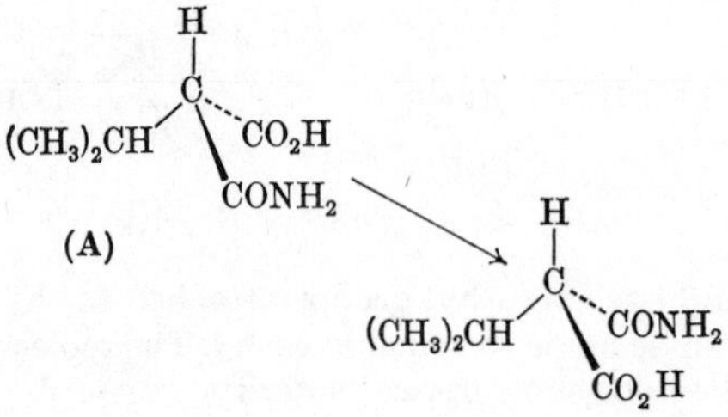

(A)

(D)

In the reaction sequence **A → D** the CO_2H and $CONH_2$ groups have been interchanged. This exchange has given us the mirror image of **A**, i.e. **D** could be written

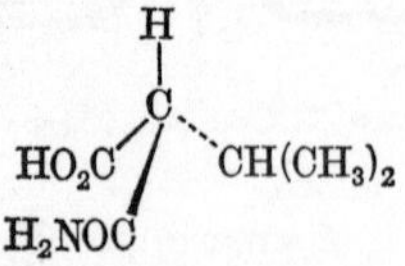

and will have a specific rotation of $-49° 40'$.

Chapter 16

1. (*a*)

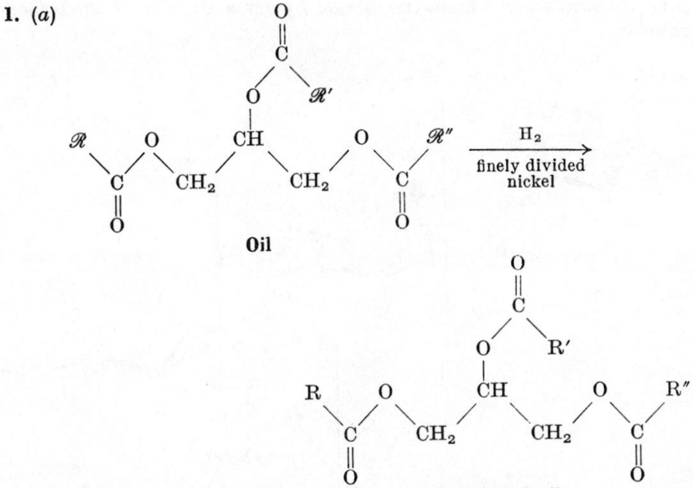

Oil

Hardened oil
(fat)

$\mathscr{R}, \mathscr{R}', \mathscr{R}''$ are hydrocarbon chains containing 15, 17, and 19 carbon atoms and one or two, possibly three, double bonds per chain. R. R', and R'' are hydrocarbon chains, partly saturated by the hydrogenation.

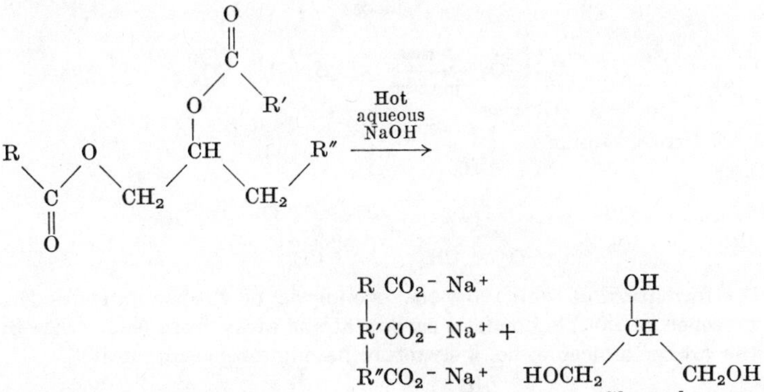

$$R\ CO_2^-\ Na^+$$
$$R'CO_2^-\ Na^+\ +$$
$$R''CO_2^-\ Na^+$$
Soap

$$HOCH_2 \quad \overset{\overset{\displaystyle OH}{|}}{CH} \quad CH_2OH$$
Glycerol

Sodium chloride is added to the aqueous solution containing the soap and glycerol. The soap is precipitated and filtered off and refined by

16

washing, adding perfume and finally formed into tablets. The glycerol is recovered from the filtrate by concentration of the aqueous solution.

(b)

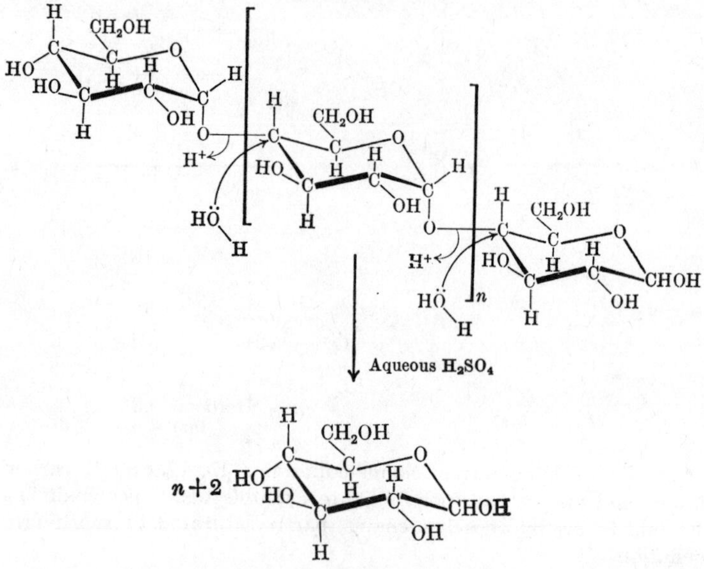

Aqueous H_2SO_4

$$n+2$$

Glucose

$$C_6H_{12}O_6 \xrightarrow[\text{in yeast}]{\text{Zymase}} 2\,C_2H_5OH + CO_2$$

Glucose

2. Pentan-4-onal

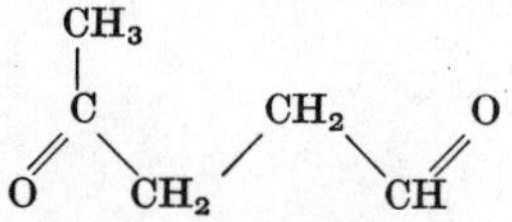

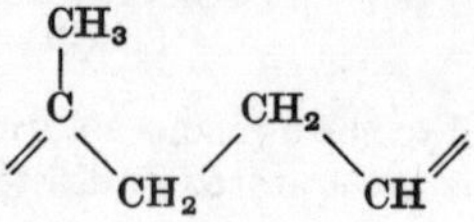

the formation of which by the ozonolysis of rubber indicates the presence of double bonds, 4 carbon atoms away from each other in the rubber molecule, i.e. a structure having a repeating unit and one double bond per 5 carbon atoms joined this way:

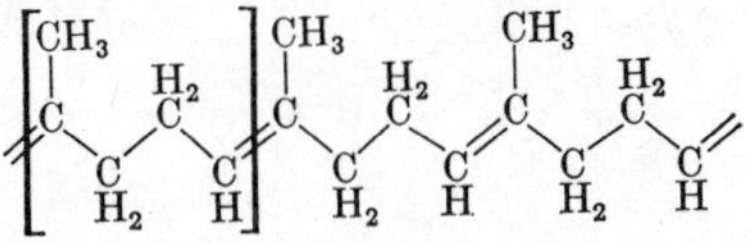

rather than:

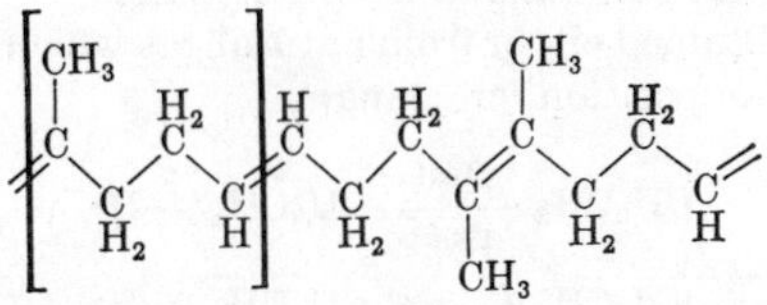

as isoprene is formed by destructive distillation of rubber.

A cyclic structure, e.g.

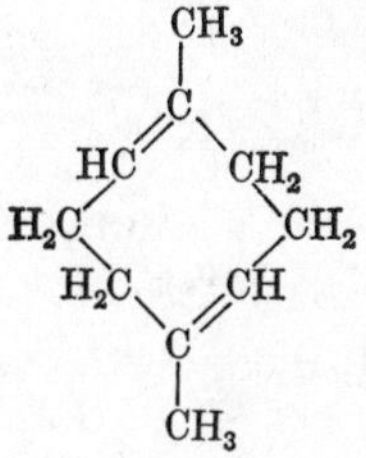

also fits the evidence given, but the high 'molecular' weight of rubber indicates that the molecule is a polymer rather than a cyclic molecule.

3. (a)

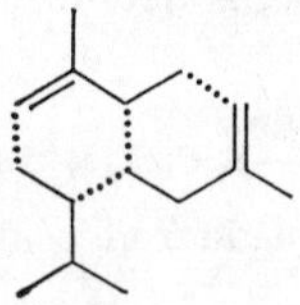

3 isopentane units; a sesqiterpene

(b)

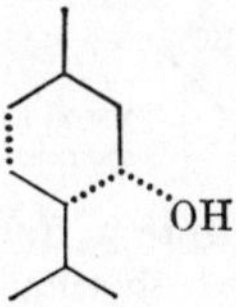

2 isopentane units; a terpene

(c)

3 isopentane units:
a sesquiterpene

Chapter 17

1. (a), (b), (c) Tetraethyllead, polyethylene, ethyl alcohol, and acetic acid may all be prepared from ethylene.

Ethylene is obtained either from natural gas which contains ethane by thermal decomposition (cracking):

$$CH_3CH_3 \xrightarrow[1000°]{\text{Heat}} CH_3\overset{\bullet}{C}H_2 + H\cdot$$

$$CH_3\overset{\bullet}{C}H_2 \longrightarrow CH_2CH_2 + H\cdot$$

or as a by-product in the cracking of higher hydrocarbons:

(e), (f) Polyvinyl chloride and acetic acid may be obtained from acetylene, which, like ethylene, is obtained by the thermal decomposition of natural gas:

$$C_2H_6 \xrightarrow{1000°} C_2H_2 + 2H_2$$

(In Britain most acetylene is made from coal via calcium carbide.)

(d) Toluene may be prepared from a fraction of petroleum containing about 7 carbon atoms by a thermal decomposition reaction which dehydrogenates and cyclizes the heptane molecules in the C_7 fraction:

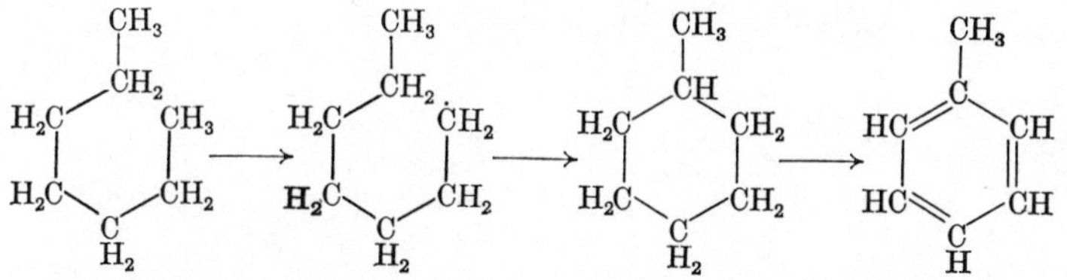

2. (*a*) Phenol is the starting material for Nylon 66. The light oil fraction of coal tar contains phenol. Sodium hydroxide solution is used to extract the phenol from this fraction (see page 169).

(*b*) *p*-Xylene, a neutral component of the light oil fraction of coal tar, is converted into Terylene by the steps shown on p. 170. (The ethane-1,2-diol used can most conveniently be obtained from ethylene, i.e. from petroleum rather than coal (see page 61).)

[Insufficient xylene occurs in coal tar, and it is prepared by the alkylation of benzene.]

(*c*) Bakelite is a condensation polymer of phenol and formaldehyde. Methane is a component of coal gas and could serve as a source of formaldehyde by controlled oxidation:

$$CH_4 + O_2 \longrightarrow CH_2{=}O + H_2O$$

(In Britain most formaldehyde is made by the catalytic oxidation of methanol.)

The condensation of phenol and formaldehyde is depicted on page 171.

(*d*) An azo dye. Starting materials:

> Benzene (light oil fraction)
> Phenol (light oil fraction)

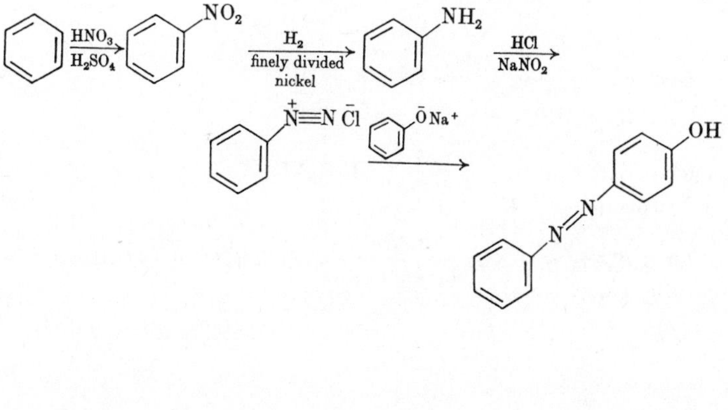

Chapter 18

1. (a) $3 C_2H_5OH + PBr_3 \longrightarrow 3 C_2H_5Br + H_3PO_3$

    or $C_2H_5OH + Na^+Br^- + H_2SO_4 \longrightarrow$
    $$C_2H_5Br + Na^+ + H_3O^+ + HSO_4^-$$

(b)

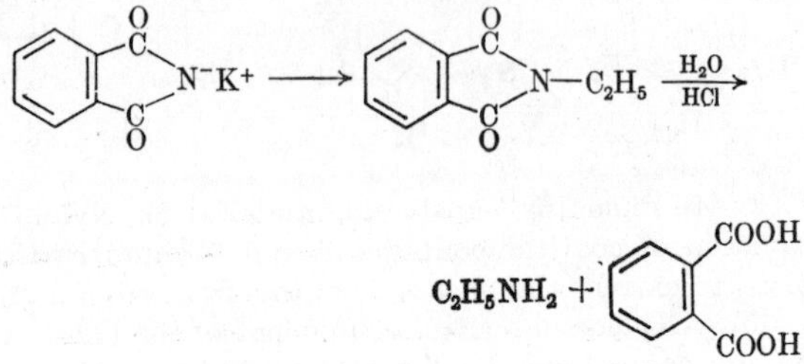

    from (a)

(c) $C_2H_5OH + Na \longrightarrow C_2H_5O^-Na^+ + \frac{1}{2} H_2$
    $C_2H_5O^-Na^+ + C_2H_5Br \longrightarrow (C_2H_5)_2O + Na^+Br^-$
    from (a)

(d) $C_2H_5Br + Mg \xrightarrow[\text{ether}]{\text{Dry}} C_2H_5MgBr$
    from (a)

    $C_2H_5MgBr + CH_2{=}O \longrightarrow C_2H_5{-}CH_2{-}OMgBr \xrightarrow[\text{acid}]{\text{Dilute}}$
    $$C_2H_5CH_2OH$$

(e) Either $C_2H_5Br + Mg \longrightarrow C_2H_5MgBr \xrightarrow{CO_2} C_2H_5CO_2H$

    or $C_2H_5Br + KCN \xrightarrow{C_2H_5OH} C_2H_5CN \xrightarrow[\text{hydrolysis}]{\text{Acid}} C_2H_5CO_2H$

    $C_2H_5CO_2H + C_2H_5OH \xrightarrow{(H_2SO_4)} C_2H_5CO_2C_2H_5$

2. (a) $C_6H_6 + Br_2 \xrightarrow{FeBr_3} C_6H_5Br + HBr$

(b) $C_6H_6 + HNO_3 + H_2SO_4 \longrightarrow C_6H_5NO_2$

(c) $C_6H_5NO_2 + H_2 \xrightarrow[\text{or Sn/HCl}]{\text{Catalyst (Ni)}} C_6H_5NH_2$
    from (b)

(d) $C_6H_5NH_2 + HNO_2 \xrightarrow[\text{aqueous } H_2SO_4]{\text{In dilute}} C_6H_5N_2{}^+ Cl^- \xrightarrow{CuCN} C_6H_5CN + N_2$
    from (c)

3.

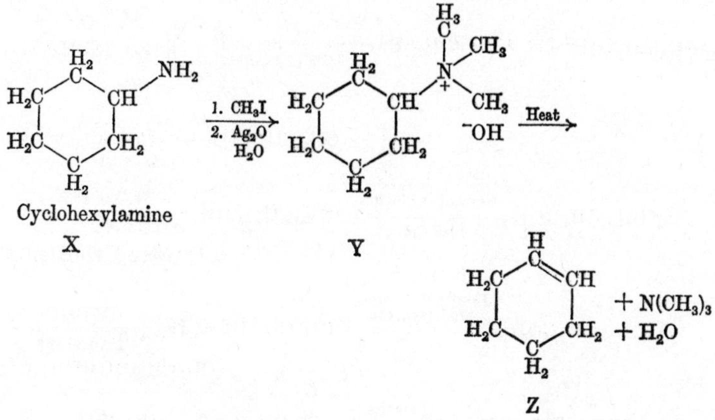
1. CH_3I
2. Ag_2O
H_2O
Heat
Cyclohexylamine
X
Y
Z
$+ N(CH_3)_3$
$+ H_2O$

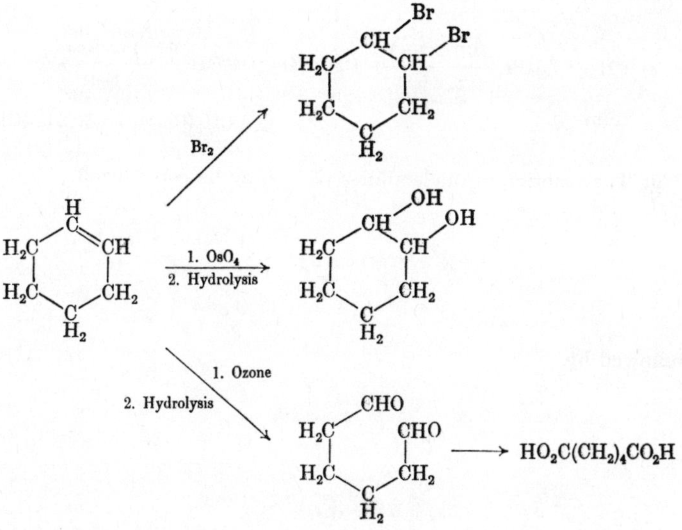
Br_2
1. OsO_4
2. Hydrolysis
1. Ozone
2. Hydrolysis
$HO_2C(CH_2)_4CO_2H$

4. (*a*)

$$CH_3(CH_2)_4OH \xrightarrow{PBr_3} CH_3(CH_2)_4Br \xrightarrow{\text{(phthalimide } N^-K^+)} \text{(N-substituted phthalimide)}$$

$$\xrightarrow[H_2O]{HCl} CH_3(CH_2)_4NH_2 \text{ (as sequence for } \mathbf{1}(b))$$

(*b*) $CH_3(CH_2)_4OH \xrightarrow[\text{with } CrO_3]{\text{Careful oxidation}} CH_3(CH_2)_3CHO \xrightarrow[\text{2. Dil. acid}]{\text{1. } CH_3MgI}$
$$CH_3(CH_2)_3CH(CH_3)OH$$

(*c*) $CH_3(CH_2)_4OH \xrightarrow[\text{acid catalyst}]{\text{Heat with strong}} CH_3CH_2CH{=}CH_2 \xrightarrow[\text{2. Hydrolysis}]{\text{1. } OsO_4}$
$$CH_3CH_2CHOHCH_2OH$$

(*d*) $CH_3CH_2CH{=}CH_2 \xrightarrow[\substack{\text{2. Oxidative}\\\text{hydrolysis}}]{\text{1. Ozone}} CH_3CH_2CO_2H + HO_2CH$
from (*c*)   Propionic   Formic
                                              acid   acid

The more volatile formic acid may be separated from the propionic acid by fractional distillation.

(*e*) $CH_3(CH_2)_3Br \xrightarrow[\substack{\text{in liquid}\\\text{ammonia}}]{CH{\equiv}\overset{-}{C}Na^+} CH_3(CH_2)_3C{\equiv}CH \xrightarrow[\substack{\text{2. 1 mole}\\CH_3(CH_2)_3Br}]{\substack{\text{1. NaNH}_2 \text{ in}\\\text{liquid ammonia}}}$
from (*a*) $CH_3(CH_2)_3C{\equiv}C(CH_2)_3CH_3$

5. The reaction of nucleophiles (X^-) may be generalized:

$$X^- \; \overset{\displaystyle C}{\underset{\displaystyle \underset{O}{\|}}{\diagdown}} \longrightarrow \overset{\displaystyle X}{\underset{\displaystyle \underset{O^-}{|}}{\overset{|}{C}}}$$

followed by

$$\overset{\displaystyle X}{\underset{\displaystyle \underset{O^-}{|} \; Y^+}{\overset{|}{C}}} \longrightarrow \overset{\displaystyle X}{\underset{\displaystyle \underset{O}{|}\;_{Y}}{\overset{|}{C}}}$$

if the nucleophile X^- was formed by the ionization of the compound XY.

(a)

$$(CH_3)_2C{=}O + HCN \longrightarrow \underset{\underset{OH}{|}}{\overset{\overset{NC \quad CH_3}{\diagdown\,\diagup}}{\underset{}{C}}}\overset{CH_3}{}\ \xrightarrow[\text{dilute acid}]{\text{Hydrolysis with}}\ \underset{\underset{OH}{|}}{\overset{\overset{HO_2C \quad CH_3}{\diagdown\,\diagup}}{C}}\overset{CH_3}{}$$

(b) $(CH_3)_2C{=}O \xrightarrow{H_2NOH} (CH_3)_2C{=}NOH \xrightarrow{\text{Hydrogenation}} (CH_3)_2CHNH_2$

(c) $(CH_3)_2C{=}O \xrightarrow[\text{2. Acid hydrolysis}]{\text{1. } C_2H_5MgBr} (CH_3)_2COHC_2H_5$

(d) $(CH_3)_2C{=}O \xrightarrow{\text{Reduce}} (CH_3)_2CHOH \xrightarrow{PBr_3} (CH_3)_2CHBr$

Subject Index

233